Blackboard Learn Administration

Discover how to administrate your Blackboard Learn platform through step-by-step tutorials

Terry Patterson

PUBLISHING

BIRMINGHAM - MUMBAI

Blackboard Learn Administration

First published: May 2013

Production Reference: 1170513

Published by Packt Publishing Ltd.
Livery Place
35 Livery Street
Birmingham B3 2PB, UK.

ISBN 978-1-84969-306-6

www.packtpub.com

Cover Image by Neha Rajappan (neha.rajappan1@gmail.com)

Credits

Author

Terry Patterson

Reviewers

David Hopkins

Dr Malcolm Murray

Simon Roberts

Wayne Twitchell

Mike Zimmerman

Acquisition Editor

Joanne Fitzpatrick

Lead Technical Editor

Sweny M. Sukumaran

Technical Editors

Prasad Dalvi

Pushpak Poddar

Project Coordinator

Shiksha Chaturvedi

Proofreaders

Maria Gould

Amy Guest

Indexer

Rekha Nair

Graphics

Ronak Dhruv

Production Coordinator

Conidon Miranda

Cover Work

Conidon Miranda

About the Author

Terry Patterson has over ten years of experience administrating Blackboard LMS environments at various institutions. During that time, he has held numerous leadership roles in Blackboard feedback panels and customer-led user groups. In 2009, he received a Blackboard Catalyst Award for his work in the Blackboard Community. He has given presentations at state, national, and international conferences about emerging and advanced integrations with the Blackboard application. He holds certifications as a Blackboard Trainer and a Blackboard Server Administrator. When not busy in his position as LMS Application Administrator at the University of Missouri, he works to help answer questions from other system administrators and posts the issues he faces on his *Blackboard Guru* blog at http://www.blackboardguru.com/.

I would like to thank my friends and family who have been positive and encouraging throughout this process. Thanks to my colleagues at the University of Missouri, including Tanys, Guy, Michael, Ethan, and countless others who have offered their expertise and support.

I also want to thank the many Blackboard employees who always welcomed my questions no matter how long winded they were. Thanks to the Packt Publishing team for their help, as I have learned the book-writing process. Finally, thanks to you, the Blackboard administrators reading this book; I hope you find this book to be a helpful resource in your duties.

About the Reviewers

David Hopkins is a respected and experienced Learning Technologist at the University of Leicester, U.K. Working closely with administrators, managers, and academic teams, David investigates and advises on the appropriate use of technology for both classroom and distance-learning students.

David writes on aspects of learning technology and the pedagogic use of technology in (and out of) the classroom on the *Technology Enhanced Learning* blog at `www.dontwasteyourtime.co.uk`, and has a growing professional network centered around his blog and Twitter handle, `@hopkinsdavid`.

Dr Malcolm Murray has used Blackboard since Version 5.5. He has over a decade's experience in using Blackboard Learn as a system administrator, as a developer, and also to support his teaching. Currently based at Durham University in the U.K., he leads the University's Learning Technologies Team and is an Honorary Fellow of the School of Education. He holds a Ph.D. in Geography and a Postgraduate Certificate in Learning, Teaching, and Research in Higher Education. He is a member of the U.K. Heads of e-Learning Forum, a fellow of the (UK) Higher Education Academy, a certified member of the Association for Learning Technology, and the Director of OSCELOT (the Open Source Community for Educational Learning Objects and Tools). He regularly attends Blackboard conferences in the U.S. and Europe, participates in Blackboard's BugSquad and Beta initiatives, and is a past winner of the Blackboard Greenhouse Award (2005), Blackboard Innovators Award (2008), and Blackboard Catalyst Award (2010).

Simon Roberts has 30 years of experience in the IT industry, as a programmer and instructor. He teaches a variety of topics, including programming and system administration for various platforms. He enjoys the travel opportunities that come his way thanks to his work, and also acts as an FAA-certified flight instructor in his spare time. Simon lives in the Denver metro area in Colorado.

Wayne Twitchell is a leader in online teaching-and-learning for over 15 years, despite being denied admission to the prestigious Mensa club. As Blackboard administrator at Grinnell College and in his current position at the University of Northern Iowa, he has managed and supported a range of Blackboard products including Learning Management, Community, and Content management in a vertically-integrated way while integrating individual products (such as Learn) into an existing campus infrastructure. Dr. Twitchell's approach engages the visionary potential of technology both in and out of the classroom without forgetting the nuts and bolts of teaching. He currently lives in Cedar Falls Iowa with his partner (who was admitted to Mensa) and their amazing bearded dragon, Gogo, as well as their puppet sheepdog, Winston.

Mike Zimmerman has been a Blackboard system administrator at the University of Nebraska in Omaha since 2001. He is an active contributor in the Blackboard user community and ListServ, and has been a part of the Blackboard Dr. C user support forums since 2006.

www.PacktPub.com

Support files, eBooks, discount offers and more

You might want to visit www.PacktPub.com for support files and downloads related to your book.

Did you know that Packt offers eBook versions of every book published, with PDF and ePub files available? You can upgrade to the eBook version at www.PacktPub.com and as a print book customer, you are entitled to a discount on the eBook copy. Get in touch with us at service@packtpub.com for more details.

At www.PacktPub.com, you can also read a collection of free technical articles, sign up for a range of free newsletters and receive exclusive discounts and offers on Packt books and eBooks.

http://PacktLib.PacktPub.com

Do you need instant solutions to your IT questions? PacktLib is Packt's online digital book library. Here, you can access, read and search across Packt's entire library of books.

Why Subscribe?

- Fully searchable across every book published by Packt
- Copy and paste, print and bookmark content
- On demand and accessible via web browser

Free Access for Packt account holders

If you have an account with Packt at www.PacktPub.com, you can use this to access PacktLib today and view nine entirely free books. Simply use your login credentials for immediate access.

Table of Contents

Preface

Welcome to *Blackboard Learn Administration*. In this book, we will review the basic and advanced topics that make up Blackboard Learn administration. By the end of this book, we will have a better understanding of Blackboard Learn, and hopefully, have some tips and tricks to add to our "administrator's toolbox". So let's get ready to challenge ourselves as we learn more about Blackboard Learn.

What this book covers

Chapter 1, Planning a Blackboard Learn Instance, reviews the information, issues, and concerns that administrators should address before installing Blackboard Learn.

Chapter 2, Installing Blackboard Learn, will show you how to prepare, install, upgrade, and maintain a Blackboard Learn environment.

Chapter 3, Setting Up and Customizing Blackboard Learn, reviews the customization options available within Blackboard Learn.

Chapter 4, Creating Courses in Blackboard Learn, will teach you how to prepare and create Blackboard Learn courses.

Chapter 5, Administrating Courses in Blackboard Learn, will show you the options to maintain, support, back up, and remove Blackboard Learn courses.

Chapter 6, Creating Users in Blackboard Learn, reviews how to create users within a Blackboard Learn environment.

Chapter 7, Managing Roles and Users in Blackboard Learn, will help you discover how to maintain, control, and remove roles and users within Blackboard Learn.

Chapter 8, Using Tools and Utilities in Blackboard Learn, will show you how to use administrator tools within Blackboard Learn.

Chapter 9, Security, Reporting, and Configuration in Blackboard Learn, reviews how to improve security, how to create reports, and performance tuning options within Blackboard Learn environments.

Chapter 10, Authentication and Data Integration in Blackboard Learn, will teach you how to connect a Blackboard Learn environment to external authentication providers and student information systems.

Chapter 11, Implementing Building Blocks in Blackboard Learn, will show you how to add building blocks and other third-party tools to a Blackboard Learn instance.

Chapter 12, Logs, Troubleshooting, and Disaster Recovery in Blackboard Learn, reviews what logs can help troubleshoot issues within a Blackboard Learn environment, and how to develop a disaster-recovery plan.

Appendix shows the default actions for eight major system roles.

What you need for this book

Access to a Blackboard Learn environment is essential to gaining experience and following along as we discuss the different parts of the application. This environment is preferably a test or development instance. If you plan to use this book to build that environment, then that will work as well. We will also need a text editor, an XML editor, and an optional HTML editor.

Who this book is for

Most novice and advanced Blackboard Learn administrators will find this book helpful. It covers many of the basic skills that will be used on a regular basis, along with advanced topics such as performance tuning, external authentication, and data integration.

Conventions

In this book, you will find a number of styles of text that distinguish between different kinds of information. Here are some examples of these styles, and an explanation of their meaning.

Code words in text are shown as follows: "Once completed, check that the DB_ BLOCK_SIZE value is set to 8192."

A block of code is set as follows:

```
TEST-COURSE-001,Test Course A
TEST-COURSE-002,Test Course B,This is the course description
TEST-COURSE-003,Test Course C,This is the course
description,#CCCC00/#003300
TEST-COURSE-004,Test Course - Marketing,This is the course description
,#CCCC00/#003300,Welcome to this course.,Course Welcome,
TEST-COURSE-005,Test Course - Marketing,This is the course
description, #CCCC00/#003300,Welcome to this course.,Course
Welcome,Marketing
```

Any command-line input or output is written as follows:

```
SELECT tablespace_name, block_size FROM dba_tablespaces;
```

New terms and **important words** are shown in bold. Words that you see on the screen, in menus or dialog boxes for example, appear in the text like this: "We click on the **Downloads** link that is found under the **Self Service** heading on the Behind the Blackboard website."

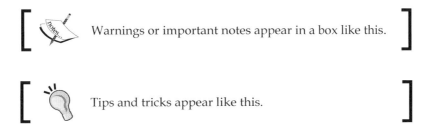

Warnings or important notes appear in a box like this.

Tips and tricks appear like this.

Reader feedback

Feedback from our readers is always welcome. Let us know what you think about this book—what you liked or may have disliked. Reader feedback is important for us to develop titles that you really get the most out of.

To send us general feedback, simply send an e-mail to feedback@packtpub.com, and mention the book title via the subject of your message.

If there is a topic that you have expertise in and you are interested in either writing or contributing to a book, see our author guide on www.packtpub.com/authors.

Customer support

Now that you are the proud owner of a Packt book, we have a number of things to help you to get the most from your purchase.

Downloading the example code

You can download the example code files for all Packt books you have purchased from your account at `http://www.packtpub.com`. If you purchased this book elsewhere, you can visit `http://www.packtpub.com/support` and register to have the files e-mailed directly to you.

Errata

Although we have taken every care to ensure the accuracy of our content, mistakes do happen. If you find a mistake in one of our books—maybe a mistake in the text or the code—we would be grateful if you would report this to us. By doing so, you can save other readers from frustration and help us improve subsequent versions of this book. If you find any errata, please report them by visiting `http://www.packtpub.com/submit-errata`, selecting your book, clicking on the **errata submission form** link, and entering the details of your errata. Once your errata are verified, your submission will be accepted and the errata will be uploaded on our website, or added to any list of existing errata, under the Errata section of that title. Any existing errata can be viewed by selecting your title from `http://www.packtpub.com/support`.

Piracy

Piracy of copyright material on the Internet is an ongoing problem across all media. At Packt, we take the protection of our copyright and licenses very seriously. If you come across any illegal copies of our works, in any form, on the Internet, please provide us with the location address or website name immediately so that we can pursue a remedy.

Please contact us at `copyright@packtpub.com` with a link to the suspected pirated material.

We appreciate your help in protecting our authors, and our ability to bring you valuable content.

Questions

You can contact us at `questions@packtpub.com` if you are having a problem with any aspect of the book, and we will do our best to address it.

1
Planning a Blackboard Learn Instance

Blackboard can be an overwhelming environment for any user when they first login, and it can be the same for administrators. Many administrators find the Blackboard environment assigned to us with little training and lots of documents to read. When family and friends ask me what Blackboard is, I normally compare the software to a virtual community. We as administrators play dog catcher, city plumber, master planner, police officer, garbage collector, fire fighter, and even the mayor. With all these different hats that we wear, it's time that we spend time learning more about how we can improve the ways in which we serve our virtual community.

In this chapter we will work to become familiar and comfortable with what Blackboard is and how we are going to set up our new Blackboard Learn instance.

What is Blackboard Learn?

Blackboard Learn is an enterprise-level learning management system similar to other products such as Desire2Learn, Canvas, Moodle, and Sakai. The software uses web tools to create content-based web pages that allow for a secure online environment for users to complete training or courses via the internet. Many organizations use Blackboard Learn for government entities, private companies, along with K12 and higher educational institutions.

Over the past few years, Blackboard has acquired many competitors including WebCT and Angel Learning. While both these product lines may be used within some organizations, Blackboard plans to end these product lines. We will spend this book concentrating on the product line entitled Blackboard Learn which combines Blackboard's WebCT line and the Blackboard Academic Suite line.

How does Blackboard Learn work?

The heart of Blackboard Learn is made up of multiple components. When installed on the Windows operating system, Blackboard uses the IIS web server. While on Linux and Solaris, Blackboard uses the Apache web server. Apart from the web servers, Blackboard Learn runs its own version of Tomcat, a web container that uses Blackboard's servlets to dynamically create web pages (called JavaServer Pages or .JSP files) to deliver course content and complete tasks. Tomcat creates these pages by accessing information stored within a database.

Blackboard also includes a collaboration server. This server creates a text-based environment which allows interaction between users in a basic form. Most administrators will initially have the collaboration server run beside Tomcat, however it can be installed to run on a separate server.

Blackboard Learn's databases run within Microsoft SQL or Oracle depending on some internal factors, such as if our organization contains a majority of Windows, Linux, or Solaris servers, database administrator experience, or application cost and support. The specific versions required by our Blackboard instance can be found in the release notes that accompany the Blackboard Learn installer. Each Blackboard Learn version may change what operating system and database application it supports.

The following diagram suggests the structure of a Blackboard Learn instance:

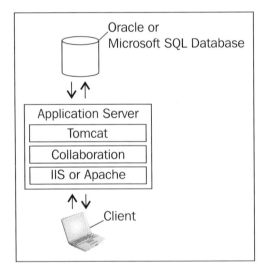

Blackboard Learn architecture

Most Blackboard administrators would agree that they strive to develop and maintain a stable Blackboard Learn environment. One of the most important factors to achieve that goal is a good foundation.

Earlier we used the example of a community, having good streets along with enough power and water will allow a community to support many residents. In this case, we need to examine the hardware and software requirements along with the different architecture options for our Blackboard Learn instance or virtual community. After we review our options, we can create a decision diagram that can help us decide what architecture options are right for our plans.

One server / Two server architecture

A one server architecture is the simplest installation of Blackboard Learn for an organization. A one server instance means that your database, application, and collaboration servers all reside on the same server.

The following diagram shows the structure of a one server architecture:

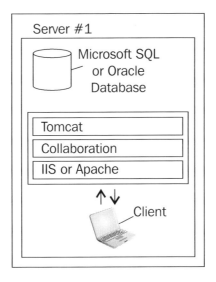

This can be a great option if we only have a few classes and a limited number of users. It's also ideal if you don't expect increased class or user growth in the near future. Many small organizations or developers use a one server architecture.

The drawback of a one server instance is the one point of failure. If any hardware or software issues occur, the Blackboard Learn environment is down for users. This environment also creates issues when your organization needs to expand their environment for growing users and course offerings. If the instance grows too big for the hardware and software it operates on, then it will require a move that will bring more server downtime. More downtime means users' work and course development is delayed.

A two server architecture is very similar to a one server, however the database has moved to a new server. This allows our server to use more processor time on Tomcat and our IIS or Apache server. The issues we brought up earlier in a one server architecture still remain the same.

The following diagram shows the structure of a two server architecture:

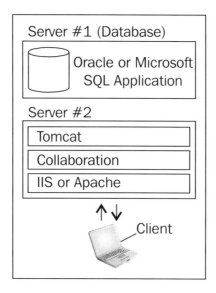

Multiple server architecture

A multiple server instance offers the best starting point for any organization. Multiple servers split Blackboard services into a server for our database, multiple servers host our Tomcat and IIS or Apache servers, and even a server that hosts our collaboration server. This architecture requires additional hardware. All the servers will need to put course and user files in one central location for every server to have access. We can accomplish this with the use of a network storage device or SAN.

This design also requires a load balancer to be added as well. It creates a single point of access, so when our user types `http://blackboard.myorganization.com` into their browser, the load balancer will direct the response to one of our application servers, bbapp1, bbapp2, or bbapp3.

Most Blackboard administrators would recommend an organization with plans to expand users and course offerings to implement this type of instance. When the organization grows, additional application servers can be added to meet increased load with little effect on the experience of our users. The diagram below offers us a view of how a two server instance can grow into a much larger instance:

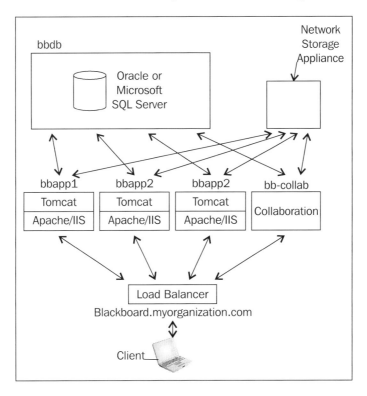

While the multiple server structure does allow the easy expansion of Blackboard Learn, it doesn't completely address issues with a single point of failure. If the database server or storage device fails, the system will be down. Some organizations may turn to adding another database server or additional backup storage devices. We will address planning for a disaster and disaster recovery in *Chapter 12, Logs, Troubleshooting, and Disaster Recovery in Blackboard Learn*.

Blackboard instance environments

While Blackboard Learn instances can be created using different types of configurations, the one thing we should also examine would be where those configurations thrive. When we think of any web service, we think of servers in a rack that do one or two different things. However, with the increase in hardware loads and costs, many organizations are looking to use the latest technology options to meet their needs and stretch their budgets.

The first option that many organizations use would be virtual servers. These software created servers reside on a hardware server; however, multiple virtual servers can be on one hardware server. This option allows for the maximum use of purchased hardware to meet the needs of the organization. Blackboard Inc. does support the installation of its product on virtual server software. The two main manufacturers are VMWare and Microsoft's Hyper V.

While most of the organizations I have worked with have used some type of virtualization, we may need to convince administration to use virtual servers. One of the biggest reasons I have shared with administrators is the ease of duplicating the server and the ability to bring the system back up. When built correctly, you can bring a virtual server back up in another location within minutes instead of hours. While we won't cover the installation and setup of virtual servers in our discussions, it is important that we understand that it is an option when planning our Blackboard Learn architecture.

Blackboard does offer managed hosting for clients. This service has Blackboard's engineering teams to take care of your instance. However, according to some clients, the service does limit the amount of control administrators have to the backend.

How do I decide what architecture to build?

Now that we reviewed the types of instances and options for our Blackboard Learn instance, let's discuss what instance we should build. If we currently are looking to have a small user pilot to test our Blackboard Learn, we can start with a single server instance that can make it easy for us to collect helpful data on how instructors and students will use Blackboard Learn. If we are migrating from another LMS product, we can use course and user storage amounts, user activity, or any other data to provide additional insight.

In *Chapter 9, Security, Reporting, and Configuration in Blackboard Learn* we discuss the collection of different types of data to improve the performance of our Blackboard Learn environment and the use of the BbStats tool that can greatly help collect data from within a Blackboard Learn pilot. When collecting our data we should work to find the averages based on multiple weeks when our environment has peak usage.

We also need to review some major questions that will help us plan what installation we will implement. First we should review how much growth our instance will see in the coming years:

- If Blackboard Learn is replacing another learning management system (or LMS), and how many users were there in the previous LMS?
- How many users do we expect will be in the LMS three years in the future?

Now we should look at course growth:

- How many courses will be on this instance?
- Will Blackboard Learn be only used for online courses or both online and supplementing face-to-face?
- If we are moving from another LMS, how much disk space did an average course use?
- Will instructors actively use the tools within Blackboard Learn?
- Do we plan to allow video and multimedia files?
- Will our instance also host the organization's internal committee and communication groups along with courses?
- How quickly will your organization be developing new courses and how many will there be in three years?

Then we look at what requirements come from your IT department:

- How mission critical is Blackboard Learn to the organization?
- How much has the IT department/organization budgeted for a Blackboard Learn implementation?

Now that we have covered all these questions and hopefully collected some data from our previous LMS or pilot project, let's look at some tables to help us analyze our information:

Title	One Server Candidate	Two Server Candidate	Multiple Server Candidate
Current Active Users	<5,000	5,000 - 20,000	20,000+
Course & User Storage	<1 Terabyte	1 - 5 Terabyte	5+ Terabyte
Five Year Growth Rate	<5%	10 - 15%	15+%
Number of Courses or Organizations	<5,000	5,000 - 10,000	10,000+
Course Retention	<18 Months	2 - 4 years	5+ years
Online In Class Assessment Usage	No	Possibly	Yes

This table will help us review the current data sets that we have. Based on that information we can understand what type of instance we currently need. The first row, Current Active Users, compares the number of users who have logged into our system or we expect to login to our system over a 90 day period. The second row looks at the combined file storage for course and user files. These files are normally associated with courses and student submitted content within them. Our third row discusses the growth or adoption rate over the next five years of the Blackboard Learn environment.

The next two rows review the number of courses created and kept on the system for an instructional term and how long these courses are kept within our environment. Some courses may never go away or some institutions create new ones each term. Our course retention normally follows a set institutional policy. The next row asks about the use of Blackboard Learn's assessment tool with face-to-face or on campus courses. The assessment tool is the heaviest process on our Blackboard Learn environment. If the tool is used to give an assessment to over 50 students at once in a lab setting, our architecture may create an unacceptable experience for users. Now let's review the broader questions we mentioned earlier by using this table:

Questions	Small and Stable	Small and Growing	Large and Stable	Large and Growing
If Blackboard Learn is replacing another LMS at your organization, the LMS user growth would have been classified as:				
In three years, you anticipate the use of Blackboard Learn at your organization to be:				
In three years, the number of courses on the organization's Blackboard Learn instance will be:				
The number of online and other courses that may use the organization's Blackboard Learn instance in the first year will be				
The number of online and other courses that may use the organization's Blackboard Learn instance in the third year will be				
How would you classify the importance of your Blackboard Learn instance at your organization				
How would you classify the budget for your Blackboard learn instance at your organization				

While our first table reviewed the current data we have, our discussion here is about the expected use and growth. Select answers to the questions in our form. If most of them are classified in the Small and Stable or Large and Stable columns, our environment will probably not see any growth so planning for expanding the Blackboard Learn instance is not a high priority. Our organization might look at a one or two server instance due to this fact. If most of our selections are within the Small and Growing or Large and Growing columns we will want to plan for some expansion and may want initially implement a multiple server architecture that will allow for the addition of application servers when needed.

While deciding the architecture of the Blackboard Learn environment for our organization we have many variables like server types, processors, memory, and organizational budgets. Even with these variables, this discussion should offer some clarity. In *Chapter 9*, *Security, Reporting, and Configuration in Blackboard Learn* we will learn how to improve the current architecture by tuning the Blackboard Learn, Apache or IIS, and Tomcat settings to get the most out of our architecture.

Summary

In this chapter, our initial discussion introduced us to Blackboard Learn and gave us a broad overview of its components. We also discussed planning the architecture of a Blackboard Learn instance. We can build our instance on one, two, or multiple server architectures. These servers can be hardware based, virtual, or even in the cloud. When we plan to create a Blackboard Learn instance, we must look at multiple factors around our organization including its use, the number of users, and how it may grow in the future. Once we create a plan on what type of instance we need to build, the creation of our Blackboard Learn instance can begin.

Our next chapter takes the planning we have done for our virtual community and puts it into motion. We will learn how to install Blackboard Learn and how to prepare our server or servers for it. Our discussions will also address how to upgrade and patch our instance to fix problems or security issues. Our construction team has been given the green light. Let's get to it!

2
Installing Blackboard Learn

Our earlier chapter took us through the process of planning and reviewing what type of Blackboard Learn instance we need to create for our users and what hardware components we need to meet their expectations. The chapter laid out the blueprints required for our virtual community. In this chapter we strap on our hard hats, grab our shovels, charge up our power tools, and maybe even drive a bulldozer to start building on our blueprints. In this chapter we will discuss:

- Configuration settings within the operating system and database required for Blackboard Learn
- How to install and configure **Java Development Kit (JDK)** within our operating system
- The Blackboard Learn installation process step by step
- How to upgrade a Blackboard Learn instance
- How to use the Blackboard Learn Patch Utility tool

So grab your coffee-filled travel mug; it's time to start constructing!

Operating systems

As mentioned earlier, Blackboard Learn runs on three different operating systems: Microsoft Windows, Red Hat Enterprise Linux, and Solaris. The operating system used will often decide what other software items you will require during the installation process. We will have two examples in this chapter; one will be for those users who plan to use Microsoft Windows, and the other covers Red Hat and Solaris. Why would we put Red Hat and Solaris together? Well, both are different flavors of the Linux operating system, but the installation of Blackboard Learn requires the same steps.

The first thing we must do is familiarize ourselves with the resources available to Blackboard Learn system administrators. We can find many of these resources within Blackboard Inc.'s support website, called Behind the Blackboard (`http://behind.blackboard.com`). This website contains documentation, support bulletins, **Knowledge Base Articles (KBAs)**, information about known issues, and a location from where we can download Blackboard Learn Installer. It is also the site where we can create support tickets for our environment. However, we must have login credentials from Blackboard Inc. to access these materials. For now, we need to go to the website, Behind the Blackboard, and download the release notes for the version of Blackboard Learn we will install. The release notes will be found in the same location as the installer. We click on the **Downloads** link that is found under the **Self Service** tab on the Behind the Blackboard website, as shown in the following screenshot:

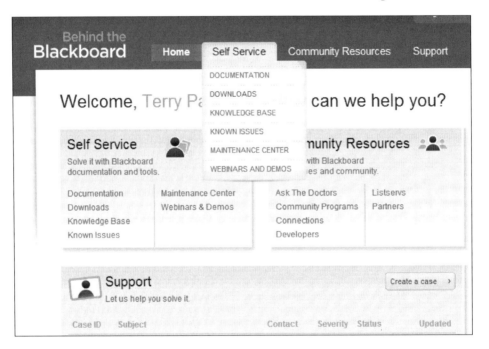

Then select the Blackboard version we want to install, such as Blackboard Learn 9.1. Our next page tells us about this version of Blackboard Learn and at the bottom of the page we find the links to the various Service Packs. At the bottom of this page we find the **Download Files** and **Release Notes** links. When we click on the **Download Files** link, a page loads that displays the links to download our installer file and also all the documentation that relates to this version of Blackboard Learn. We can click on the link to download the release notes which are normally in the PDF format. The following screenshot illustrates this process:

These release notes give us information about what hardware and software this version of Blackboard Learn supports. These also list the possible steps to fix issues. We will want to take a print of these notes, so we can refer back to them during our installation process.

Based on the information contained within the release notes, we know the architectures and the operating systems that will work with our selected Blackboard Learn version. We should also make sure that our server or servers use 64-bit environments. The latest versions of Blackboard Learn only support installations in these environments. Once we have checked that, we need to make sure our server or servers are up-to-date. Do this by starting your update managers (either Windows Update or the yum utility) to ensure the operating system is updated. If your organization has specific rules about updates, make sure to discuss which items should be allowed in the update.

Space requirements

We also need to discuss the file structure and storage of our Blackboard Learn files. Our discussions in *Chapter 1, Planning a Blackboard Learn Instance*, briefly mentioned the file-structure needs and that our Blackboard Learn environment needs large storage areas for files from the course, the users, and the system itself. Most Blackboard administrators will put the Blackboard folder on a different drive than the server's operating system, either by creating a new drive in the Windows server, such as F:/Blackboard for application files, or G:/Bb-Content/ for content files. In Linux or Solaris, we add an additional hard drive mounted to the /usr/local/ blackboard/ and /usr/local/blackboard/content/ subdirectories. We will also want to make sure that we understand the sizing issues of the application and log files. In the following table, we see the average folder sizes for a medium Blackboard Learn instance. This information, along with our discussion in *Chapter 1, Planning a Blackboard Learn Instance*, helps us plan our storage expectations.

File Types within Blackboard Learn	Size
Blackboard application Files	3GB
Daily log file size	3GB - 5GB
Log file archives	30GB - 40GB
Course and Users Files (located in /usr/local/blackboard/content)	1TB - 2TB

Installing the database

When it comes to databases, we must use Oracle if we use the RedHat or Solaris operating system, or Microsoft SQL Server if we choose to use the Windows operating system. This design requirement comes from Blackboard Learn and the specific instance designs they will support. We can find this information within the release notes. Most institutions have an experienced database administrator who will perform the installation process of our database application. If our organization doesn't have such a person, we should invest in a book that can help us with the installation process and essential support issues. Either operating system follows its typical installation process; however, there are a few options that you could review and change.

Installing an Oracle database for Blackboard Learn

During an Oracle installation, we should make sure that we have the application and the initial database installed to allow full functionality with Blackboard Learn. Once completed, check that the DB_BLOCK_SIZE value is set to 8192. We do this by running the following query using a query command-line tool such as SQLPlus or Oracle SQL Developer:

```
SELECT tablespace_name, block_size FROM dba_tablespaces;
```

Most versions of Oracle (10*g* and later) use this setting by default. If it is not set to the correct size, we should consult with our database administrator or contact Oracle support.

Oracle database users should also make sure that the character set and the national character set values match those required for Blackboard Learn. These sets for Oracle should be WE8ISO8859P1 and AL16UTF16 respectively. We can check this by running the following set of queries. Our results should be similar to the ones given here:

```
$ sqlplus '/ as sysdba'
SQL> select parameter, value from v$nls_parameters where parameter =
'NLS_CHARACTERSET';

PARAMETER                          Value
----------------------------       ----------------------------NLS_
CHARACTERSET                       WE8ISO8859P1

SQL> select parameter, value from v$nls_parameters where parameter =
'NLS_NCHAR_CHARACTERSET';

PARAMETER                          Value
----------------------------       ----------------------------NLS_
NCHAR_CHARACTERSET                 AL16UTF16
```

If we don't find the WE8ISO8859P1 or AL16UTF16 values in our results, as seen in the previous example, we need to run the following queries within SQLPlus, which is an Oracle command-line utility:

```
SQL> SHUTDOWN;
SQL> STARTUP MOUNT;
SQL> ALTER SYSTEM ENABLE RESTRICTED SESSION;
SQL> ALTER SYSTEM SET JOB_QUEUE_PROCESSES=0;
```

```
SQL> ALTER DATABASE OPEN;

SQL> ALTER DATABASE CHARACTER SET INTERNAL_USE WE8ISO8859P1;

SQL> ALTER DATABASE NATIONAL CHARACTER SET INTERNAL_USE AL16UTF16;

SQL> SHUTDOWN IMMEDIATE;

SQL> STARTUP;
```

We should also address a security change in Oracle 10*g* R2 and later versions. Starting with this version, Oracle made changes which disabled some privileges for the CONNECT role. When getting ready to install or upgrade, we must run the following commands to allow Blackboard Learn to install properly:

```
sqlplus "/as sysdba"

SQL> @$ORACLE_HOME/rdbms/admin/rstrconn.sql

SQL> GRANT create session, create table TO CONNECT;

SQL> commit;

SQL> exit
```

We can remove these granted permissions after installing or upgrading Blackboard Learn if there are security concerns. When our Oracle installation ends, we should make sure that the database and Oracle listener are running. This should address most of the issues that Oracle could offer for our installation, but as always we should check the release notes for our version of Blackboard Learn. The release notes may show changes and further issues that we may need to address before our installation starts.

Installing a Microsoft SQL Server database

Our Microsoft SQL installation should be smoother in comparison to the one in Oracle. However, we do have a few areas where changes need to be made during our installation process. First, we need to make sure that the installation is at the root of the drive, such as C:\MS-SQL-SERVER. We should install the software as a local user and use Mixed Mode Security Authentication. This Mixed Mode will create a database administrator username, sa. We will have to create a password for this sa user and have this information available. Blackboard recommends that we use the default SQL Server instance name, but if you must change it, use only alphanumeric characters and make sure the instance name is not case sensitive. Once the installation is done, we need to make sure that we set the SQL Server Agent to start automatically:

1. Right-click on **Computer** and select **Manage**.

2. Within the Server Manager, click on **Configuration** and then click on **Services**.

3. Right-click on **SQL Server Agent** (instance name) and select **Properties**.

4. From the **Startup type** drop-down list, select **Automatic**.

5. Click on **OK**.

Now if we ever restart our server, the SQL Server Agent will start automatically. If we don't install our application server on the same machine as our database, we will have to install the Microsoft SQL Client tools on each application server separately.

Installing JDK

In *Chapter 1, Planning a Blackboard Learn Instance*, we discussed that Blackboard Learn runs on Tomcat, which uses Java to create the pages that users will see on their browser. Many times we hear the term Java being used in a variety of different places; in a discussion about desktops and laptops, servers, or even some electronic devices. So let's take a moment to understand what type of Java affects us and our Blackboard Learn environment. **Java Runtime Environment** (**JRE**) will normally be found installed on your desktop or laptop. It allows Java applets to run within a browser or a Java application on your device. JDK helps to create and compile Java applets.

Blackboard Learn can be very specific about which version of Java it uses, and most operating systems don't include the correct version of Java during the operating-system installation. Because of this, we will install JDK, which allows Blackboard Learn to create the pages and files we need.

First we must download the JDK software package for our operating system. Our release notes should tell us which version we need to install. You should find the JDK package by going to the Java SE Downloads website at `http://www.oracle.com/technetwork/java/javase/downloads/index.html`. In this case, we are downloading the latest version of Java SE7, which is **Java SE 7u17** (Update 17), as shown in the following screenshot.

Now we click on the JDK download image. On the JDK download page, we will need to accept the licensing agreement and download the JDK package appropriate to our operating system.

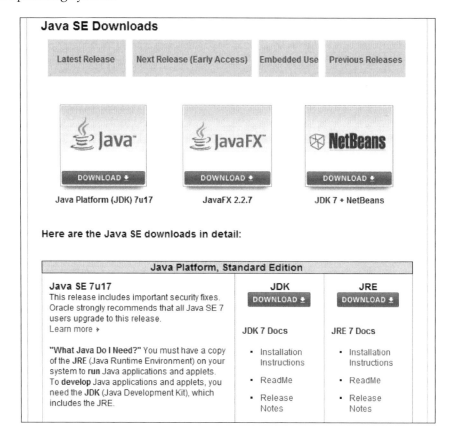

Once we have downloaded the appropriate version, we need to install JDK onto our application server. If we have more than one application server, we will need to install this same version on the others as well. If you are installing your Blackboard Learn instance on Linux, I would recommend the JDK RPM-based installation, since RPM is the base installation package for Red Hat Linux operating system.

Our installation of JDK should be standard on Linux and Windows, but we might want to change the installation location. For installations on Linux, we can install JDK at the location /usr/local/java/ while for installations on Windows, we must change its default location. Blackboard Learn Installer requires that the path must not have a whitespace in any folder name as this causes an issue when it's installed within the Program Files folder. Most administrators will create a folder at the root of the drive, such as C:\Java; this should be the only change you will need to make during this installation process.

Preparing a Windows Server environment

We need to get Windows Server ready for the Blackboard Learn installation process. Our first task is to set the JAVA_HOME environment variable within our application server. Here are some simple steps to set this variable to the location of your Java installation:

1. Right-click on **Computer** and select **Properties**.

2. Click on **Environment Variables** in the **Advanced** tab in **System Properties**.

3. In the **System variables** list, find **JAVA_HOME** and click on **Edit**. If **JAVA_HOME** doesn't exist in the **System variables** list, click on **New**. A new window will appear. The **Variable name** field should read JAVA_HOME.

4. Enter the full path to our JDK installation in the **Variable value** field, for example, C:\Java\jdk1.7.0_17\bin.

5. Click on **OK**.

The following screenshot illustrates these steps:

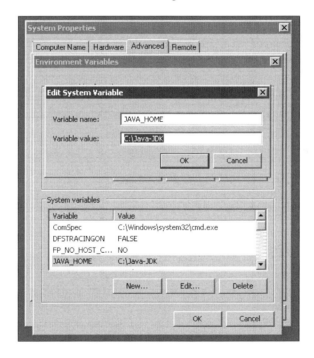

If we are installing Blackboard Learn on Windows Server 2008, we should refer to the Blackboard Learn document titled *Configuring Windows Server 2008 IIS 7 Roles and Features*. Other prior versions of Windows Server do not require this setup. The simple directions help make IIS 7 compatible with Blackboard Learn.

Now we need to create a domain user, which might require the help of your user administrator. This user allows the Blackboard Learn instance to use the same username on the different servers we might be using. In our case, the username has access to the application and database servers. This user will need to be placed in the Administrators group during the installation of Blackboard Learn. You should use this domain user when logging in to the application server to begin your Blackboard Learn installation and whenever you need to run any of the Blackboard services.

Preparing a Red Hat or Solaris server for Blackboard Learn

We need to prepare our Red Hat or Solaris server for our Blackboard Learn installation. These specific environments will require the installation of additional libraries, which include the following:

- apr-1.2.7.11.el5_3.1 (or possible newer version)
- e2fsprogs-libs-1.39-23.el5 (or possible newer version)
- gdbm-1.8.0-26.2.1 (or possible newer version)
- glibc-2.5-24 (or possible newer version)
- libaio-0.3.106-3.2 (or possible newer version)
- libgcc-4.1.2-46.el5 (or possible newer version)
- libstdc++-4.1.2-46.el5 (or possible newer version)

The Apache and Tomcat applications will be installed with our Blackboard instance. So we don't need to install these prior to Blackboard Learn Installer. Currently, Blackboard Learn installs Apache 1.3, which is no longer supported by its community. After the installation we can replace this version with Apache 2. We will discuss this in detail in *Chapter 9, Security, Reporting, and Configuration in Blackboard Learn*.

Next we need to create a user within our Red Hat or Solaris installation. The username must be called bbuser. This user must have permissions on the directory where we install blackboard (for example, /usr/local/blackboard). This username should also have a home directory such as /home/bbuser for Red Hat instances or /export/home/bbuser for Solaris instances.

Final preparations before installing

We need to make sure the clocks on our servers are synchronized. We should also set our clocks to the appropriate time zone for our users. Blackboard Learn allows users to disable tasks and content access based on the server time. We should set our server clocks to the location where most of our users reside to prevent any major issues.

We also need to make sure the ports that Blackboard Learn uses are open:

- Ports 80 and 443 are web server ports, both unsecure and secure
- Ports 8010 and 8011 allow users to connect to the collaboration server
- If you enable SSL encryption on your collaboration server, you will need to open port 8443 as well

Other points to consider before we start the installation process are as follows:

- Make sure you have not used an underscore in the name for any of the servers that will host Blackboard Learn
- Make sure your DNS server will resolve the server names used in your Blackboard Learn instance

Now we will move on to the installation of Blackboard Learn.

Installing the Blackboard Learn application

Let's start with the installation:

1. Blackboard Learn Installer can be started by opening a command window and going into the folder where our installer resides. The following commands are executed:

   Here's the command for Windows:

   ```
   C:\Bb-Installers>java -jar bb-as-windows-[version#].jar
   ```

   Here's the command for Linux and Solaris:

   ```
   root@blackboard:home/bbuser/bb-installers$ java -jar bb-as-
     unix-[version#].jar
   ```

So there are three different options. Windows users and those Linux and Solaris users who are logged in to a GUI desktop, will get the installer window. Linux and Solaris users who are using command line, will receive a text-based installer. This makes it sound like only Linux and Solaris users get the text-based installer, which isn't true. Please note that the text-based installer follows the same basic steps, and requires the same information. The first step in the installation process, as seen in the following screenshot, welcomes us to the installation process. As mentioned earlier in this chapter, it is recommended that we review the release notes for this version before we start the installation process.

2. The next item in the installation process asks us to point to the location where we would like to install our Blackboard Learn application. We can browse to that location, such as `F:\blackboard` for Windows, as shown in the following screenshot,, or `/usr/local/blackboard` for Linux and Solaris. Then submit it to the application. Remember that in our Linux and Solaris instances the `bbuser` username must have permissions to this directory.

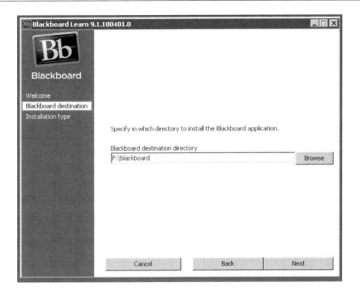

3. Now we need to select what type of installation we are completing on our server. Since this marks our first installation for this server environment, we will use the **Full installation** option, as shown in the following screenshot. If we plan to install additional servers, we will go to the other app servers and use the **Appserver-only installation** option. Either option will have the same steps; the **Appserver-only installation** option does not make changes to the database since that was completed in the full installation.

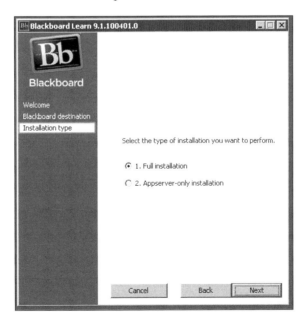

4. Moving ahead, we need to accept the software license agreement from Blackboard. The following screen will ask you to enter the location of the Blackboard Learn license file. You should have a copy of this from your account representative. It is an XML file that tells the software what items within the Blackboard Learn environment should be available in your instance. We simply find the file and direct the installer to it.

5. We now need to let the installer know where our version of JDK resides within the server for Blackboard Learn. The following screenshot illustrates this. Remember that in Windows instances we placed this into a folder at the root of the drive (C:\Java\jdk1.7.0_17\bin) or /usr/local/java/bin for Linux and Solaris instances.

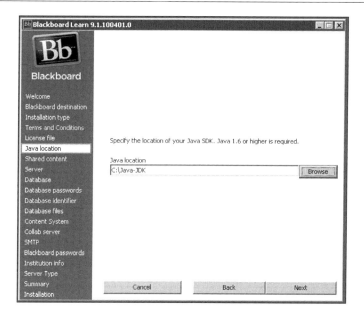

6. Now the installer asks us to specify where we want the content of our Blackboard Learn instance to reside, shown in the following screenshot. If we are installing a one- or two-server architecture, this can reside on a local drive, but we may also use a network drive on a storage area network (or SAN) device. However, if we have more than a two-server architecture, we must use a network drive.

7. After putting in our content location, we need to insert our server information. This should be the machine name of our server and the domain of our organization. Our example shows that the machine name is `blackboard` and the domain is `myorganization.com`. This is shown in the following screenshot. We also need to make sure we don't have other web services running on the server. We should make sure that IIS Web Services in Windows instances or Apache in Linux and Solaris instances are stopped.

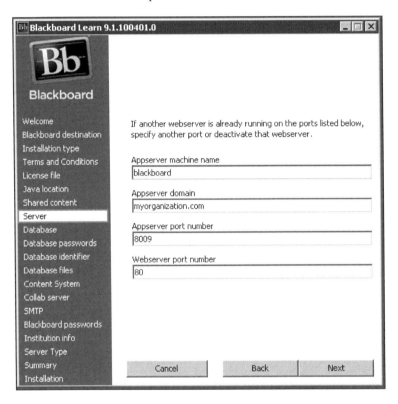

8. Following the information for our application server, we should get the information for our database server. If our instance is all on one server, the database hostname will be the same as our application server. If we have more than one, we should use the machine and domain name to connect the database hostname. Our example (shown in the following screenshot) shows the `Database hostname` as `bbdb.myorganization.com`. We can leave the `Database instance name` field blank if we use the default instance in Microsoft SQL Server. If we use Oracle or a different database instance, we must add this information. Finally we add the `Database administrator password`.

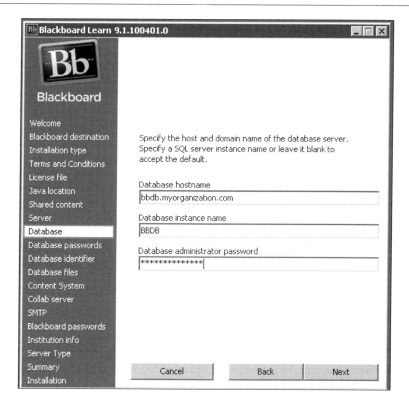

9. Next we need to set the passwords for our database.

10. The upcoming item requires us to set our database identifier. Most common installations will automatically fill this in with the default name BBLEARN. However, if there is already a database with that name, we must use a different identifier.

After setting the identifier, we need to point the installer to the directory or directories that will hold our data files and log files on the database server, as shown in the following screenshot. If we are completing a single server instance, these folders should be on our local drives. If we are installing an instance with two or more servers, we must type in the remote location of our directory or directories for the database data files and log files. We must make sure they are created before we start the installation process or our installation will fail. This is important; it has stumped a few administrators.

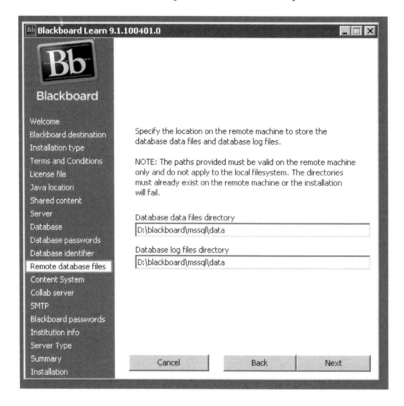

11. Our installation process asks us put in a password for the file storage database used if we have licensed the content system for our Blackboard Learn instance. We must also tell the installer the directory which will be home to the file storage system for the content system. This will normally be a directory that is inside our main content storage location. The following screenshot illustrates this:

12. The installer now asks for information about where our collaboration server, also called **Collab server**, will reside. In a one- or two-server instance, the collaboration server resides on the application server. If we plan to install more than one application server, we will need to decide which application server it will reside on or if it will be kept on its own standalone server. The collaboration server also uses the **TCP port number**, **8010** and the **HTTP port number**, **8011** by default (shown in the following screenshot). We should normally never have to change this for our instance.

13. The window, shown in the following screenshot, requests for the **SMTP server** of our organization. We need this information if we expect the instance to send e-mails to users about their courses on Blackboard Learn. We should speak with the administrator that supports our organization's e-mail. Our Blackboard Learn instance can send a large number of e-mails into the organization's e-mail server and we will need to make sure that e-mails from our instance are never labeled as spam.

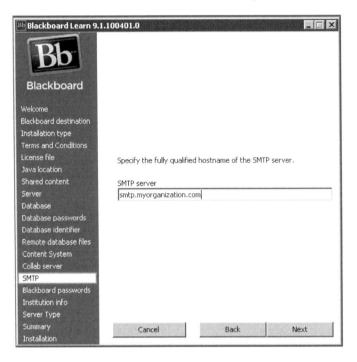

14. Next we must set up passwords for the administrator user, the integration service, and the Blackboard root administrator, as shown in the following screenshot. These should follow our organization's security policy, if one is available for administrator passwords and accounts. Once we create an additional system-administrator user, we can disable the administrator user account. Many organizations disable the administrator login because this account's username, administrator, is widely implemented and could be the starting point for a non-administrator to gain access to our entire system.

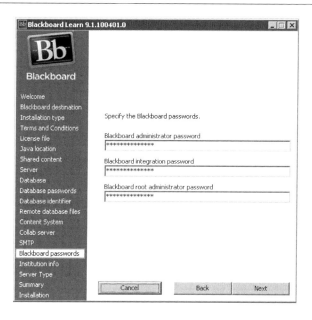

15. The last piece of information, which we type in now, gives our organizational data to the installer. When filling out the **Administrator name** and **Administrator email** fields (shown in the following screenshot), it should be noted that these will be displayed when e-mails are sent from our Blackboard Learn instance. Normally we can use a generic name and e-mail ID such as `Blackboard Administrator` and `blackboard@myorganization.com`. Fill out all the information and we move on.

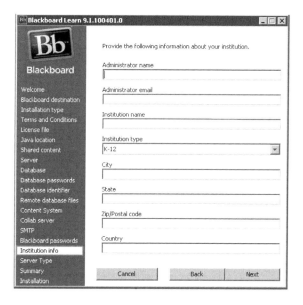

16. Our Blackboard Learn instance needs to be categorized into one of the many different server types. If we plan to use our server for developing training materials or building blocks for our organization, we can select Development from the **Server type** drop-down list, as shown in the following screenshot. If this server will be used for delivering courses to our users, we should classify it as **Production**. These choices, in the previous versions, are located within the `bb-config.properties` file and have had little impact on the functionality and integration options available. However, with the addition of cloud and mobile services, this information may be used to control different parts of our environment.

17. Great job so far. We have put all the information in to get our Blackboard Learn instance ready to install. We simply click on the **Next** button to start the process, as shown in the following screenshot:

18. As the installation begins, a text will appear wthin our installer as **checking the ports on the server**. Then it moves on to **moving files into the new locations**. Once that wraps up, the installer will show a bar moving across the screen. During this time the installer is creating the databases, database logins, and database items for our instance. This process can take several minutes, but at the end you will get a statement that the installation was successful or unsuccessful. If it is the latter case, go to the `logs` subdirectory of our `blackboard` folder and open the `bb-installer.log` file to review the process. If the issue isn't apparent within that log file, we need to contact Blackboard Support.

Wow, that was a lot of data we just went through. It can be a big task. When preparing to complete an installation process as tedious as this, I always recommend that the admins have a test environment to try it out in. It can make things go smoothly during a lengthy installation process. Take a deep breath and review any of the steps we just discussed, if needed. Our next stop takes us on the upgrade of a Blackboard Learn instance.

Upgrading our Blackboard Learn instance

Blackboard always seems to be updating its Learn environments, either because of the issues it finds in the code, or because of the enhancement requests made from within the company or by the user community. Administrators face the task of upgrading the Blackboard Learn instances to meet the needs of its users. This section will guide you through the steps to upgrade a Blackboard Learn instance. Now we should note that before starting an upgrade, a backup of the current instance should be available, if for some reason there is a failure or corruption. We will cover these operations in *Chapter 12, Logs, Troubleshooting, and Disaster Recovery in Blackboard Learn*.

Before we move ahead, we should discuss any unique changes that we may have done. Items such as a customized login page, custom themes, custom brands, configuration files, and other changes we may have made to our instance could be overwritten during the installation process. We should back up these documents off our server to ensure we don't lose our work. We will talk about how we back up some of these files in *Chapter 3, Setting Up and Customizing Blackboard Learn*.

The first few steps in the upgrading process mirror the installation steps we covered in the previous section. The change comes after we select where our Blackboard Learn instance should be installed. The installer finds the config directory and locates our bb-config.properties file, which holds all our installation information. The installer gives us many options, including the ability to upgrade Blackboard Learn, or just our app server; put in a new license file; get a pre-upgrade change report; and uninstall Blackboard Learn. Perform the following steps to accomplish the upgrading process:

1. Select the first option, **Upgrade Blackboard Learn**. This is shown in the following screenshot:

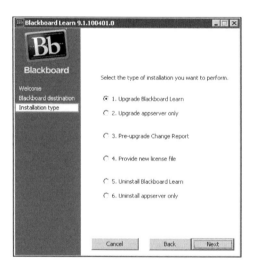

2. Next the installer presents the changes that will be made during the upgrade process. We click on the **Next** button and the installer begins, as shown in the following screenshot:

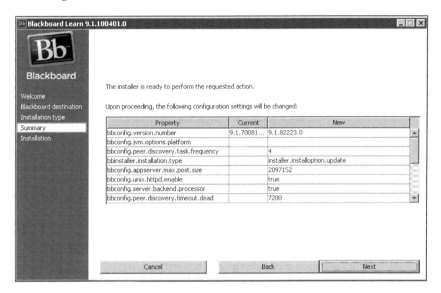

3. The installer will move through its processes and we should get a confirmation that the upgrade was successful or unsuccessful. If it was unsuccessful, review the steps and try again. If that does not fix our instance, we should contact Blackboard Support.

Managing Blackboard Learn services

Now we have completed the installation or upgrade of our Blackboard Learn instance. Blackboard has on-board ability to manage its services. These allow you to control when Bb-Tomcat, Bb-Collab, and the web service (either Apache or IIS) are available to users. These three services start the different components we mentioned in *Chapter 1, Planning a Blackboard Learn Instance*. For clarification, Bb-Tomcat is the service that oversees the starting and stopping of the Tomcat server and Bb-Collab controls the collaboration server. The utilities that we will discuss should be run by the user that we created during the installation of our instance. The two biggest options we need to discuss would be ServiceController and PushConfigUpdates.

The ServiceController utility available to administrators resides in the tools\ admin subfolder of the Blackboard home folder. If you are working on an application server, such as making changes or fixing a bug, this will stop users from being able to access the server. We can consider this option as similar to putting our instance into maintenance mode. This utility is a .bat file for Windows users and a .sh file for Linux and Solaris users. It allows users to stop, start, and restart Bb-Tomcat, Bb-Collab, and the web service, using arguments. Here are some examples showing how to use the utility:

- ServiceController.bat services.stop: This argument stops the Blackboard services currently running.

- ServiceController.sh services.start: This argument starts the Blackboard services currently stopped.

- ServiceController.bat services.restart: This argument stops the Blackboard services currently running, then starts them back.

The PushConfigUpdates utility available to administrators resides in the same location (the tools\admin subfolder) as its sibling, the ServiceController utility. While it has parallels to the ServiceController utility, it will push the updated files to the Blackboard services. An example would be updating the authentication. properties file to add a new server. After we have made the changes to the file on all the affected servers, we must run the PushConfigUpdates utility on each one to have Blackboard Learn load our new file for its use. We may also run this after making changes to the server to fix issues and improve performance. As with the ServiceController utility, the .bat file is available for Windows instances and the .sh file is available for Linux and Solaris instances.

These two utilities only control the services on each server. If we have multiple application servers, we must run the utility on each server. This allows the other application server to serve user requests, while we take one down and address the issue found. Then run our utility to make that server available to users once the services are back up and running. Then we follow the same steps for the other server or servers. This is commonly known as a rolling restart.

The Blackboard Learn Patch Utility tool

Most experienced administrators know that any piece of software or hardware will have bugs. Operating systems use update managers to fix issues and hardware manufacturers to create firmware updates for their products. Blackboard uses a software it calls **Blackboard Learn Patch Utility**, to apply patches within different Blackboard Learn instances. Patches come from Blackboard Support to fix major issues, which cannot wait for a service pack or hot fix, that customers face. These patches fall into different categories. Patches fix critical Blackboard Learn issues that are normally built for individual issues for specific organizations. Patch Sets put numerous patches together and, unlike a single patch, receive more testing to fix common issues that customers report. Security Update patches specifically fix security issues reported in a security bulletin by Blackboard. Utility patches fix database, support scripts, and other utilities built into Blackboard Learn. This utility allows us to fix issues while not having to go deep into the server to make those changes to the files. Let's review the utility.

Getting Blackboard Learn Patch Utility

The Blackboard Learn Patch Utility tool doesn't come preinstalled with our Blackboard Learn environment. We have two options on how to get the Patch Utility tool for our Blackboard Learn environment. We can download a ZIP file, which contains the utility and its supporting files, and unzip it within each of our application servers. However most administrators use the second option, which is installing and enabling the utility as a building block from the Blackboard Extensions catalog. This building block puts the patch utility commands within the `tools/ admin` subdirectory, such as the `ServiceController` and `PushConfigUpdates` commands. We will learn more about building blocks, the Blackboard Extensions catalog, and installing a building block, in *Chapter 11, Implementing Building Blocks in Blackboard Learn*.

Getting Blackboard patches

The patches used for the Blackboard Learn Patch Utility tool normally come from Blackboard Support in two ways. The tool can download these patches from a secure online repository that Blackboard Support keeps up to date, or Blackboard Support will attach a patch to an open support ticket. This patch file must be located on the server for the utility to install it. Many times we will learn about patch availability via the **Software Update** module within the **Administrator** panel. Any patch, (such as the Security Update patches and Patch Sets) will be displayed when we click on the icon titled **Blackboard Learn Updates Available** (shown in the following screenshot) to see what patches may be available. This area will allow us to download the patch as well; however, we must still run the utility from the command line to apply it.

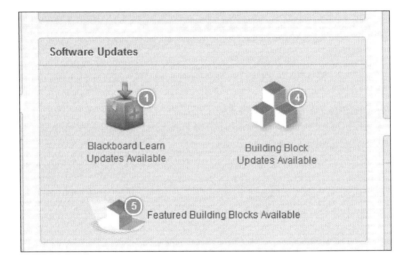

Managing Blackboard patches with the Blackboard Learn Patch Utility tool

Now that we understand the background and usage of the Patch Utility tool, we should review with an example how to use it within our instance. After opening a ticket with Blackboard Support about an issue we have found with our Blackboard Learn instance, Support tells us that the issue is resolved in the patch LRNSI-123456, which is available. We can download the patch file using the utility, or we can download the patch file attached to our open support ticket. If we download the patch file using the utility, we will need to run the following command from the directory where the patch utility is installed, which is normally in the subfolder tools/admin of the Blackboard home folder:

```
/filepath/bbpatch.sh download LRNSI-123456
```

If we decide to download the file, we will need to place it into a folder on the server. In this case we can use `bbpatches` as the folder name.

When applying some patches, it might be important to know what changes will be made for your documentation. The utility allows this by using the `describe` action:

```
C:/filepath/bbpatch.bat describe C:/bbpatches/LRNSI-123456.bbp
```

This action will display information similar to the previous example:

```
Identifier : AS-162070

Description : Text and images are displayed distorted while navigating
with IE9 and Arabic

Language Pack

Resolves bugs : AS-162027

Date built : 2011-07-12 15:46:53 +0100

Compatible with : 9.1.60230.0

Platform : Any

File operations:

Update frameset_jsp.class -> webapps/portal/WEB-INF/classes/blackboard/
web/frameset_jsp.class

Update frameset_jsp.class ->

webapps/searchwidgets/WEB-INF/classes/blackboard/web/course/frameset_jsp.
class

Update frameset_jsp.class ->

webapps/searchwidgets/WEB-INF/classes/blackboard/web/ext/frameset_jsp.
class

Update subtabFrame_jsp.class ->

webapps/portal/WEB-INF/classes/blackboard/web/portal_005fjsp/layout/
subtabFrame_jsp.class

Update viewPortfolio_jsp.class ->

webapps/bbcms/WEB-INF/classes/blackboard/web/portfolio/viewPortfolio_jsp.
class

Update courseFrameset_jsp.class ->

webapps/blackboard/WEB-INF/classes/blackboard/web/course/courseFrameset_
jsp.class

Update downloadWrapper_jsp.class ->

webapps/blackboard/WEB-INF/classes/blackboard/web/content/
downloadWrapper_jsp.class
```

```
Update integrationFrameWrapper_jsp.class ->
```

```
webapps/xythoswfs/WEB-INF/classes/blackboard/web/IntegrationFilePicker/
integrationFrameWrapper_jsp.class
```

```
Update filesframeset_jsp.class ->
```

```
webapps/xythoswfs/WEB-INF/classes/blackboard/web/filesframeset_jsp.class
```

```
Update gradecenter_005fframeset_jsp.class ->
```

```
webapps/gradebook/WEB-INF/classes/blackboard/web/gradebook2/instructor/
gradecenter_005fframeset_jsp.class
```

```
Update contentWrapper_jsp.class ->
```

```
webapps/blackboard/WEB-INF/classes/blackboard/web/content/contentWrapper_
jsp.class
```

```
Update frameset_jsp.class ->
```

```
webapps/searchwidgets/WEB-INF/classes/blackboard/web/user/frameset_jsp.
class
```

```
Package deployment guidance:
```

```
Package scope: Host-only. Apply/rollback on all hosts
```

```
Downtime requirement: This host. Stop application before apply and
rollback on this host
```

This displays which specific files will be affected by the application of the patch, and also shares if the patch is for a specific version or platform, and how much downtime will be required when it is applied. If we have made changes to any files to address issues within our organization, they could be removed if the patch is replacing a file that we have edited. Make sure that you carefully review this information if you have done so.

We now know what is going to be changed when we apply our patch. It's now time to apply it to our Blackboard Learn instance. This requires us to use the apply action with our bbpatch utility. When you apply a local patch file, simply use the following command:

```
C:/filepath/bbpatch.bat apply C:/bbpatches/LRNSI-123456.bbp
```

When applying a patch file that you downloaded using the patch repository, you will run the following command:

```
/filepath/bbpatch.bat apply LRNSI-123456
```

This command will load the patch that you have in a predefined folder. You have the following two actions that you can use with this command:

- `-f, --force`: This command action removes any other patches that conflict with the one you are currently installing.
- `-s, --silent`: This command action stops any prompts for confirmation while installing this patch.

Sometimes we may apply a patch, then learn that it causes more issues than it fixes. This kind of situation can happen, so we have the `rollback` command in the Patch Utility tool, which allows us to remove a patch we applied previously. This command looks like the following:

```
C:/filepath/bbpatch.bat rollback LRNSI-123456
```

We can use the `--silent` option with the `rollback` option as well.

If we ever forget what patches we have installed onto our Blackboard Learn instance, we can use the `list` action to find out exactly what patches have been installed and when. Just use the following command:

```
/filepath/bbpatch.bat list
```

This action will display something similar to the following on the screen:

```
Blackboard Learn, Version 9.1.60230.0, C:\blackboard

Packages installed on this host:

Identifier Date Installed          Date Built            Bugs
  Resolved

AS-163058  2011-08-11 15:37:43 +0100 2011-08-09 01:00:16 +0100 AS-
  148787

AS-163080  2011-08-11 15:31:47 +0100 2011-08-08 20:28:57 +0100 AS-
  156226

Packages installed globally:

Identifier Date Installed          Date Built            Bugs
  Resolved

AS-162340  2011-08-11 15:32:31 +0100 2011-07-12 18:28:07 +0100 AS-
  157908
```

This command comes with the following two options:

- `-a, --all`: This option shows the details for all Blackboard Learn hosts
- `-v, --verbose`: This option will display additional information about the patches that have been applied

Summary

We started this chapter by talking about the construction of our virtual community by building our Blackboard Learn instance. Like any big construction project, we had to spend a lot of time getting the site ready before starting the building of our Blackboard Learn instance. We also used the information and resources of our database, operating systems, and e-mail systems to complete our project. We also reviewed how to keep our system up and running, and deploy patches and upgrades as well.

We might be done with the construction, but our virtual community needs to be given some flair. Our next chapter moves into the design and appearance of our virtual community to its residents. So get out your hex colors and background designs. We are going to learn how to make our Blackboard Learn instance shine.

3
Setting Up and Customizing Blackboard Learn

If we put down this book for a moment and think about the buildings and homes that surround the place where we currently are, we probably would find that the home or building next door isn't the same as the one a few blocks or miles away. It might be the color, the coverings, the windows, or the look of each one. They all have something that makes them unique over the ones to the left and right of them. Our virtual community is the same way and we need to make our Blackboard Learn instance unique to our users' needs along with creating the welcoming and informative atmosphere that we want to convey to our users.

In this chapter we are going to learn how we can do this—by changing the theme, branding, login page, and many other options—to make our Blackboard Learn instance a home sweet home for our virtual community.

Branding Blackboard Learn

For those of us who have never studied marketing in school, **branding** describes a specific design, based on layout, fonts, and colors, that make something unique. A good example would be when you see a national flag. The colors and layout of the flag quickly set your expectations without saying a word. Many organizations have very specific branding for their online presence—whether it's a website or a Facebook page. Just use a search engine to find the Blackboard Learn login pages from organizations around the world. In the result, we can see how these organizations brand the entry point for their Blackboard Learn environments. We should make sure we include our organization's marketing or communications department in the branding discussions. These departments have experienced members branding the organization's online presence, and can work with us to bring that branding into our Blackboard Learn environment.

The branding work we will do in this chapter will require us to use our web-development skills—specifically, editing **cascading style sheets (CSS)** and HTML files using any familiar text editor or software to edit CSS and HTML files.

Blackboard Learn offers multiple ways to brand the instance. We can use images to share our logo and other organizational branding, develop themes that mimic the look and feel of other websites, and change the color palette that users see on a regular basis. Let's begin by looking at a basic **landing page** in Blackboard Learn and understand its different parts.

Many Blackboard Learn administrators use the term landing page to describe the first page a user sees after logging in to the Blackboard Learn environment. Here you can see a default layout which shows a small area at the top of the webpage. This area, called the **Header** (marked in the next screenshot), will normally show the user the organization's logo, possibly a background image or color, and tabs to access other pages within Blackboard Learn. This header page appears virtually the same to all users and offers a consistent navigational area for the user. This area also offers links to help and allows the user to log out of the Blackboard Learn environment.

The other part of the webpage is called the **Content Frame** (marked in the following screenshot). It is appropriately named, because the content that we as administrators, along with users, will interact with, resides here. We should remember these definitions, as we work to make changes to our Blackboard Learn instance's look and feel. We can see the header and the content frame in the following screenshot:

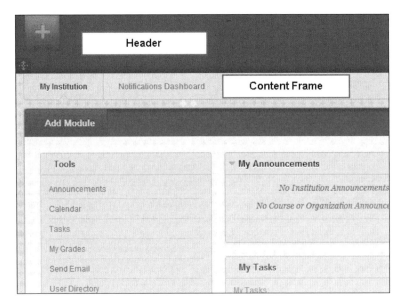

While we are discussing the different parts of our Blackboard Learn environment, let's review how to navigate it.

 Some of the options we will discuss in this chapter may be available only to the organizations that license the Blackboard Community system. This system resides within Blackboard Learn and gives administrators additional tools to support organizations and the institutional community as a whole. These may include detailed customizations and controls, however, organizations that don't have this system will find themselves still able to brand their Blackboard Learn environment.

Blackboard Learn themes

The first place to start our discussion about branding Blackboard Learn would be on the **System Admin** tab. Under the **Communities** section of the **Administrator** panel we find many options, but we will start with **Brands and Themes**. First let's look at the **Theme and Palette Catalog** page.

The term **theme** in Blackboard Learn describes the cascading style sheets, images, and other files that create the look and functional environment of our Blackboard Learn instance. Blackboard offers many different themes installed by default that capture the look and feel of other **learning management systems (LMS)** that the organizations may have used previously. One of the best ways to start thinking about how we might want to customize our theme is by looking at the themes built into the Blackboard Learn environment by default.

In the previous screenshot, we can see within the **Theme and Palette Catalog** area a list of different built-in themes. These themes give us some great examples of how we can change our Blackboard Learn environment. However, we may not want to deploy each of these themes within our instance just to view the theme itself. We can see an example of each of them by hovering over the theme name and clicking on the small chevron that appears to the right of our theme's title. If we click on the chevron, an action menu appears and we can either **Preview** or **Download** the selected theme as seen in the following screenshot. In this example, let's select the **Preview** option.

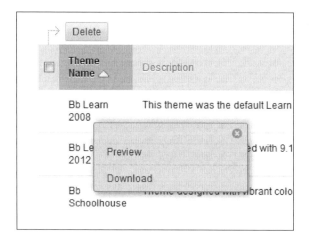

The **Preview** option will display the layout and the default color scheme for our selected theme. Within this preview page, we can see how this theme displays navigation, data collection, course menus, and inventory lists (or item lists). Each theme will vary, but keep the same layout design. We can see the similarities and differences between the Bb Schoolhouse theme and our current one in the following screenshot:

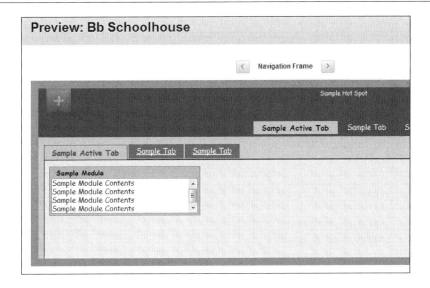

Blackboard Learn color palettes

We have now had the chance to review the themes that come with Blackboard Learn. We also have another piece of the branding puzzle. Color palettes control how pages and modules look within our environment. We can preview all the built-in color palettes by going back to the **Theme and Palette Catalog** page and clicking on the **Manage Color Palettes** button in the upper-right corner of the page. This takes us to the **Color Palettes** page, where we find 15 different color palettes available to us. As shown in the following screenshot, we can see our options, which are similar to those we found for themes, within this page. We can **Download** each of the color palettes and also see a preview within our environment. At the top of the page, we have the ability to create a color palette by clicking on the **Create Color Palette** button.

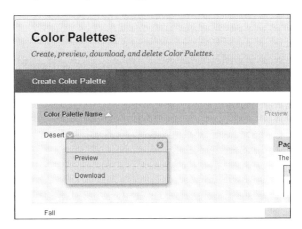

Some Blackboard Learn administrators will want to make minor changes to customize their instance's brand while some may want to make major changes by editing the theme itself. Many of the minor changes can be made using the options we have within our environment; however, some will require advanced web-development skills. Let's look at how we can change our brand using the tools within Blackboard Learn.

Basic branding within Blackboard Learn

Let's learn about the ways by which we can customize our brand within Blackboard Learn. Back on the **Brands and Themes** page, click on the **Customize Default Brand** option, shown in the following screenshot:

The **Customize Default Brand** page appears with three different tabs. Let's learn about each of them. Our initial tab, titled **Themes and Colors**, gives us the ability to select one of the themes and color palettes we saw in our previous discussions. This page, shown in the following screenshot, also provides us the ability to preview and download both options as well.

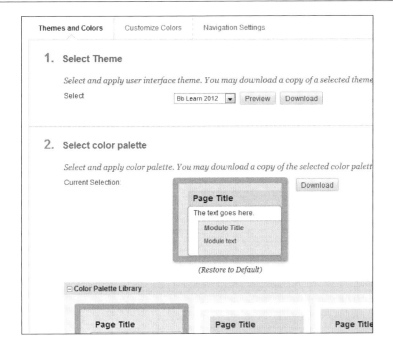

Let's move on to the next tab, **Customize Colors**. This tab really should be called Customize Color Palette, because any changes you make here will override the color palette we selected on the **Themes and Colors** tab. The **Top Frame** section sets how elements appear within the header of the Blackboard Learn website. As seen in the following screenshot, we can set three different options:

- **Background Color**: This option sets the background color of our header
- **Text Color**: Here we can select the color of any text that appears within the heade.
- **Background Image**: If we have an image that we want to be our header background, we can click on the **Browse** button and upload the image from our computer

If we wish to change the top frame's background color, simply click on the chevron to the right of the color block. We then see our menu of colors, demonstrated in the following screenshot. We can select a color by simply clicking on one of them. If we want to be more exact in our choice, we have the ability to put in the HEX color value at the top and then click on **Preview**. **HEX color** is a six-digit number preceded by a # sign that tells our browser what color should be displayed. We then see the color we have selected in the **Color Preview** area. Once we have found the right color, just click on **Apply**, and that element is set.

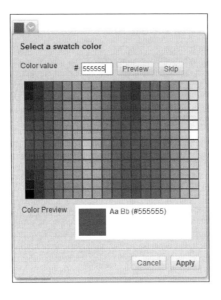

Customizing the header

We should be aware that it is important to have contrasting colors between the background and the text in this area. A text color that blends into the background will make the text and the links very difficult for the users to see.

If we decide to upload an image for our background, make sure to test it. If we plan to put text or images into our background banner, we should remember the top frame is about 90 pixels in height. If we use a background image, we must make sure that we understand the top frame's constraints.

Our next set of options deals with the tabs we find within the header. The tabs at the top give us options to colorize and control how the tabs in the top frame look. Each tab is classified as either active or not active. If we look at the tabs in the following screenshot, we see the **System Admin** tab is **Active** — this means we are currently working within that tab, and not within the other tabs, which makes them **Inactive**.

The following screenshot shows the elements we can control in the **System Admin** tab:

Let's have a look at each of these options:

- **Background Color**: This option sets the background color for inactive tabs
- **Text Color**: Our inactive tab titles will appear in this color
- **Active Tab Color**: We can give the active tab a different color than the inactive tabs
- **Active Tab Text Color**: This option gives us the ability to have a different text color for the tab we are currently on

We've dealt with the elements within the header or top frame, now we can deal with the elements within the content frame. Our first elements deal with the **Content Frame** (marked in the following screenshot) itself, by setting the **Background Color** and **Text Color** options. We can also set a background image but be aware that the image will be repeated across and down each content frame. So let's review our options:

- **Background Color**: This option sets the background color of our content frame
- **Text Color**: Here we can select the color of our content-frame text

- **Background Image**: If we have an image that we want as our content-frame background, we can click on the **Browse** button and upload the image from our computer

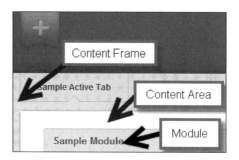

The next element is the **Content Area**, marked in the previous screenshot. Think about this as setting what color paper you will use in your printer. It could be white, off white, or grey, but make sure that the background color and the text color contrast one another. We can also set a background image that you may want to experiment with; however, some patterns might make it difficult for users to read the content text on top of it. The following list described the options available for the content area:

- **Background Color**: This option enables us to change the color of our content-area background

- **Text Color**: This option controls the color of our text within the content area

- **Background Image**: Using this option, we can set an image to be the background for our content area by clicking on the **Browse** button and uploading the image from our computer

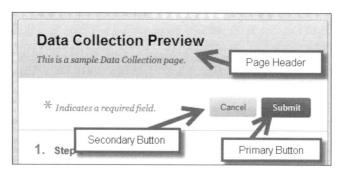

The top part of the content area is called the **Page Header** (marked in the previous screenshot), which displays the title and many helpful directions. As in the content area, we have the options to change the background to a color or to an image along with changing the text color.

This is shown in the following screenshot:

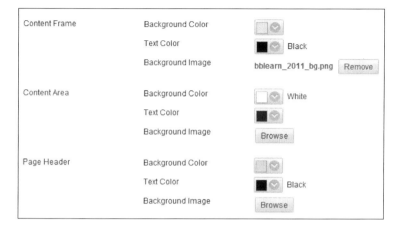

Let's look at the options available to us in detail:

- **Background Color**: This option controls the background color for every page header within our Blackboard Learn environment.

- **Text Color**: This option enables us to change the text color within the page header.

- **Background Image**: Using this option, an image can be uploaded; it will be the background within the page header. We upload the image by clicking on the **Browse** button and upload the image from our computer.

The next elements we find are the **Primary Buttons** and **Secondary Buttons** elements. As we saw in the screenshot with the page header **Data Collection Preview**, primary buttons are normally buttons that are committing or starting a process. An example of primary button would be the Submit button. A secondary button is an additional option. An example of this would be the Cancel button. As seen in the following screenshot, both button elements offer the ability to change the background and text colors:

Let's look at the options here:

- **Primary Buttons**:
  - ○ **Background Color**: This option sets the background color for every primary button within our Blackboard Learn environment
  - ○ **Text Color**: This option sets the text color for every primary button

- **Secondary Buttons**:
  - ○ **Background Color**: This option sets the background color for our secondary buttons
  - ○ **Text Color**: The color we select in this option will be the text color for all the secondary buttons within our environment

The **Module** element is the last configurable option on this page. Modules are the small window-like boxes that reside within our main landing page and other locations in Blackboard Learn. We can control the **Title Color**, **Title Text Color**, **Background Color**, **Text Color**, and **Border Color**, as shown in the following screenshot:

The Module element has the following options:

- **Title Color**: This option sets the background color of the module title
- **Title Text Color**: Our selection sets the text color within the module title
- **Background Color**: This setting changes the the background color of the module body
- **Text Color**: The color of text within every module is controlled by this option
- **Border Color**: The outline color of every module will be set by this selection

After we have made these changes, we can immediately review what our changes will look like without applying them to the entire instance. We do this by clicking on the **Preview Pane** button in the right-hand corner of the page. The top of our page expands and we see our proposed changes along with the buttons to see the different page types, as shown in the following screenshot:

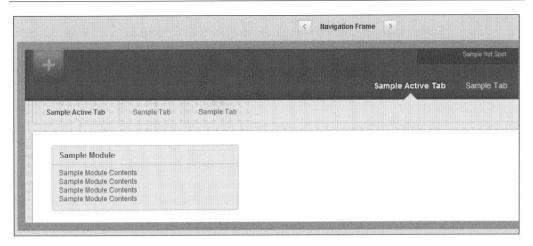

We can also reset our changes back to the defaults by clicking on the **Reset Custom Colors** button as seen in the following screenshot. If we like the changes we make, we can also save them as a new color palette by checking the checkbox beside **Save as New Color Palette**. If we check that checkbox, we must add a **Palette Name**, which will be displayed, and a **Reference Name** for internal use within our Blackboard Learn environment.

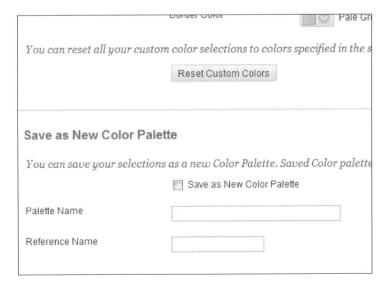

Our final tab reviews the options for the navigation settings with our Blackboard Learn environment. This area allows us to change the navigational elements of Blackboard Learn. Our first option gives us the ability to stylize and align the tabs that appear in the header frame of our instance. We can set how the tabs will appear in most browsers by setting the **Tab Style** option. However, Internet Explorer will display the tabs with square corners no matter what we set. A sample of some of the tab options are shown in the following screenshot:

The **Tab Alignment** option sets where our tabs appear within the header area, that is, whether on the left, right, or center. As seen in the following screenshot, we select our tab options by selecting the radio button beside our preferred option:

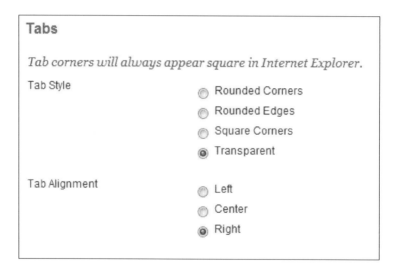

Our next navigational item sets the size of the header, also called **Top Frame**. The header has two sizes, which are referenced as large and small. The following screenshot shows we can select to use either the small or the large frame at all times, or use the large frame at all times except when we are accessing a course within the content area:

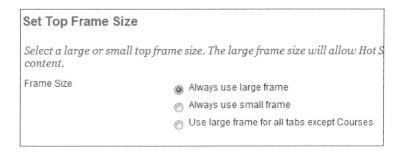

The next option configures the banner image. This image will be displayed on the left side of the header. In our earlier screenshots, we can see the default banner image, which is a teal graphic with a centered **+** (plus) symbol. This image is linkable, which allows users to click on the image and be taken to a website we specify. If we do add a banner image, we should also fill in the **Alt Text for Banner Image** field, shown in the following screenshot, to describe our banner image. Some administrators that use header background images will create a transparent GIF image. This allows them to make a part of the background image linkable.

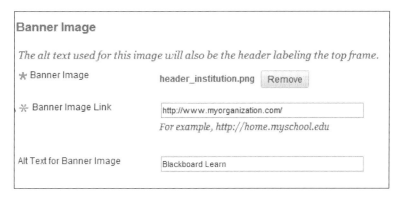

If we look in the header area, we may find our name along with some icons. This icon set corresponds to different links (from left to right): the home page, the support page, and logout. These are shown in the following screenshot:

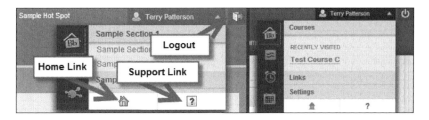

Some themes allow us to change the icon sets. We also have the ability to set the websites when users click on the home or support icon. We can set our support link to go either to a custom website or webpage, or Blackboards default help website, `http://help.blackboard.com/`. This is shown in the following screenshot:

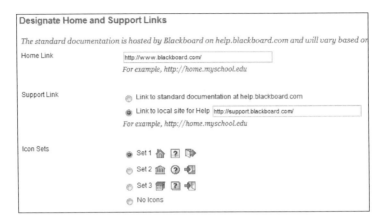

The next option affects those institutions that have licensed the Blackboard Community system. The **Direct Access Tab and Module Content** window (such as the Login tab and module) will normally appear to a specific role. By default, this is **Guest** (shown in the following screenshot), but here we have the ability to change the **Institution Role**.

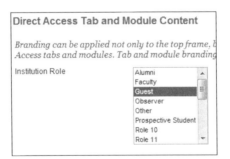

Our last element sets how the course name in each course or organization shell will be displayed. We can select the radio buttons for **Show Course Name**, **Show Course ID**, **Show Course Name followed by Course ID**, and **Show Course ID followed by Course Name**, to let users see the respective things. We haven't discussed the differences between course name and course ID, but we will, in our next chapter. Once we understand this, we can make this decision. We can also reset our navigation settings by clicking on the **Reset Navigation Settings** button.

This is shown in the following screenshot:

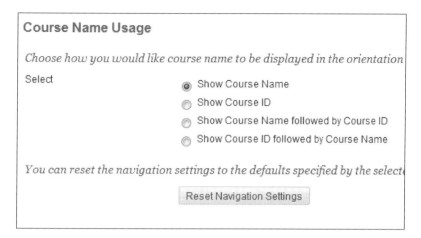

Once we have made the changes, we can click on **Apply All Changes**. Before we apply the changes, we can see what our changes look like by clicking on the **Preview Pane** button at the top of the content page. Even if we don't preview our changes with the **Preview Pane** button, when we apply the changes, we will see a preview pane to review them before submission. We also have the option to **Go Back** or **Cancel** all these changes entirely, as shown in the following screenshot:

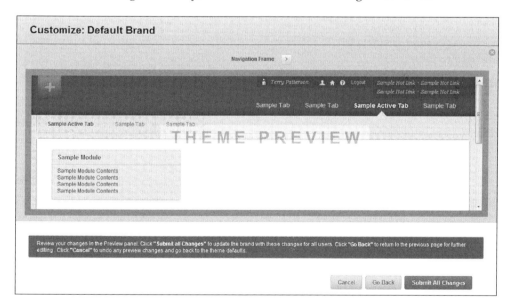

Advanced branding of our Blackboard Learn instance

As we just discussed, we have the ability to make changes to the branding used in our Blackboard Learn instance. These tools give administrators like us the basic tools to give our instance a custom look and feel. However, if we have some experience with CSS, Blackboard offers the ability to do more advanced styling to our instance.

If we want to do some advanced styling, it will require us to download the theme we want to customize and re-upload it. Let's discuss this first step and learn how to download a theme.

When we discussed the ability to preview a theme earlier, that menu gave us the option to download the selected theme. Let's get back to this location by moving our mouse pointer over the theme name, and click on the chevron. Here we find the menu once again; now click on the **Download** option. Once we click on it, our browser will download a compressed (.zip) file to our local computer. Once we decide where to save the file, the download starts and we find our ZIP file, such as the as_2012.zip file saved on our local computer, as seen in the following screenshot:

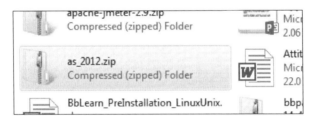

Now that we have understood the steps to download a theme from our Blackboard Learn instance, let's learn about some of the CSS files within the zipped file. When it is unzipped, we find several different cascading style sheets. Each sheet helps to stylize a different part of our Blackboard Learn instance. Here are some of the files we might find, along with how each file corresponds to our instance:

- assessment.css: This style sheet controls how tests and surveys are displayed in our Blackboard Learn instance.
- core.css: Administrators and developers should avoid making changes to this file unless told to do so by Blackboard Support. This controls the basic display settings within Blackboard Learn.

- `external.css`: This sheet helps to style the on-demand module that users can view.

- `gradebook.css`: As the name implies, changes within this sheet will affect the look of the Grade Center in Blackboard courses and organizations.

- `interactive.css`: We can change the look and feel of blogs, discussion boards, and wikis within this style sheet.

- `login.css`: This file gives use the ability to enhance the look and feel of our login page. We will discuss more about the login page later in this chapter.

- `outcomes.css`: If you have the Blackboard Outcomes system, this sheet will give you styling control over those components.

- `sp6.css` and `sp8.css`: These two style sheets deal with the changes made in Service Pack 6 (`sp6.css`) and Service Pack 8 (`sp8.css`).

- `theme.css`: Instead of calling each CSS file when needed, Blackboard's development team created this style sheet to call all the other style sheets.

- `theme_rtl.css`: This file sets style formats for those languages that require right to left justification.

- `theme_specific.css`: While each theme controls the same basic items, there are some specific enhancements used; those are listed in this file.

- `wizard.css`: Blackboard offers several different "wizards" that guide the users through different processes. This sheet controls this styling and formatting.

Different themes may have different files, so we shouldn't be surprised if there are additional files. We also need to remember that the changes made in these style sheets can create major issues if we don't test the themes before putting them into production. Upgrades can also cause issues with edited themes. Until recent versions, Blackboard would provide administrators a ZIP file that would explain any changes between the different versions. This information would be found in the same area where we would find the release notes; however, Blackboard Inc. no longer posts this information.

Customizing the Blackboard login page

So we have reviewed the branding options within our Blackboard Learn environment. We changed the look and feel of our Blackboard Learn instance, but we have an additional place to apply our branding—the application's login page.

Earlier we learned that if we are a licensed user of the Blackboard Community system, we are allowed direct access. If the **Direct Access** tab is on, a user who hasn't logged in will see a page with tabs and modules with the ability to log in. This differs from the default login or gateway page in Blackboard Learn. In the following screenshot, we can see a comparison of the two different options side by side. We can configure the settings how users will log in to our Blackboard Learn environment within the **Gateway Options** area under the **Security** module on the **System Admin** tab. If we don't have Blackboard Community we will be directed to the gateway page by default.

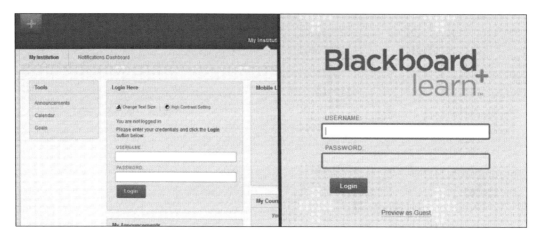

The **Login Page** (also called gateway page) is pretty plain by default. However, we might want to put information on this page. Some administrators put links to help resources, access to tutorial videos, live chat options, request forms, and so on. We could also add text to explain planned downtimes or performance issues. Under the **Brands and Themes** area we were in earlier, click on the **Customize Login Page** link. In the following screenshot, we see the options within our page—which are to use the **Default Login Page** (under **Use System Default**), or **Upload Custom Page** (under **Use Custom Page**). Before we upload a customized login page, we need to create one. Our best option would be to click on the **Download** button and use the default login page to start creating one.

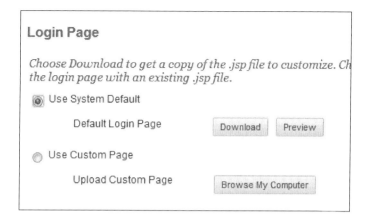

We can use our HTML coding skills or a website developer, to create a login page that meets our branding found on our organization's other websites. To do this, we need to understand what elements and guidelines Blackboard requires in the login page.

Some tag elements in the login page begin with bbNG:. These elements tell us that this is a Blackboard-created element. The first tag element we run into is bbNG:genericPage, which is a standard wrapping element for all pages in Blackboard. Blackboard recommends keeping this tag in place for the page; it should not interfere with the rest of the page.

The login page uses multiple cascading style sheets to set its look and functionality. We can add our own custom style tags into the page by using the bbNG:cssBlock tag. It is recommended that you put your CSS styling into this area and not direct it to another page.

The other tag that we will see in the login page is loginUI. This tag refers to the different parts of the login page that will need to be displayed. We should review each of these:

- loginUI:accessibility: This tag will display the text resizing and high contrast options that are present on the login page.

- `loginUI:localPicker`: We may allow our users to use different languages to interact with our Blackboard Learn instance. This tag allows the user to see the login page in a different language. Beware that this only changes the Blackboard-created content on the webpage. Any content placed there by us or the web developer will not change. We will learn more about how Blackboard interacts with different languages in *Chapter 8, Tools and Utilities in Blackboard Learn*.

- `loginUI:errorMessage`: If a user tries to log in with an incorrect username or password, the webpage will display the error in this location.

- `loginUI:loginForm`: This tag contains the most important item; it creates the login form so that our users can access the system.

- `loginUI:gatewayButtons`: This tag refers to the options in the **Gateway Options** area under **Security**. If we allow guest access, account creation, course-catalog access, or users to reset their password within Blackboard, the links would be displayed where this tag resides.

- `loginUI:welcomeArea`: This tag inserts a default welcome statement created by Blackboard.

- `loginUI:systemAnnouncements`: We have the ability to create system announcements, which we will discuss in *Chapter 8, Tools and Utilities in Blackboard Learn*. This tag will be replaced with any administrator-created announcements that are pushed to the login page.

Blackboard states that these tags can be moved around the login page to match our organization's branding. We now have a basic blank canvas to create a login page with a few required elements. By using the tags mentioned here, along with customizing the `login.css` file within our theme, we can really make this login page meet our organization's needs. This task, however, can be more than an experienced admin might feel comfortable starting. We can find inspiration by using our favorite search engine and find other Blackboard Learn login pages from other organizations to give us ideas.

Summary

This chapter took us on a review of how to improve the look of our Blackboard Learn instance and how to make it into one that matches the look and feel of other websites within our organization. We defined the parts that make up Blackboard and reviewed the simple and advanced options to make branding changes. Blackboard also gives us the ability to customize the login page to match our organization's branding.

Now that we have the street signs painted, flowers on the sidewalks, and a nice welcoming area for our users, we need to create places for the users to do their work in. We need to create courses that will be the virtual classrooms for our users. We should get to work before the school bell rings.

4

Creating Courses in Blackboard Learn

The previous chapters in this book discussed how to make our Blackboard instance ready for users. We've gotten our virtual community up and running, and given it a look and feel that makes its users comfortable to work with. Before we cut the ribbon and open our doors to the users, we need to create homes and apartments where they can work and communicate with one another. In Blackboard Learn, these areas are referred as **courses**.

In this chapter we will:

- Learn how to configure default course settings and organize courses within our Blackboard Learn environment
- Understand the different ways to create courses
- Know how to bring content into our newly created courses

We have quite a bit of information to review in this chapter, so let's start creating courses.

Courses in Blackboard Learn

The basic structure of any learning management system relies on the basic course, or course shell. A **course shell** holds all the information and communication that goes on within our course and is the central location for all activities between students and instructors.

Let's think about our course shell as a virtual house or apartment. A house or apartment is made up of different rooms where we put things that we use in our everyday life. These rooms such as the living room, kitchen, or bedrooms can be compared to content areas within our course shell. Within each of these content areas, there are items such as telephones, dishwashers, computers, or televisions that we use to interact, communicate, or complete tasks. These items would be called **course tools** within the course shell. These content areas and tools are available within our course shells and we can use them in the same ways. While as administrators, we won't take a deep dive into all these tools; we should know that they are available and instructors use them within their courses.

Blackboard Learn offers many different ways to create courses, but to help simplify our discussion, we will classify those ways in two categories, basic and advanced. This chapter will discuss the course creation options that we classify as basic. No need to worry though, we will talk about the advanced options in *Chapter 10, Authentication and Data Integration in Blackboard Learn.*

Course names and course IDs

When we get ready to create a course in Blackboard Learn, the system requires a few items. It requires a course name and a course ID. The first one should be self-explanatory. If you are teaching a course on "Underwater Basket Weaving" (a hobby I highly recommend), you would simply place this information into the course name. Now the course ID is a bit trickier. Think of it like a barcode that you can find on your favorite cereal. That barcode is unique and tells the checkout scanner the item you have purchased. The course ID has a similar function in Blackboard Learn. It must be unique; so if you plan to have multiple courses on "Underwater Basket Weaving", you will need to figure out a way to express the differences in each course ID.

We just talked about how each course ID in Blackboard has to be unique. We as administrators will find that most Blackboard Learn instances we deal with have numerous course shells. Providing multiple courses to the users might become difficult. So we should consider creating a course ID naming convention if one isn't already in place. Our conversation will not tell you which naming convention will be best for your organization, but here are some helpful tips for us to start with:

- Use a symbol to separate words, acronyms, and numbers from one another. Some admins may use an underscore, period, or dash. However, whitespace, percent, ampersand, less than, greater than, equals, or plus characters are not accepted within course IDs.

- If you plan to collect reporting data from your instance, make sure to include the term or session and department in the course ID.

- Collect input from people and teams within your organization who will enroll and support users. Their feedback about a course's naming convention will help it be successful.

 Many organizations use a **Student Information System, (SIS)**, which manages the enrollment process. If you are interested in integrating it with our Blackboard Learn environment, you can review this discussion in *Chapter 10, Authentication and Data Integration in Blackboard Learn*.

Most administrators who have worked with multiple instances of Blackboard during their career, normally find similar naming conventions for many organizations. They tend to look something like [DepartmentCode.CourseNumber.SectionNumber. Term or Session] or [Term or Session-DepartmentCode-CourseNumber-SectionNumber]. Remember the input you get from people within your organization may create something completely different from what you see here. A good course ID naming convention allows Blackboard Learn administrators and support personnel to quickly find a course and assist users when they request support.

New shells versus recycling

Many times, instructors will make some slight changes to their courses between semesters while some will make major ones. Some courses may have students complete the course after its end due to personal issues. When these topics come up, it brings many administrators to a central question about course shell. Is it better to create new shells or recycle the ones just used?

After having this discussion with Blackboard Inc., it recommended creating new course shells for new courses and then copying course material from the old course shell into the new one. Administrators who agree with Blackboard's recommendation have found several reasons for this.

- Recycling the same shell over and over again can create corruption. When working with a course that has an issue, check to see how old the course is and has it been recycled. Data loss occurred when trying to "scrub" a course by removing student content (also called **bulk delete**) can create orphaned information and issues when reused.

- Many organizations would like to automate course creation and enrollment process in their Blackboard Learn instance. The recommended way to make this happen quickly and easily requires new course shells to be created for every new course.

- Administrators may wish to keep students' work and grade information intact. This information, while it can be archived, may be kept intact for administrative purposes.

- Storage costs have gone down dramatically in the recent years and many instances have many storage options available. Courses can be copied, and then the older courses can be archived to keep the course's content and other important data that Blackboard courses hold.

This requires us to use the **Course Import** or **Course Copy** tools, which we will discuss later in this chapter.

Course settings in Blackboard

As we start creating courses, we must first set up how each course will function in our Blackboard instance. When the course can be accessed, the structure, images, and other settings are just some of the options available. The default settings for these options can be configured in the **Course Settings** area within the **Courses** module in our **System Admin** tab, as shown in the following screenshot:

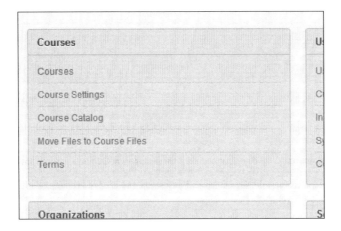

Default course properties

The first item in our **Course Settings** area allows us to set up several of the default access options within our courses. The **Default Course Properties** page covers when and who has access to a course by default.

- **Available by Default**: This option gives us the ability to have a course available to enrolled students when it is created. Most administrators will have this set to **No**, since the instructor may not want to immediately give access to the course.

- **Allow Guests by Default** and **Allow Observers by Default**: The next options allow us to set guest and observer access to created courses by default. We will discuss the guest and observer roles in *Chapter 7, Managing Roles and Users in Blackboard Learn*. Most administrators normally set these to **No** because the guest access and observer role aren't used by their organizations.

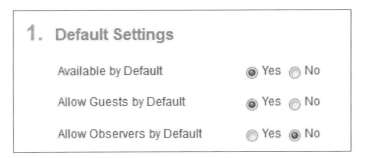

- **Default Enrollment Options**: We can set default enrollment options to either allow the instructor or system administrator to enroll students or allow the student to self enroll. If we choose the former, we can give the student the ability to e-mail the instructor to request access. If we set **Self Enrollment**, we can set dates when this option is available and even set a default access code for students to use when they can self enroll. Now that we have these two options for default enrollment, most administrators would suggest setting the default course enrollment option to instructors or system administrators, which will allow instructors to set self enrollment within their own course.

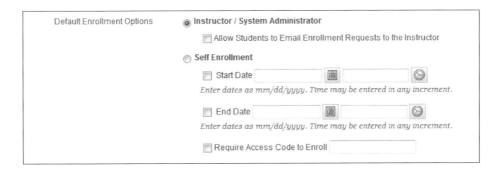

- **Default Duration**: The **Continuous** option allows the course to run continuously with no start or end date set. **Select Dates** sets specific start and end dates for all courses. The last option called **Days from the Date of Enrollment** sets courses to run for a specific number of days after the student was enrolled within our Blackboard Learn environment. This is helpful if a student self enrolls in a self-paced course with a set number of days to complete it.

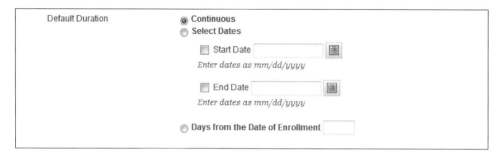

 Pitfalls of setting start and end dates
When using the Start and End dates to control course duration, we may find that all users enrolled within the course will lose access.

Course themes and icons

If we are using the Blackboard 2012 theme, we have the ability to enable course themes within our Blackboard instance. These themes are created by Blackboard and can be applied to an instructor's course by clicking on the theme icon, seen in the following screenshot, in the upper-right corner of the content area while in a course. They have a wide variety of options, but currently administrators cannot create custom course themes.

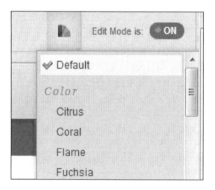

We can also select which icon sets courses will use by default in our Blackboard instance. These icon themes are created by Blackboard and will appear beside different content items and tools within the course. In the following screenshot, we can see some of the icons that make up one of the sets. Unlike the course themes, these icons will be enforced across the entire instance.

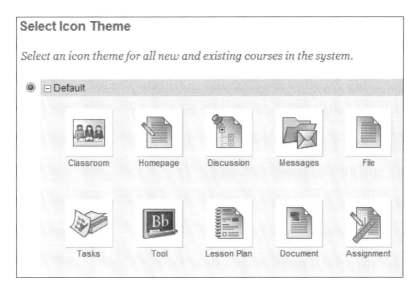

Course Tools

The **Course Tools** area offers us the ability to set what tools and content items are available within courses by default. We can also control these settings along with organizations and system tools by clicking on the **Tools** link under the **Tools and Utilities** module. Let's review what tools are available and how to enable and disable them within our courses.

 The options we use to set course tools are exactly same as those used in the **Tools** area we just mentioned. Use the information provided here to set tool availability with a page.

We can set different availability options for each tool based on where they are used. Blackboard also allows administrators to give tool access to guests or observers within a course or organization by checking the boxes within a tool's row.

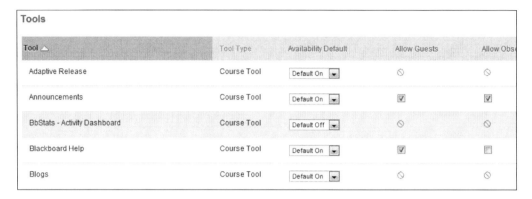

Let's take a more detailed look into the default availability setting within this page. We have four options for each tool. Every tool has the same options.

- **Default On**: A course automatically has this tool available to users, but an instructor or leader can disable the tool within it
- **Default Off**: Users in a course will not have access to this tool by default, but the instructor or leader can enable it
- **Always On**: Instructors or leaders are unable to turn this tool off in their course or organization
- **Always Off**: Users do not see this tool in a course or organization, nor can the instructor or leader turn it on within the course

Once we make the changes, we must click on the **Submit** button.

Quick Setup Guide

The **Quick Setup Guide** page was introduced into Blackboard 9.1 Service Pack 8. As seen in the following screenshot, it offers instructors the basic introduction into the course if they have never used Blackboard before. Most of the links are to the content from the **On Demand** area of the Blackboard website. We as administrators can disable this from appearing when an instructor enters the course. If we leave the guide enabled, we can add custom text to the guide, which can help educate instructors about changes, help, and support available from our organization.

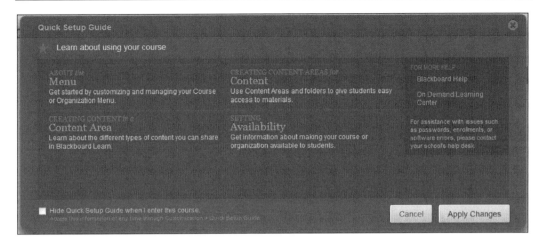

Custom images

We can continue to customize default look and feel of our course shells with images in the course entry point and at the top of the menu. We might use these images to spotlight that our organization has been honored with an award. Here we find an example of how these images would look.

Two images can be located at the bottom of the course entry page, which is the page we see after entering a course. Another image can be located at the top of the course menu. This area also allows us to make these images linkable to a website. Here's an example.

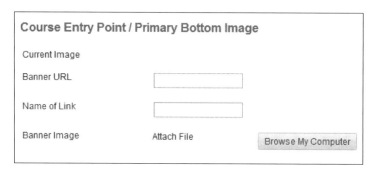

Default course size limits

We can also create a default course size limit for the course and the course export and archive packages within this area. **Course Size Limits** allows administrators to control storage space, which may be limited in some instances. When a course size limit is within 10 percent of being reached, the administrator and instructor get an e-mail notification. This notification is triggered by the disk usage task that runs once a day. After getting the notification, the instructor can remove content from the course, or the administrator can increase the course quota for that specific course.

- **Maximum Course disk size**: This option sets the amount of disk space a course shell can use for storage. This includes all course and student files within the course shell.

- **Maximum Course Package Size**: This sets the maximum amount of content from the **Course Files** area included in a course copy, export, or archive.

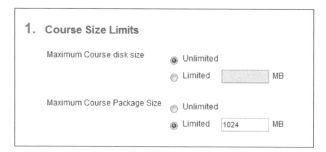

Grade Center settings

This area allows us to set default controls over the **Grade History** portion of the **Grade Center**. Grade history is exactly what it says. It keeps a history of the changes within the Grade Center. Most administrators recommend having grade history enabled by default because of the historical benefits. There may be a discussion within your organization to permit instructors to disable this feature within their course or clear the history altogether.

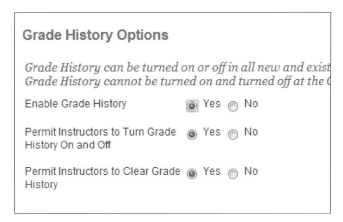

Course menu and structures

The course menu offers the main navigation for any course user. Our organization can create a default course menu layout for all new course shells created based on the input from instructional designers and pedagogical experts. As seen in the following screenshot, we simply edit the default menu that appears on this page.

As administrators, we should pay close attention when creating a default course menu. Any additions or removals to the default menu are automatically changed without clicking on the **Submit** or **Cancel** buttons, and are applied to any courses created from that point forward.

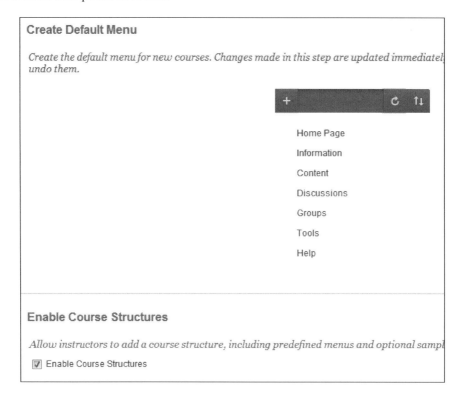

Blackboard recently introduced course structures. If enabled, these pre-built course menus are available to the instructor within their course's control panel. The course structures fall into a number of different course instruction scenarios. An example of the course structure selection interface is shown in the following screenshot:

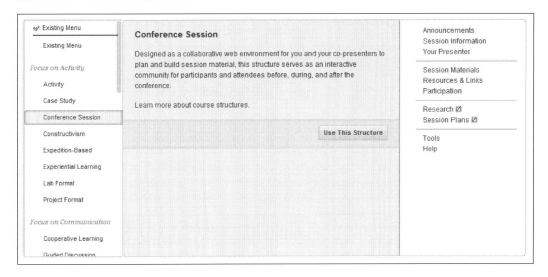

Default notification settings

As administrators, this area gives us the ability to set up how notifications are sent out system wide. These notifications are based on course actions or due dates such as when a new assignment in the course is available or a test is nearing its due date for completion. These notifications can be sent to a user by an e-mail or text, or displayed in the users's dashboard module. The system defaults have every option turned on by default in the student's dashboard. We will discuss these options in more details in *Chapter 8*, *Using Tools and Utilities in Blackboard Learn*. We can make changes to these options as we see fit.

Default grading schema

Many institutions use different grading scales or schemas for their instructions. This area allows you to set a default schema that is available to all courses globally. So if we make a change to this schema, it will be applied to all courses created from that point forward, but not to courses already created. Any changes can greatly affect students' grades and instructor's grading options within current courses, which requires caution.

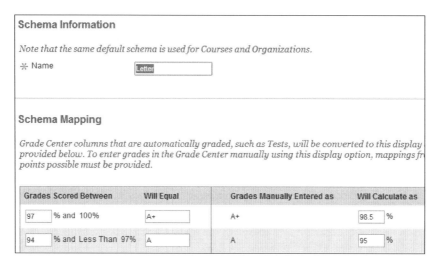

Creating a course catalog structure

Some organizations list and group their courses by departments or other internal structures. Sometimes, a possible student may want to look at the different courses our organization offers online with Blackboard Learn. He or she might even want to look within a course to see what makes up an online course. The **Course Catalog** tool allows us to create a structure similar to folders, which can contain courses. This is the primary way that the Blackboard Learn environment allows anyone without a username and password to look around and possibly see course content available to guests.

We can start by going into the **Course Catalog** area by clicking on its link within the **Courses** module. We then click on the **Create Category** button to open the following page.

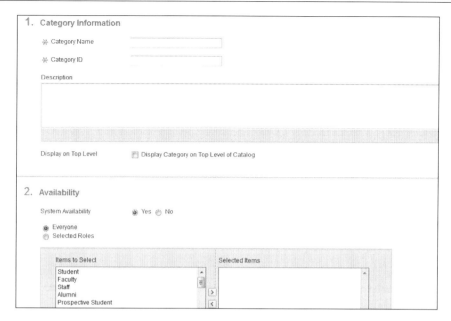

Now, we will add a new category that will be displayed in our **Course Catalog**. We will put in our **Category Name**, which will be a broad topic; it might be the name of a school, department, or training topic within your organization. We will then put in a category ID, which will be internally used by our Blackboard instance. We also have the option to add a description that will be displayed with our category. We can force our category to be displayed in the top level of the catalog instead of having a user to search through sub-categories to find our course listing. We also have the ability to make this category unavailable system wide and can use institutional role permissions within our Blackboard instance to restrict or permit access to this category. If we want to create a sub-category, we would simply click on the name of the category we just created and use the same process to create it. Later in this chapter, we will learn how to put our courses into these categories. In the following screenshot, we can see the **Widget Making** course category is a sub-category of **Engineering**, which is a top-level category.

Terms

The **Terms** option offers the ability for administrators to group and control the availability of courses being offered. This is done by creating term identifiers based on a time frame. We can create terms in a way similar to the process of creating course categories. In our example, we will create two terms for our courses. Courses that are currently being taught and courses that were taught in the last term.

A term is a set time such as a semester, session, or academic year that courses within our Blackboard Learn instance are associated with. For example, spring, summer, fall, or winter terms at a college or university.

To create a new term within our instance, we click on the **Terms** link within the **Courses** module. Simply click on the **Create Term** button to begin and we see the page similar to the following screenshot:

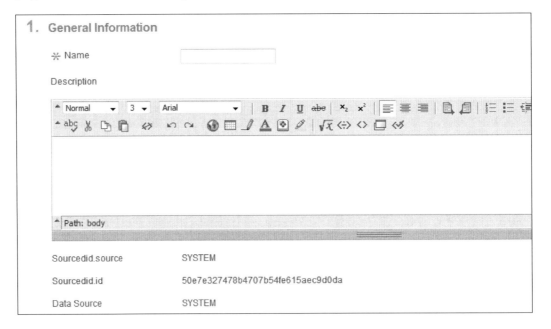

We must first give the term a name. This name will be displayed in the **My Courses** module to help aggregate courses by our term. Here we can also add a description for this term. Below the description, there are three lines of information.

The next options allow the term to have control over the availability and duration of courses. The following screenshot shows our first option to set the duration of the term. It can be continuous, based on a date range, or set on the days after the user's initial enrollment. Once our options are set, simply click on **Submit**. We will discuss how to associate our manually created courses later in this chapter.

Searching for courses in Blackboard

Now that we have reviewed all the course settings, we'll start with the **Courses** link. This link within the **Courses** module gives us the ability to find and search for any course within the system. It doesn't matter whether it's available to users or not, we can use multiple options to search for course shells within our Blackboard instance. We can search by:

- **Course ID**: A set of numbers, letters, and symbols that create a unique identifier to a course shell within Blackboard Learn
- **Course Name**: The name, such as "Underwater Basket Weaving", that a course shell is given within Blackboard Learn
- **Description**: A few sentences that describe the course to users
- **Instructor**: The user ID of the user or users who teach the course within Blackboard Learn
- **Data Source Key**: A set of numbers, letters, and symbols used in snapshot and SIS integrations
- **Term**: The time frame that a course maybe associated with

Our next search option allows the user to set how the search criteria will be used:

- **Contains**: The search term appears anywhere within the selected field
- **Equal to**: The search term matches the selected field
- **Starts with**: The search term appears at the start of the selected field
- **Not blank**: When selected and the search term is left blank, the search returns all courses in Blackboard Learn

We can also set what courses are returned in our search by setting the **Date Created** option. We have an option to select before or after a specific date.

Creating single courses in Blackboard

Now that we have reviewed how to search for courses, we need to create a course to search. This requires us to click on the **Create Course** button and select the **New** option as shown in the following screenshot:

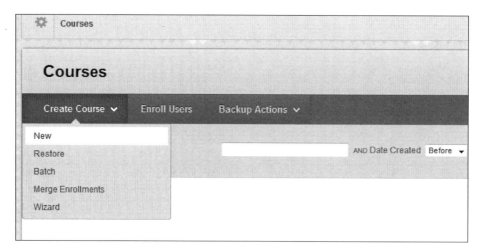

We arrive at the page shown in the following screenshot. This page asks for a course ID (which we talked about earlier), a course name (this is the name users will see and click on in their **My Courses** and **Course List** modules to access the course), and an optional description. We also have the ability to select a subject area and discipline for the course that some long-term Blackboard environments might have customized, but may have been ignored by some organizations. We can also set the term for the course using the drop-down menu.

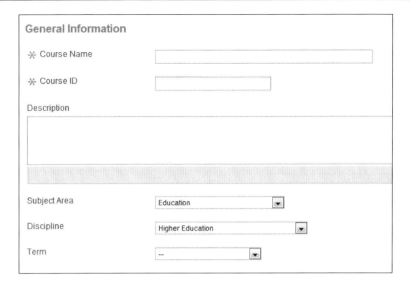

Courses also have to be made available for users to access them. These settings should mirror our default course settings we learned about earlier, but we can change them here as well. We can go ahead and make the course available when the course is created, if we wish. The duration of the course can also be set using the following options:

- **Continuous**: This duration allows the course to be available and not tied to any date

- **Select Dates**: This option will keep the course open to student users from the selected start and end dates

- **Days from the Date of Enrollment**: This allows student users to have course access for a specified number of days from their enrollment within the course. Courses can also give guest users access to review a course before enrolling by setting **Guest Permitted** to **Yes**. Our course can also be categorized using the course catalog that we created earlier. Here we can click on the category or categories we want our course to be associated with and then click on the button pointing to the right between the two columns to move the selected category or categories over.

The next option allows us to add a banner to our course. A banner is a graphic image that appears at the top of the announcements or homepage. The banner can give student users a visual clue telling them which course they are in; see an example of a banner in the following screenshot:

Next, we can insert a course cartridge download key. A course cartridge normally comes from a publisher and adds content to a course. The content can vary greatly from publisher to publisher, but it can include PowerPoint files, games, or simulations. Student users must have an access code that can be purchased separately or with their textbooks. Some instructors find this content valuable to students, however sometimes the content lacks the interactivity that many online users want. An excellent suggestion when discussing course cartridges with instructors is to create a temporary course shell where they can review what content will be added to the course. They can then make a decision on if that content will benefit their instructions and students. In the following screenshot, we can see how to add a banner and course cartridge key to our course creation process.

Our course can also select from two different options when it comes to enrollments. The first option is to have the instructor or system administrator to enroll student users into a course. This option is how the majority of enrollments are done. We will talk about how administrators enroll users into courses in *Chapter 7, Managing Roles and Users in Blackboard Learn*. The other option, called **Self Enrollment**, requires users to go and search for the course. Users can do this by using the course catalog or the course search module. They then will have to click on the **Enroll** button to be enrolled in the course. We can add an additional requirement for this self-enrollment option by adding an access code.

The **Language Pack** option allows us to apply a language to our course. If we select a new language, this will only change the titles and instructions that the Blackboard application controls. We also have the ability to enforce the course language pack, which overrides the user's language pack and the system language pack. Many times instructors use this option when teaching courses in foreign languages. The following screenshot shows how the enrollment and language pack options appear on the webpage:

Now that we have dealt with many of the items, with the delivery of this course we can move onto the visual layout of our course menu. The course menu will show our instance's default style, however we can change the style to use either buttons or text and select the color or style of either option. When doing this, we must make sure that every student will be able to read the text clearly. So when using a dark colored background, we should use white- or light-colored text and those colors should be visible to color blind users.

The final option on our new course page is for setting the default content view. These options control how items in a course content area are displayed.

- **Icon Only**: This option will display just the icon and the title. If you have ever used WebCT, this option mimics the look of that application. If the users wants to read the description, they can simply click on the icon.

- **Text Only**: This option displays the same information as icon and text, but without the icon.

- **Icon and Text**: This is the default option. When selected, it displays the icon, text, and description in the content area.

Most instructors find the icon as a key visual cue to student users, so we would want to suggest using either the icon or icon and text. In the following screenshot, we can see how the menu style and content view options appear on the page:

Now that we have selected all our options, we can now click on the **Submit** button. The course has been created in our Blackboard instance. Our instance takes us back to the courses page and a green success bar appears letting us know the course has been created. We can see an example of this bar in the following screenshot:

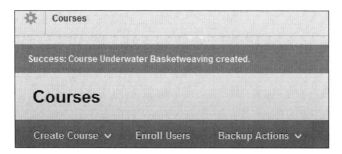

Creating courses using the batch course creation tool

We have walked through the process to create a single course, however we as administrators normally need to create more than one course at a time. This situation requires the use of the batch course creation tool within Blackboard. Before we create our courses using this tool, we must create the file that lists these courses.

The file will be delimited using a comma, tab, or colon to separate the different fields within our file. Using our file, we can add information such as COURSE ID, course name, course description, button style/color, initial announcement, announcement title, and course category. Each of our courses may not require all this information and we can leave some of these items blank. The only items required by our instance are the course id and course name. Here is a sample of a batch course creation file that is comma delimited.

```
TEST-COURSE-001,Test Course A
TEST-COURSE-002,Test Course B,This is the course description
TEST-COURSE-003,Test Course C,This is the course
description,#CCCC00/#003300
TEST-COURSE-004,Test Course - Marketing,This is the course description
,#CCCC00/#003300,Welcome to this course.,Course Welcome,
TEST-COURSE-005,Test Course - Marketing,This is the course
description, #CCCC00/#003300,Welcome to this course.,Course
Welcome,Marketing
```

As you can see, each course has a different configuration for each line, but this will
not be a problem for the tool. However, if we use different delimiters in the file,
that would cause errors. Once we have created our file, we click on the **Courses** link
within the **Courses** module in our **System Admin** tab. Under the **Create Courses**
button, we will find **Batch**. Simply click on that link and our **Batch Course Creation**
page will load.

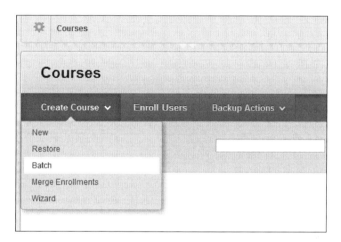

The following screenshot shows the first options we have on our **Batch Enrollment**
page. Here we should browse and select our file to create batch courses. Then we
should select the delimiter type, or just leave it to **Automatic**.

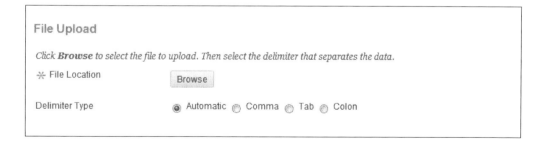

Our next option, seen in the following screenshot, allows us to set the course menu style if one hasn't been set within the batch file. Now, we can click on **Submit** and the file will be processed.

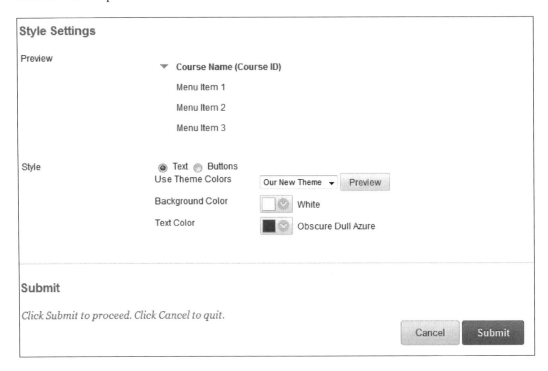

The process then will display any errors that occurred. Note any issues that might have caused a course not to be created properly, and then click on **OK**. An example of the error is shown in the following screenshot:

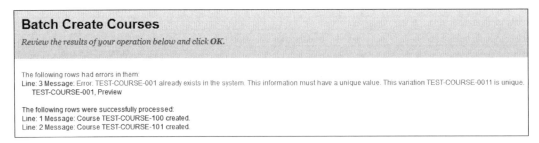

We should address another option to create courses within our Blackboard instance. This option is called the **course wizard**. It offers a six-step process, which breaks up the options used when we created a single course earlier. Most administrators don't use this tool because it is easier to use the other processes we have as administrators, however we as Blackboard Learn admins can allow instructors to use **Create Course Wizard**.

Importing content into a new course

Now that we know how to create blank course shells, let's move on to learn how to add or include content that may come from a previously taught course. We can import content that has been exported from a previous course and saved in the common cartridge or Blackboard Learn formats. The common cartridge format was created to promote sharing across learning management systems by the IMS Global Learning Consortium. Either of these export formats from a previous course will work in the same manner when importing content into a new or existing course shell.

 We will discuss how to export and archive course content into the common cartridge format (`.imscc`) and Blackboard Learn format (`.zip`) in our next chapter. We might want to skip to this chapter and create an export if we want to practice the process we are about to review.

The import process begins in the **Courses** area. On the right side of the header, we find the **Import Package** button.

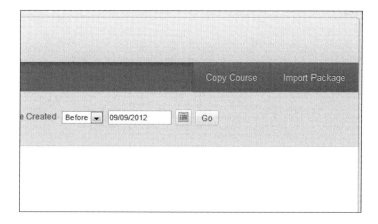

We can use **Import Package** to create a new course using the package content, or import the package content into an existing course. Our first option asks for **Destination Course ID**. If we are importing this information for a new course, we can put our new course ID in this box. If we want to import content into an existing course, we can simply type or paste it into the textbox or click on the **Browse** button where we get options similar to those in our course search area to find the course. After our search, simply click on the radio button beside the course ID and course name, and then click on **Submit** as shown in the following screenshot:

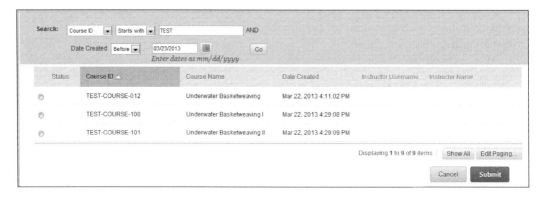

The next step requires us to select the `.zip` or `.imscc` file that contains our course content from a previously taught course that we exported. Simply click on the **Choose File** button and search your filesystem. Once selected, click on **Open** and the file will be displayed on the page. We should use caution when trying to import a very large course. If the file is larger than two gigabytes, the upload may fail. Files larger than this should use the command-line import tool. We will discuss how to use this tool in the next chapter.

After selecting the file, we must decide what imported content needs to come into the new Blackboard course. We simply select the items we want to add from our file. Most administrators use the **Select All** button to make sure all the content that the instructor wants will be there. Then the user can remove unwanted content.

Importing or copying content for disabled tools

If a tool, such as announcements, has been disabled within our Blackboard Learn environment, we will not see the option to import or copy that content into our instance.

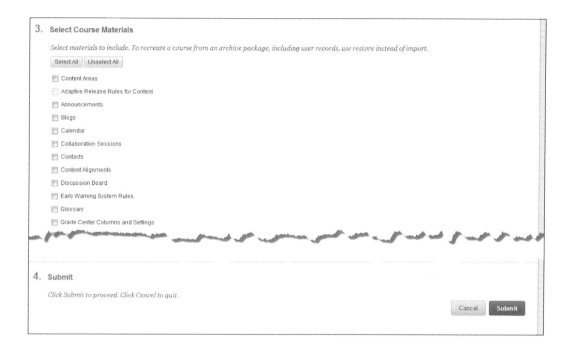

Then click on **Submit** to start the process. The import process will then be put into a queue to run as a background task within Blackboard Learn. This allows our instance to control how much load is given to these tasks. Once our import finishes, our instance sends an e-mail to the task creator. This e-mail informs the creator that the import has finished and will include information about the import process. The process might have generated some errors; those errors will be listed in the e-mail for us to review and troubleshoot. When you enter our newly imported course, you will find an orange bar at the top of the content area; it gives the same information found in the e-mail along with an option to download the detailed log of the course import.

Copying content into a new or existing course

At times, we may want to copy some or all of the content from one course to another course. Blackboard offers the **Copy Course** tool for this situation. The copy course tool is available in the **Courses** area under the **Courses** module in our **System Admin** tab. We start the process by clicking on the **Copy Course** button at the top of the page beside the **Import Package** button.

Our first option in this process requires us to select the copy type. We can copy course content into a new course or existing one. These options will only copy selected content and configuration of tools from the source course to the destination one; we will learn how to select those items in a bit. The last option allows us to copy all content and configuration settings, including the student users and their content. Blackboard Learn calls this option an **exact copy**.

Once we select the copy type, our next option requires us to find the source and destination course ID. We have the same options found when we selected the course ID when we were importing content into a new course. Either we can type or paste the course ID into the source course ID and the destination course ID. If we don't know either of these, we can simply click on the **Browse** button and our **Search** window will open up. After selecting these two options, click on **Submit** to move on.

The next step in the copying process requires us to select what content, tools, and settings we want to copy from our source course into the destination course. Let's review what items we can copy over to our new course.

- **Content Areas**: When selecting this option, the process will copy course materials such as uploaded files, learning modules, and links. We have the ability to specify what content areas we want to copy over.

- **Adaptive Release Rules for Content**: This option allows us to copy adaptive release rules, however the rules that require user or assignment submissions will only work when the Grade Center is copied over as well.

- **Announcements**: The process will copy over all announcements from the source course.

- **Tests, Surveys, and Pools**: All tests and surveys are copied over from the source course including the questions and deployment options. Pools are all copied over as well.

- **Calendar**: All calendar items are copied to the destination course.

- **Discussion Board**: The forums are copied along with threads and replies within in each forum.

- **Grade Center Items and Settings**: This option copies items in the Grade Center along with the settings for each one.

- **Group Settings**: Group names, tools availability settings, and discussion board forum names are copied over when this option is selected.

- **Contacts**: All contacts are copied over to the destination course.

- **Course Settings**: These items are copied when selected: tools (both Blackboard and building block), content tools, course registry, and proxy tools. When copying into a new course, the course name and description will be copied over along with the items previously listed.

- **Availability**: This option copies the availability status and term association of the source course.

- **Banner Image**: The process will copy the course banner to our destination course.

- **Course Guest Access**: The course guest access settings from the source course will be copied over.

- **Course Observer Access**: The access settings for course observers will be copied to the destination course.

- **Duration**: The duration properties such as continuous, start and end dates, days from date of enrolment, and term association will be copied.

- **Enrollment Options**: The source options for enrollment in the source course will be applied to the destination course.

- **Language Pack**: The selected and enforced language pack settings are copied from the source course.

- **Navigation Settings**: This option copies the background and text colors along with the button types from the source course.

- **Course Cartridge Materials**: Content imported from a course cartridge will be copied from the source course. This option appears when the source course contains a course cartridge and the destination course does not.

We can simply select the items we want to copy over or click on the **Select All** button at the top of the list.

Now that we have selected what items we want to bring over in the copy process, we can calculate the size of the new course. This can be very helpful if course quotas are enforced. Sometimes a faculty member may have many items in the course filesystem and some of those files may no longer be needed. We can remove specific files from the copy by clicking on the **Manage Package Contents** button. This will open a new window that shows us the files within our source course. Here we can select what files and directories should be copied. When we check the box to the right of the **Manage Package Contents** button, any files within our source course that aren't linked within any course content area being copied will not be brought over.

Our final option, as shown in the following screenshot, gives us the ability to copy the users that are enrolled in our source course. This does not bring grades or other user content, however only an exact course copy is brought. We can now click on the **Submit** button and just as the course import, the copy goes into the queue of background tasks. We will be notified via an e-mail once the course copy completes.

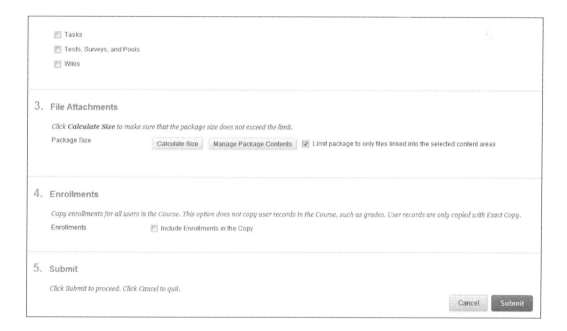

The import and copy processes offer the administrator the ability to bring specific content into a new or existing course. However, there are a few items we should learn about that could affect our results and also the expectations of instructors.

- Copying a course time and time again can create corruption issues. We mentioned this issue in our *New shells versus. recycling* conversation. The more number of times an item is copied, the greater is a chance for this. As an administrator, we need to be careful of this issue.

- When user enrollments are not copied over, information posted within tools such as discussion boards and announcements will be shown as posted by the user who ran the course copy or import process or it will display anonymous in the name fields.

- Course copies and imports will copy over all due date and date restrictive information as well and will not change based on the course's start or end dates.

Summary

As we learned in this chapter, creating courses in our Blackboard Learn instance can require a lot of planning and configuring. As administrators, we need to create a standard naming convention for our courses to help us find and access them easily. Then courses require us to create default settings that dictate what tools are available and how the course appears to the student user. Once we are ready to make a course, we have several ways to do so. We also have the ability to move contents and settings from one course to another within Blackboard Learn or bring content from another Blackboard instance or other LMS using the common cartridge format.

While we reviewed many course items in this chapter, we have only scratched the surface. Our next chapter really starts to dive into the administration of courses within our Blackboard Learn environment. These topics cover how to enroll users, making courses accessible to students, along with archiving and removing courses. So let's continue learning more about courses within Blackboard Learn.

5
Administrating Courses in Blackboard Learn

In the previous chapter, we reviewed how to create courses in Blackboard Learn. We now know how to create course shells, or virtual homes, and apartments that allow our virtual community to communicate and start the learning process. We, as administrators, act as landlords for the homes and apartments within our virtual community. We are responsible for keeping the tools and content areas within these spaces working. It's these tasks that we will discuss in this chapter. We will address the following topics:

- How we, as administrators, can enroll users and make courses available to student users

- How to quickly access courses as an instructor

- The ways to back up course and student data from Blackboard Learn

- How to remove student data and entire courses from Blackboard Learn

Enrolling users into Blackboard Learn courses

So we've created courses. Our next step is to add users to a course. Blackboard Learn calls this step **enrolling**; this gives users the key to access the virtual home or apartment within our Blackboard Learn environment that we will use for a course. While instructors have the ability to provide access to users, administrators are also given the same ability. Our enroll options are listed in the course search area when we click on the **Courses** link in the **Courses** module in our **System Admin** tab. When we want to enroll users we have two different options—either add users one at a time, or batch-enroll users using a text file.

Most organizations that use enrollment software such as **Student Information System (SIS)** or **Student Records Systems (SRS)** enroll users with the Blackboard Snapshot or SIS Framework integrations. These processes allow us to automate the enrollment process and keep enrollments up to date. We will discuss these options in *Chapter 10, Authentication and Data Integration in Blackboard Learn.*

When we want to add users into a course one at a time, we have to follow a few steps:

1. First we must find the course to which we need to enroll a user. Simply search for the course using one of the many types of search options we discussed in the previous chapter. Once we have the course listed in our search results we simply click on the action button, which appears to the right of the course ID. The **action button** looks like a chevron and will only appear when we move our cursor over the course name in the search results. When we click on the action button, a menu appears; we call this **action menu**, and the options it displays will vary from item to item. More about the items in this menu will be discussed a little later, but one of the many options we have in the action menu is **Enrollments** (shown in the following screenshot), which we need to select for our next step.

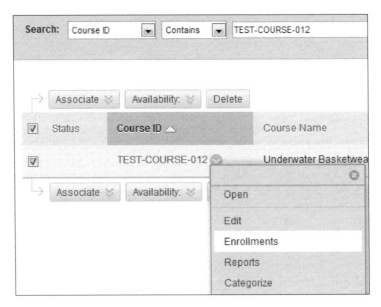

   ○ Enroll new users into this course

   ○ Remove existing enrolled users from this course

   We will discuss about removing users later in this chapter, but for now, let's continue with our enrollment conversation. We continue by clicking on the **Enroll Users** button, seen in the following screenshot. This takes us to the **Add Enrollments** page, and here we have different ways to enroll a user.

3. If we know the username or group of usernames to add into this course, we can just type it into the **Username** textbox. In the following screenshot, we see that a group of usernames have been typed in, with a comma separating each one. If we don't know the username, we simply click on the **Browse...** button, which opens a new window.

4. This window, which opens when we click on the **Browse...** button, allows us to search for a user by the **Username**, **First Name**, **Last Name**, and **Email address** (these options are present in the drop-down list located next to **Search**.). When Blackboard Learn returns our search results, we can select the user we want to enroll by checking the checkboxes on the left side of the page. Once we have selected our users to enroll, as seen in the following screenshot, we click on **Submit**. Our window is closed and our selected username or usernames appear within the **Username** textbox on the **Add Enrollments** page.

5. The next option requires us to set the course role for the user or set of users we want to enroll. The **course role** is a set of privileges within Blackboard Learn that can be associated with a user within a course shell. We have several default course roles; so let's review each one:

   ○ **Student**: This role normally has access to view content and course assignments. It does not have access to create new content areas, disable tools within the entire course, neither does this role have access to other users' information such as submitted homework and grades.

   ○ **Instructor**: This role has the ability to do all permissions allowed within a course. Users under this role can create content, enable and disable available tools, customize the course's look and feel, and access the grades of all **Student** role users in the course.

- ○ **Teaching Assistant**: This user role, by default, has the same permissions as **Instructor**, except this role isn't listed in Blackboard's course catalog. Also, users with this role cannot enroll and remove users within the course, nor can this user archive the course.

- ○ **Course Builder**: This role gives the user permissions to create, edit, and remove content and tools in a course. This role doesn't have access to Grade Center, the ability to grade many of the tools, and the user will not receive course e-mails.

- ○ **Grader**: While the Course Builder role had the option to create content, this role can only grade students' work within the course by default and will not get course e-mails.

- ○ **Guest**: This role may be disabled globally, but if not, it allows the user to review documents that have been given guest privileges. Only content items and web links can be made available this way.

We can change the privileges for these default course roles using the privileges tool. We will discuss how to use this tool in *Chapter 7, Manage Users in Blackboard Learn*.

If we have the Blackboard Community system, we can create new course roles and manage the privileges for those.

This information may seem a bit much, so here's a table to use as a reference for the default configuration of these roles:

	Student	Instructor	Teaching Assistant	Course Builder	Grader	Guest
View Content	Yes	Yes	Yes	Yes	Yes	Yes, if permitted
Access Available Course Tools	Yes	Yes	Yes	Yes	Yes	No
Control Course Tool Availability	No	Yes	Yes	Yes	No	No
Add, Edit, Remove Content	No	Yes	Yes	Yes	No	No
Enroll Users	No	Yes	No	No	No	No
Remove Users	No	Yes	No	No	No	No
View My Grades	Yes	No	No	No	No	No
Edit Grade Center	No	Yes	Yes	No	Yes	No
Grade Submitted Assignments / Assessments	No	Yes	Yes	No	Yes	No
Send and Receive Course Emails	Yes	Yes	Yes	No	No	No

6. Once we select the role our user or users will have in the course, we need to set the **Enrollment Availability** option (shown in the following screenshot) for the user or users. **Enrollment Availability** controls if a user's enrollment is active or not. If set to **Yes**, the user can log in to our Blackboard Learn environment and if the course is available, see it listed within their course list. If set to **No**, it will not appear. Once we have set these options, we simply click on the **Submit** button. The user or users are now enrolled in our course.

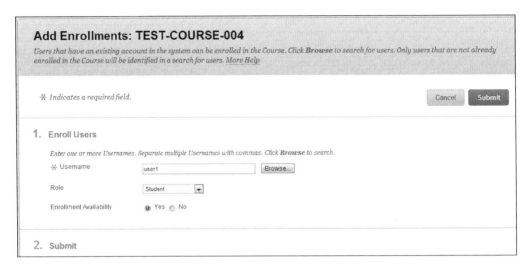

7. We as administrator can change a user's enrollment availability. This is done on the **Enrollments** page. We mouse over the username and click on the action button. The action menu appears and we select **Edit**. This takes us to the **Edit Enrollment** page for this course. We can change the user's course role and also change the **Enrollment Availability** option. Then we click on the **Submit** button to apply our changes. The **Edit Enrollment** page is shown in the following screenshot:

If we need to add one or two users into a course, the process we just discussed seems simple, but what about enrolling a hundred or a thousand users into a course or courses? Blackboard offers us an option to enroll in large groups or batches, called the **batch enrollment** process. On the course page, we simply click on the **Enroll Users** button at the top of the page. The new page allows us to use a formatted file to enroll users.

Creating a batch enrollment file

Our batch enrollment file has some required and some optional fields. Many of the fields in this file match the ones we have discussed in the previous chapters. Each line can have all these fields: Course ID, Username, Course Role, System Availability, and Course Availability.

> Two fields we haven't discussed are System Availability and Course Availability. Here's a brief description:
>
> - System Availability: This yes or no setting allows us to turn on or off a user's ability to log in to our Blackboard Learn instance.
> - Course Availability: This yes or no setting allows the user to have access to the course we enroll them in and if set to **No**, it will not allow access even if the course is currently available. This operates the same way as the **Enrollment Availability** option we discussed in the previous section, but it points out a lack of continuity within the Blackboard Learn environment.

Course ID, Username, and Course Role are the only required fields in this file, while System Availability and Course Availability are optional. The Course Role field uses a single character to represent the different roles:

- S: Student
- P: Instructor (We can also use Professor to help us remember)
- T: Teaching Assistant
- B: Course Builder
- G: Grader
- U: Guest.

We are using two user IDs, user1 and user2, in this batch enrollment process. We discuss how to create users within our Blackboard Learn environment in *Chapter 6, Creating Users in Blackboard Learn*.

Let's use the courses we created in the previous chapter and enroll two example users into them:

```
TEST-COURSE-001,user1,P

TEST-COURSE-001,user2,S

TEST-COURSE-002,user1,P

TEST-COURSE-002,user2,S

TEST-COURSE-003,user1,P

TEST-COURSE-003,user2,S

TEST-COURSE-004,user1,P

TEST-COURSE-004,user2,S

TEST-COURSE-005,user1,P

TEST-COURSE-005,user2,S
```

While we used a comma to separate our fields in the first example, we can use a semicolon (;), colon (:), or a pipe (|).

Enrolling users using the Batch Enrollment process

Now that we have created our file it's time to upload and process it within Blackboard Learn. We should be in our **Courses** page with our course search option and notice the **Enroll Users** button. Simply click on this button to begin our batch enrollment process, as shown in the following screenshot:

We notice that this page looks very similar to the one we saw during the batch create-courses process. The first step requires us to browse and find our batch enrollment file on our local computer. This file should be in text format (.txt) to make sure Blackboard Learn will be able to understand it. Our next option requires us to tell our instance the character (comma, tab, or colon) we are using to separate our fields. Once we have selected that, we click on **Submit** and the file will be processed. This is shown in the following screenshot:

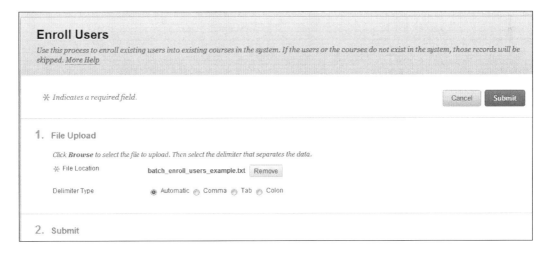

Possible issues with the batch enrollment process

Now that we know the process, let's look at some of the issues we might face while using this process.

If a user is already enrolled in a course we will get an error stating that fact. The application will continue to read the file, but sometimes an incorrect character in a line will throw the system off. We can correct the error within our file and rerun it. The process will skip previously-processed enrollments. We will also see errors in the log output, as shown in the next screenshot.

Another issue we need to discuss is the limitation of this process. If we try to batch-enroll more than 500 users at one time within the system, the process will not be able to handle it, and simply fail. If we want to use this batch process and we have more than 500 enrollments, we will need to break our enrollments into smaller files.

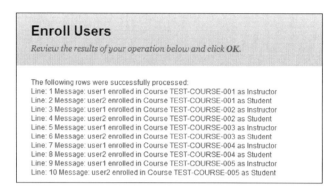

Using Quick Enroll in Blackboard Learn

Now that we have users enrolled in our courses, we should learn how we can put ourselves into a course. Many times an instructor or a student will report an issue within a course, and we need to be an enrolled user to see the issue. When such situations happen, we, as administrators, have the **Quick Enroll** button. This button appears in every course below **Control Panel** when someone with the system administrator role accesses it. This is shown in the following screenshot. When entering a course, we scroll down and find the **Quick Enroll** button below **Control Panel** and click on it. This will make us an **Instructor** in the course and allow us to access the same tools that an instructor would.

If we look at a course before we click on **Quick Enroll**, most of the `Instructor` capabilities are available. What items would not be available to us we might ask? Well that can vary among the different Blackboard Learn versions, but one major example would be viewing course discussion boards which will require our account to be enrolled in the course to view any of the posts. Once we are finished reviewing an issue, we should always unenroll from that course by clicking on the **Quick Enroll** button again (which is called the **Quick Unenroll** button after using it to enroll in a course). If not, be prepared to get e-mails and notifications from the course; this could fill up our inbox.

Rights to Quick Enroll

Some administrators will give different system-support roles the ability to use the **Quick Enroll** button within Blackboard Learn. This can be done using the privileges tool and system roles we will discuss in *Chapter 7, Manage Users in Blackboard Learn*. Many organizations will use this tool in different ways and may allow many or few system administrators to use it. There are many options available and we must select the one that meets our organization's needs.

Exporting and archiving courses in Blackboard Learn

It seems like we have everything ready to go for our virtual community. We've reviewed how to build these courses, but now we need to understand how we can protect our course data from being corrupted or lost, whether by users or by technology. The first step in safeguarding our courses is exporting and archiving the courses.

Before we jump into the exporting and archiving processes, we should define what these options are and how they differ from each other:

- **Course Exports**: This process takes the contents of our course shell that the instructor has created, such as items, folders, tests, assignments, settings, grade center columns, and others, from a course. This process is similar to the Copy process discussed in the previous chapter; however, instead of putting these files into a destination course, they go into a ZIP file.

- **Course Archive**: This process creates a zip file as well. However, the archive contains not only the instructor-created files within the course, but also the student content, which include discussion-board posts, wikis, blogs, journals, assignment and assessment submissions, and messages. The archive also holds a list of all the enrolled students and their activities within the course.

We will discuss each option separately. First let's review how to export a course from our Blackboard Learn environment.

Exporting a course

While administrators can give instructors, teaching assistants, and course builders, the ability to export a course, sometimes we administrators will need to create a course export process. One example is when trying to replicate issues within a live course. Many times we need to move the content over to a new course shell to allow testing and replication. These situations allow us to give Blackboard Support the access it needs without concerns regarding the access to student information.

Currently in Blackboard we have two ways to export course content—either as a file that is native to only Blackboard Learn environments or as a file in Common Cartridge format. In the previous chapter, we talked about the Common Cartridge format and how we can import this file type into our Blackboard Learn instance. At this time, the option to export in Common Cartridge is not available in the same area as a Blackboard Learn export, so we will see two different ways to export courses—first in the Blackboard Learn format and then the Common Cartridge format.

Now that we have the two different options to export our course content, which one should we prefer? The basic answer should be determined by where the course content will be used next. If our content will be going to another course-management system such as Moodle, Sakai, Canvas, or Desire2Learn, then we should use the Common Cartridge format. If we plan to use the content in the same or another Blackboard Learn instance, use the Blackboard proprietary file format. Let's start with the directions on how to create an export file for Blackboard Learn.

Exporting a course using the Blackboard Learn format

We should start in our **System Admin** tab and click on the **Courses** link within the **Courses** module. Once there, hover over the **Backup Actions** button and select the **Export Course** option.

We will select the course we want to export by either typing in the Course ID into the textbox, or clicking on **Browse...**, which opens our search window. This step is shown in the following screenshot. We then use our search options to find our course to export. Once selected, we click on **Next** to move on to the next step.

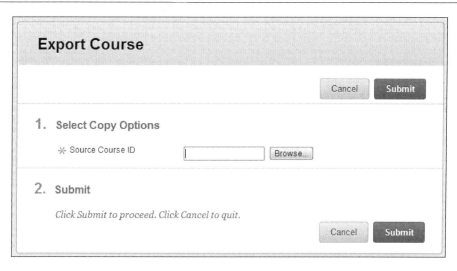

The following screenshot looks familiar because many of the options listed here are also there in the previous chapter. First we have the ability to see how big the course export will be, by clicking on the **Calculate Size** button, along with reviewing what files we want to export by clicking on the **Manage Package Contents** button. Our course export process also allows us to export only those files that are linked in the course content areas that we export by clicking on the checkbox to the right of our **Manage Package Contents** button.

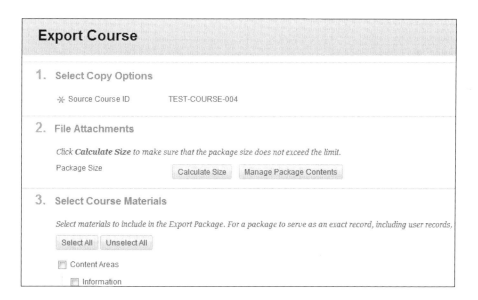

Now we really start to make decisions on what we do and don't want to export from the course. A good rule of thumb when exporting from courses would be, export everything, then import everything. This would allow our ZIP file to contain just about every item from the course and then after the import process the instructor can hide or remove what he or she doesn't want to use. Blackboard offers the ability to select all or none of our options by simply clicking on the **Select All** and **Unselect All** buttons at the top of our course materials list. We can click on the content areas and content associated (with these Blackboard Learn tools), which we want to export selectively, by checking the checkboxes to the left of every listed item. If we need to review the item descriptions, this information is available in *Chapter 4*, *Creating Courses in Blackboard Learn*, under the heading, *Copying Content into a New or Existing Course*.

Another reason to export everything out of a course would be to maintain the connections between tools and content areas. For example, if the course has a quiz deployed with a Grade Center column, not exporting any of the parts used by the quiz (the content area, Grade Center columns, Tests, Surveys, and Pools) will result in none of the connections working properly when it's imported from the export file. This will cause more work to get our course connections set back up.

Once we have selected our items to export, simply click on the **Submit** button. As in our import and course copy processes, the process is queued and we are notified that we will get an e-mail once the process is complete. This e-mail will include the export log which displays any issues with the export. Once we get the e-mail, we need to retrieve the zip file from our Blackboard Learn environment.

Our file will not be found in the area where we just created our export but is within the export/archive area of our course. Back in the courses area, we need to search for the course we just exported. Once we find that course, hover over the course name and click on the action button that appears to its right. We need to click on the **Export/Archive** option seen in the following screenshot to get our export file.

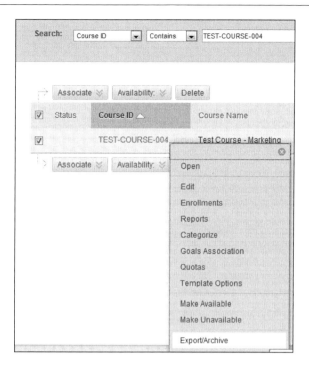

The **Export/Archive** page appears and our course export is listed. We can simply right-click on the file and save it in our computer. Back in our e-mail, we find detailed log of our export and this same log can be found if we click on the action button beside our exported file. Another item we should notice is that a set of numbers are added to the end of our zip file's name, shown in the following screenshot. In our example, the number is `20121103102710`. This means that our export file was completed on November 3, 2012 at 10:27:10 a.m., based on the server time. This allows us to know when an export was created in case we do multiple course exports or archives.

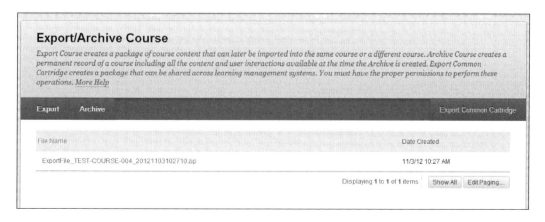

This location also allows us the ability to export and archive the selected course. The steps to export and to archive (which we will discuss in this chapter) can be completed using the **Export** and **Archive** buttons on this page. The process offers the same steps; however, we have already selected the course, so that step is skipped.

We have some options within this page also. If we hover over the name of the export file, we will see the action button appear and when clicked we will see an action menu just like the one in the following screenshot. Here we can look at the basic and detailed logs from our export process. We also can delete this export, which helps control the course's size within our Blackboard Learn environment.

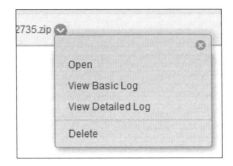

Exporting a Blackboard course into Common Cartridge format

In the previous chapter, we learned about the Common Cartridge format. We also went through the steps to import a Common Cartridge-format file into a new Blackboard course. Unlike the previous export process, we have only the Common Cartridge export option when we search for a specific course using the course search tool. Once we find our course to use in this process, we access the **Export** or the **Archive course** option by selecting it from the course action menu. The **Course Export/Archive** page appears, and on the right side we see the **Export Common Cartridge** button. We click on this button to start the export process.

The first step asks us to decide which version we want to use. The IMS Global Learning Consortium, which oversees the development of the Common Cartridge format, continually reviews how it can improve the format. This might be the time to find out if the Common Cartridge version that we plan to use is supported by the IMS Consortium. Once we have selected this option, click on **Submit**. The following screenshot illustrates this process:

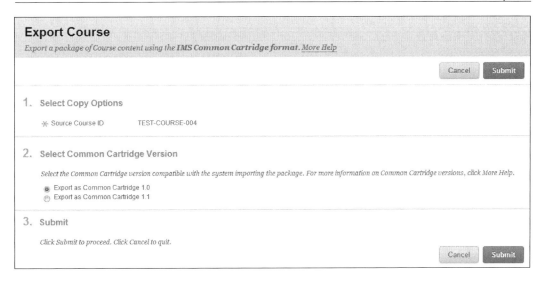

The export process begins and we will get a confirmation e-mail once it's completed. Unlike the export process using the Blackboard Learn format, this export will automatically grab all the content and tool data supported by the Common Cartridge format we selected. After we get the e-mail notification that the export process is complete, we simply go back to the **Course Export/Archive** page and the export is available for download. Notice the differences between the two exports. The Common Cartridge export includes the term in the filename along with a different file extension .imscc.

Archiving a Blackboard course

Exports can be great to move and back up course content from a Blackboard Learn instance. However, what if we want to have not only the content, but also user interactions, submissions, and grades? The archive process takes both types of content and puts it into a zip file that can be restored into the same or a different Blackboard Learn instance.

We start our archive process back in the **Course Search** page where we move our mouse pointer over the **Restore Options** button and click on the **Archive course** option. This loads the **Archive course** page where we select the course by typing in the course ID into the textbox, or clicking on **Browse...**, which opens our search window. We then use the search options to find our course to archive. Below the **Source Course ID** input box, notice the checkbox which allows us to include grade history from the course. Most administrators highly recommend that this option be checked. The grade history logs the changes made in the course's Grade Center, which could be helpful if the file is ever restored.

Our next option was also found in our course copy process. We can click on the **Calculate Size** button to see how big our archive package will be, and use the **Manage Package Contents** option to select what items might not need to be added to the archive file. This is shown in the following screenshot. However, we might not wish to remove any files from our archive since that defeats the purpose of this process. Noticeably absent from our options are the course content and tool selections that we find in a course copy and export process. Again, the purpose of our archive is to collect all files from this course. Simply click on the **Submit** button, and as with our other options, the process queues up, and an e-mail is generated when the process is completed.

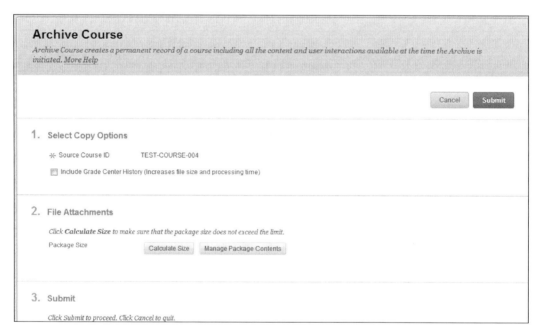

Once completed, the archive file appears in the same location where our export and Common Cartridge files appear, as shown in the following screenshot. One item that we should notice if we use external building blocks such as SafeAssign, lecture capture, or publisher websites, is that those items may not be exported or archived with the course because they may not follow the Common Cartridge guidelines. We should test those courses that we are concerned won't have some content exported or archived.

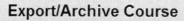

Export/Archive Course

Export Course creates a package of course content that can later be imported into the same course or a different c
permanent record of a course including all the content and user interactions available at the time the Archive is cr
Cartridge creates a package that can be shared across learning management systems. You must have the proper j
operations. More Help

Export   Archive

File Name

ExportFile_TEST-COURSE-004_20121103102710.zip

CommonCartridge_TEST-COURSE-004_20121103103001.imscc

ArchiveFile_TEST-COURSE-004_20121103104155.zip

Displaying **1** to **3** of 3 it

Batch exporting and archiving courses

We've just covered the basic process to export and archive courses from our Blackboard Learn instance one at a time. However, as administrators we may require the ability to export and archive multiple courses as a first step in a disaster-recovery or a term-ending process. Blackboard provides us with a script which uses a flat file to export a group of courses into their own separate zip files. We have a few steps to cover in this process, so let's begin with creating our flat file.

Our flat file is actually a `.txt` file that will have two different values separated by a comma, a semicolon, or a tab. If we plan to export or archive a set of courses, the process and the file will be formatted in the same (following) fashion:

```
COURSEID, /folder/
```

So if we plan to export the courses, which we created in the previous chapter, into an archives folder, our flat file would look like the following snippet if we are on a Linux or Solaris system. Note that the `myuser` folder seen in the code could be the home folder for the `bbuser` account we created during the installation process.

```
TEST-COURSE-001, /home/myuser/course_archives/

TEST-COURSE-002, /home/myuser/course_archives/
```

```
TEST-COURSE-003, /home/myuser/course_archives/
```

```
TEST-COURSE-004, /home/myuser/course_archives/
```

```
TEST-COURSE-005, /home/myuser/course_archives/
```

Or like this if we are on a Windows platform:

```
TEST-COURSE-001, C:\course_archives\
```

```
TEST-COURSE-002, C:\course_archives\
```

```
TEST-COURSE-003, C:\course_archives\
```

```
TEST-COURSE-004, C:\course_archives\
```

```
TEST-COURSE-005, C:\course_archives\
```

Unlike the batch create course and enroll users tools we used earlier that allowed only a maximum of 500 lines, this process does not have that maximum cap.

Now that we have created our flat file listing the courses to be archived, it's time to call the script to run the batch process. The script name is `batch_ImportExport.bat` for Windows platform and `batch_ImportExport.sh` for Unix and Solaris environments, and can be found in the `/apps/content-exchange/bin/` directory under the Blackboard `home` directory. While the script does not mention `archive` or `restore` in the title, we use this script for those processes as well.

When we run our script there are a few parameters that we need to give to it. The first one would be the full path to where our text file resides (`-f`). Here are some examples of file paths:

- On Windows platforms:

  ```
  C:\batch-text-files\weekly_course_export.txt
  ```

- On Linux and Solaris platforms:

  ```
  /home/myuser/batch-text-files/weekly_course_export.txt
  ```

The next parameter indicates the delimiter we used in our text file (`-l`). Unlike the batch course creation and batch enrollment files we created in *Chapter 4, Creating Courses in Blackboard Learn*, this script doesn't automatically detect which delimiter we use. Another interesting item is that this script uses numbers to designate the delimiter:

- 1 represents a comma (,) delimiter
- 2 represents a semicolon (;) delimiter
- 3 represents a tab delimiter

Another parameter our script requires is the operation we are requesting it to do. We have four different operations (listed here) to choose from, but we are only talking about two operations in this example:

- import
- export
- restore
- archive

The final parameter is only required if we are running this script on virtual installation within our Blackboard instance (-n). If so, we must add the virtual hostname as a variable. If we are not running any virtual installations, we can leave this variable off. So with all this information, let's see how we will create our single-lined script command:

- On Windows platforms:

```
C:\blackboard\apps\content-exchange\bin>batch_ImportExport.bat -f
C:\batch-text-files\weekly_course_export.txt -l 1 -t export -n
virtualhost.myorganization.com
```

- On Linux or Solaris platforms:

```
/usr/local/blackboard/apps/content-exchange/bin/batch_
ImportExport.sh -f /home/myuser/batch-text-files/weekly_course_
export.txt -l 1 -t export -n virtualhost.myorganization.com
```

What is a virtual hostname

We just learned about virtual installation and virtual hostname. One of the advanced options it provides is, it allows the creation of multiple Blackboard Learn environments to reside within one instance. For example, our corporate training, sales, or outreach departments could have different environments, with their own web addresses, courses, and users. This option is only available to organizations that license the Blackboard Community system, which is why we only mention it in passing.

Now we can start our command and begin the export or archive process. Many experienced Blackboard administrators will recommend we run a batch export or archive when the system isn't heavily used. This process can take a lot of time and some administrators have left a batch export or archive process running over an extended weekend. While any specific time frame will vary based on the content of the courses and our environment's specifications, but on an average, 1,000 courses will take about 12-16 hours to archive.

Tips for batch exporting and archiving

If we are running a load-balanced environment, we might take one application server out of our load-balanced environment to run a batch-export process like this.

We could also split the archive file among multiple application servers to allow each server to take a part of the load.

Whatever process we use, understand that a batch-export or archive process will put additional load on the application and database servers we are running the process on. Especially, if we are archiving courses, the database server will have heavy load, so remember to run these processes when there are very few users on our Blackboard Learn instance.

Once we complete our batch export or archive, we should move these files off the server to save space within our application server. These files may be kept on an available external hard drive or network storage device.

Many of the courses we want to export or archive can be rather large. If we find that our course exports or archives are not completing or giving a heap error, we can update the script to use more of the instance's heap size. Simply edit the script by adding the following line in a Windows platform:

```
OPTS="%OPTS -Xmx6g"
```

Or the following line in a Linux or Solaris environment:

```
OPTS="$OPTS -Xmx6g"
```

6g corresponds to the 6 GB of heap size that would be listed in our `bb-config.properties` file. This setting should never be larger than the heap size we have listed in our properties file and should never be larger than the amount of physical memory within our server. Once we have completed this process, we should remove this line from our script. We talk more about tuning the heap size and changing our `bb-config.properties` file in *Chapter 9, Manage Users in Blackboard Learn.*

Using the Bulk Delete function in Blackboard Learn

So we have exported or archived our course content from our instance and our instructor wants to re-use the course shell. How can we remove the users from this course, or remove parts of course content without recreating the course shell? The **Bulk Delete** option within Blackboard Learn is a great tool for this situation. Let's go through the Bulk Delete process for one of our courses.

We need to start back in the **Course Search** page, which we access by clicking on the **Courses** link within the **Courses** module on our **System Admin** tab. We then search for our course and once we find it in our search results, we click on the chevron to the right of the course name. In this menu, we click on the **Bulk Delete** option. The **Bulk Delete** page loads, shown in the following screenshot:

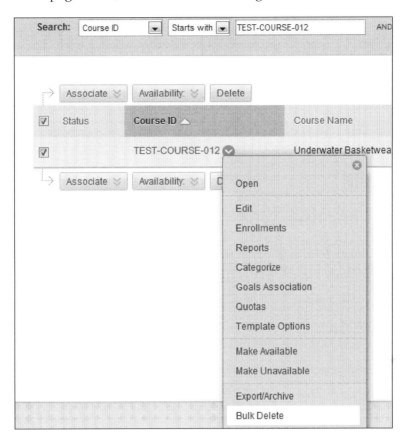

Here, on the **Bulk Delete** page we notice a few things. First, we are within the course to run this command. This is surprising because most administrator commands are run outside of the course. Hopefully this is an oversight by Blackboard. We have several areas within our course where we can remove course and user content. The page offers us the ability to delete content areas within this course—these would be areas normally displayed in the course menu. Next we can remove other content connected to the many tools used in this course; this area includes users.

Once we select all our options, we need to type in the word **Delete** into the textbox and then click on **Submit**. This is shown in the following screenshot:

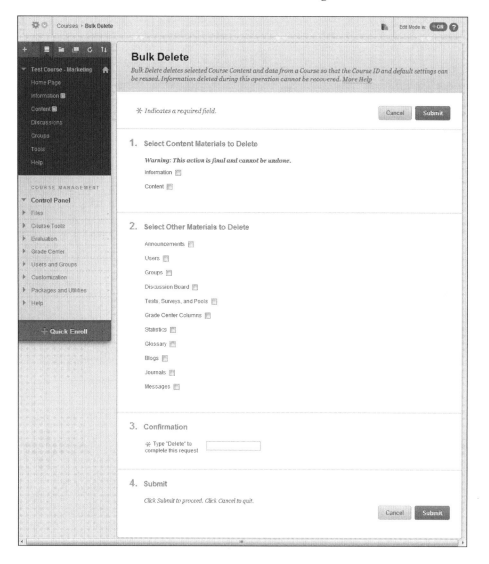

We should strongly consider how easily this tool can cause major issues if used without understanding the implications. There is no undo option; if we delete the users, announcements, or a content area (unless we have an export and/or archive of the course) we cannot get this information back. Most administrators don't give users the access to the **Bulk Delete** option for this reason and restrict it with the privileges tool that we will discuss in *Chapter 7, Manage Users in Blackboard Learn*.

Removing a course from Blackboard Learn

As we conclude this chapter and our discussion on courses in Blackboard Learn, it seems appropriate to discuss how to remove a course from our environment. Sometimes we no longer need to keep a course shell on our Blackboard instance or we have exported all the content and want to reduce the amount of used disk space. Whatever reason we might have, there are two ways to delete courses in Blackboard Learn.

The first option allows us to just search for a course using the course search tool and click on the chevron to the right of the course name. In that menu, we will find the **Delete** option, shown in the following screenshot. Once selected, we will get a pop-up box asking us to confirm if we want to delete this course. If we do, just click on the **OK** button. The course is now deleted and any course content will be marked as orphaned content. Orphaned content will be cleaned up with a regular task that runs within our Blackboard Learn environment.

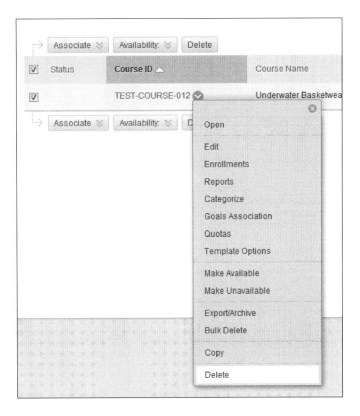

If we want to delete several courses all of which have similar searchable items such as a course ID code or the same instructor, we can use the course search tools to find these courses. Once we have them listed, just check the boxes to the left of the course ID and then click on the **Delete** button at the top or bottom of the list, shown in the following screenshot. The same pop-up warning appears and to confirm the deletion just click on the **OK** button.

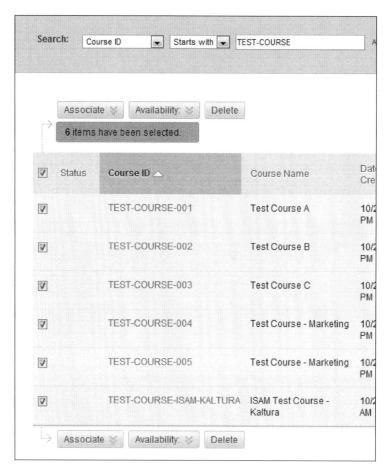

Reusing recently-deleted course IDs

Most administrators will at some point delete a course shell and then need to quickly recreate it for any, among a number of, reasons. In older Blackboard versions, this wasn't an issue, but with the introduction of the course file structure within course shells, there are a few steps we must complete before reusing the course shell. First we must go to the **Content Management** module and click on the **Content Orphaned by Location** link. This link will load a list of all the orphaned files and folders from deleted courses. We can look for the course ID we just deleted in the page's **Location** column, seen in the following screenshot. We then check the checkbox to select the folder and then click on the **Delete** button at the top or bottom of the list. A pop-up warning appears to let us know this can't be undone. If we want to go ahead and delete this, click on the **OK** button. Now we can re-use the course ID. If we want to be a bit more patient, we can normally wait about 24 hours for the system tasks to delete all the orphaned files out of our environment.

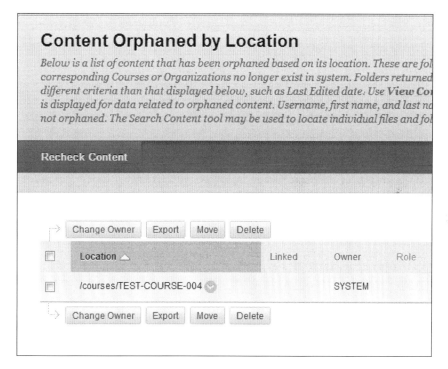

Summary

In this chapter we learned about courses in Blackboard Learn. We reviewed how to get users into our courses one by one or in a large group, and how we, as administrators, can access courses as instructors to help troubleshoot issues. Our discussion also covered how to allow those enrolled users access to the courses we create. We took a deep dive into the export and archive process—reviewing differences between the two and how to create these types of files from the website and command-line interfaces. Our final topic reviewed how to remove content or the entire course from Blackboard Learn.

Our virtual community has been created. We might call it a utopia for online learning; however, we are missing an important part. Users play a major role in the learning process and we need to allow them to have access. Without their participation, this is a virtual ghost town. So our next chapter will discuss how we can get our population to rise.

Creating Users in Blackboard Learn

Any community couldn't function without people in it. No matter if it was a cashier at the local coffee shop or the teacher at the local school. It's vital to our virtual community to allow users to access it and interact with others. This chapter will start our discussion and steps on how we develop a user creation policy and create users in Blackboard Learn. By the end of this chapter, we will have a good understanding about:

- Developing user guidelines on what information we need to create users
- Setting what user information we want to collect about users
- The process to create a single user in Blackboard Learn
- The process to create multiple users in Blackboard Learn

Let's begin our discussion by learning more about our organization's current users and usernames.

User creation policy

Before we start creating users within Blackboard Learn, there are a few considerations to take into account. Many Blackboard Learn instances use the application's ability to integrate with enrollment or authentication systems already implemented within an organization. While we will discuss these options in *Chapter 10*, *Authentication and Data Integration in Blackboard Learn*, creating users without thinking about these issues could cause problems later.

For example, if we plan to use an external authentication server such as **LDAP (Lightweight Directory Access Protocol)** to authenticate our Blackboard users, our usernames must match the LDAP requirements for our users to be allowed access to Blackboard. This means we will need to create users based on the same information used to create them within the external authentication environment. If we plan to integrate with an enrollment system, the username, student ID or employee ID, and other information will need to match this environment as well. The more we integrate our Blackboard Learn instance with other systems within our organization, the more time and thought we will need to put into how to make sure our instance and user data are accurate.

If our organization decides that our Blackboard Learn environment won't be connected to an external authentication or enrollment system, we may want to utilize the same usernames for user's ease and support. There may be a situation where you must create a new username structure for our Blackboard Learn environment. In the following examples, we will see how different administrators or organizations have dealt with creating usernames within their instance. No administrator will have the right answers for us, but we can review these tips on usernames to educate and help ourselves if we ever want to create our own username structure.

- **Base the username from the person's name**: It can be easier to remember a username if someone can associate a few letters from his/her name. If John S. Smith wanted a username, we could use jsmith.

- **Always be prepared for multiples**: We like to think that everyone is unique, however names sometimes aren't. If we have two users with the name John S. Smith at our organization, how will we designate between them? We could use jssmith and jsmith or jsmith01. We should have a plan for this situation.

- **Add differences between types of users**: Many organizations use different types of usernames for instructors and students in Blackboard Learn. Some examples might be using jsmith for instructors, but jsm0447, j546sm, or stu0447 for students. This can put some users into an odd situation where their instructor username is enrolled in a course as a student or a student username is an instructor in a course, such as a graduate assistant. In this situation, we may want to create a student account for our instructor to access courses as a student. We may find our instructors want to have a separate student user account for every student.

- **Plan for the long term**: Usernames should be long term IDs. We should take great care in the way we create and maintain them. However, we need to have the ability to deal with any changes in user's life such as marriage, divorce, or legal name changes. Make sure all departments who use our Blackboard Learn instance understand and agree to the username policy.

User Creation Planning	Yes	No
Does our organization already have a user creation policy in place?		
Do we plan to connect our Blackboard Learn environment to any external systems?		
Do we plan to make clear differences between instructor and student user names?		
How long do we plan to keep our user naming policy in place before reviewing it?		

These username tips come from many years of working experiences with Blackboard and we may find more to address this issue as we continue to work with Blackboard Learn, but now we have a better understanding about usernames and why we should have a user creation policy. Now, we need to set up what information Blackboard Learn will require to create users.

Setting Up default user information in Blackboard Learn

Any Blackboard Learn instance collects and displays information about each user. Common information includes the user's first and last name along with his/her e-mail address and maybe even their student ID number. This information can be provided by administrators (that is, ourselves) or by the user. We also have the ability to decide if this information is displayed and if it's editable by the user with Blackboard Learn. We set these options in the **Customize User Information** page.

To get to this page, go to our **System Admin** tab and find the **Users** module. Click on the **Customize User Information** link. The first option on the **Customize User Information** page is shown in the following screenshot. It allows us to create a link to a site where users can update their information. We might use this option if we use information from an external system such as an enrollment or student information system to update user data within our instance. Enabling this would direct users to the updated page for the external system.

This area allows us to put in our link, title, and instructions to users. These instructions might share the process we just mentioned and ask the user to update their information there. If you won't be using an external system, leave the box unchecked.

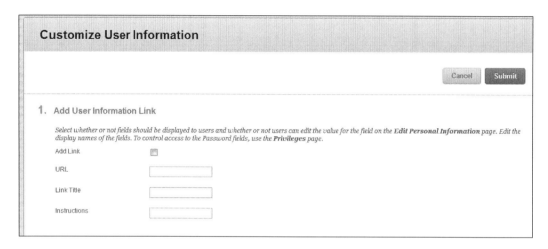

In the following screenshot, we can see all the information that Blackboard Learn, by default, collects from users. It may seem like a lot of information, however remember that most of this information is optional. The only items that are required to create a user are **First Name**, **Last Name**, **Username**, and **Password**.

These are the only four that are required by the application; however I would suggest that you consider another field as well, **Email**. If you expect a user to get e-mails about notifications, discussion board's posts, or e-mail from instructors about course progress, an e-mail address is needed. We will talk more about notifications in our next section.

Adjacent to each field name we find two checkboxes. The first checkbox option is **Display**, which if checked will allow all users to see this information. The second option is **Editable**. If this box is checked, it will allow the user to change the information displayed in this field. Our decisions to display (or not to display) user information will be based on our organization's policies along with that of other governance bodies. We should note that the only way other student users can see this information is by using the user directory, which we can disable, or via the **Roster** tool with the course.

This page also allows us to rename these fields, in order to change them to match terms used for this data within our organization. An example would be changing the field **Other Name** to **Preferred Name** for users. If we make any changes on this page, we should click on the **Submit** button to apply our changes to the application.

Creating single users in Blackboard Learn

We've now customized the user information for our Blackboard Learn environment and now it's time to create a user. Even if we plan to create users from external systems, administrators will normally keep a few local user IDs around in case the external systems fail and we need to gain access to our instance, or we need to create test or demonstration accounts that don't need to interact with the larger campus. So let's go through the steps to create a user in Blackboard Learn.

In the preceding screenshot, we saw part of the **System Admin** tab, here we click on the **Users** link. This takes us back to the **Users** page. Now click on the **Create User** button, shown in the following screenshot, to create our first user:

This takes us to the **Create User** page. We've got quite a few textboxes to fill in, but remember that there really are only five boxes that we must fill (or six if you count **Email**). Notice that the required fields have an orange asterisk beside the field name.

Create User

Information about users is stored in a User Profile. It is possible to set which the fields of data in editable by users. More Help

✻ *Indicates a required field.*

1. Personal Information

Title

✻ First Name

Middle Name

✻ Last Name

Suffix

Other Name

Email

Student ID

2. Account Information

✻ Username

✻ Password

✻ Verify Password

The first section asks for the user's personal information. The only fields that we must fill in here are **First Name** and **Last Name**, however we would also want to put in an e-mail address for reasons we discussed earlier. The next section allows us to put in the username and password. Remember earlier in this chapter we discussed a username policy and its importance. We should now have our username creation policy ready, so we should be sure to follow it. Then, we fill in the user's password twice to confirm that the password is correct. Next we can add more detailed information about the user including contact information, but this information is optional and is only used in the user directory.

Our last two options give us the ability to set institutional and system roles. If your instance doesn't include the Blackboard community, you will only see the system role. The institutional role will allow the user to see information such as modules and tabs within the community system based on the assigned role.

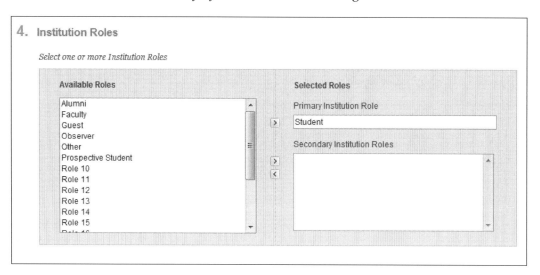

The system roles give users access to administrative controls within our Blackboard Learn instance. Each role can be assigned permissions to access areas. The only default roles that don't grant administrative access are guest, observer, and none. The system role defaults to none for every user, however we can click on a different role and then click on the **>** button. This button sets the primary system role. Users can also have secondary system roles; let's explore this with a hypothetical example. A user is the head of our help desk team but also needs to be able to create and manage user accounts for his colleagues. While his primary system role might be **Support**, he may also want the secondary system role of **User Adminstrator**. By giving him both system roles, we can better manage the privileges required by each user in our Blackboard Learn instance to complete his/her duties. Any user that is assigned a system role will see the **System Admin** tab. However, their access to the tools within this tab will be controlled by the **Privileges** tool. In the following screenshot, we see how we can assign these two system roles to a user:

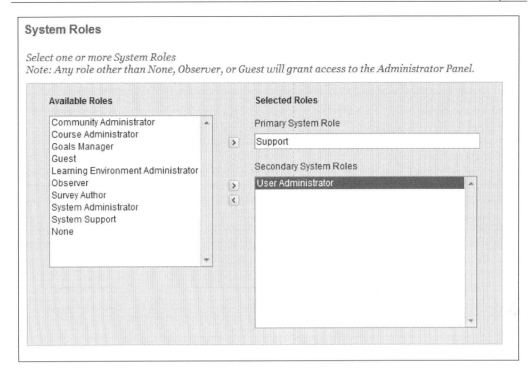

 If we want to see the default privileges for most of the system roles listed, we can find a table in the *Appendix*.

We have finished putting in our user information and now we simply click on the **Submit** button to create the user. If the username is already in the system, we will get an error stating that. It then suggests a new username with the letter a placed at the end. If not, a green success banner will appear.

Creating multiple users in Blackboard Learn

We have just reviewed how to create one user in Blackboard Learn, but most administrators won't use that creation process often. If we want to add a large amount of users, we need to use a batch process just like we did while creating courses and enrolling users. Before we start the batch user creation process, let's create our file.

As we saw when we created our user earlier, we have several different fields to fill. These include the following, in order:

- **Username**
- **Last Name**
- **First Name**
- **Email**
- **Password**
- **Student ID**
- **Middle Name**
- **Job Title**
- **Department**
- **Company**
- **Street 1**
- **Street 2**
- **City**
- **State / Province**
- **Zip / Postal Code**
- **Country**
- **Work Phone**
- **Home Phone**
- **Work Fax**
- **Mobile Phone**
- **Website**
- **Primary Institution Role**
- **System Availability**
- **Other Name**
- **Suffix**
- **Title**

While we might use all these fields when creating some users, our example will concentrate on the required fields (**Username**, **Last Name**, **First Name**, and **Password**) along with the very strongly advised **Email**. If we don't set fields such as **Primary Institution Role** or **System Availability** within our batch file, they will be set to system defaults. As with other batch files in Blackboard Learn, we can use comma, tab, or colon as delimiters in our batch file. In our example we will use comma.

Now if we wish to create three users in our Blackboard Learn instance. First we would create a batch file, which would look like the following.

```
User5, Smith, John, jsmith@myorganization.com, jsmith5
User6, Nice, Suzy, snice@myorganization.com, snice6
User7, Kline, Ted, tkline@myorganization.com, tkline7
```

Then we would save the file in a `.txt` format. Now these three users can be created using the batch user creation process.

The process is similar to our other batch processes. Go to the **Users** page in the **Users** module, mouse over the batch actions, and click on the **Create Users** link. This will take us to the **Batch Create Users** page.

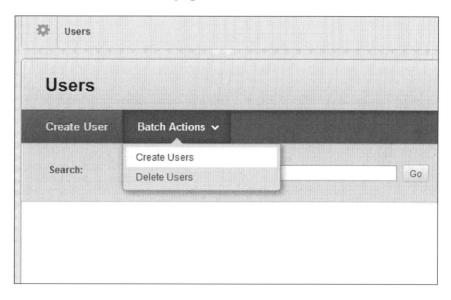

Here we click on the **Browse** button to find our text file on our computer. Then we can select our delimiter or leave the automatic setting. Finally, we click on the **Submit** button.

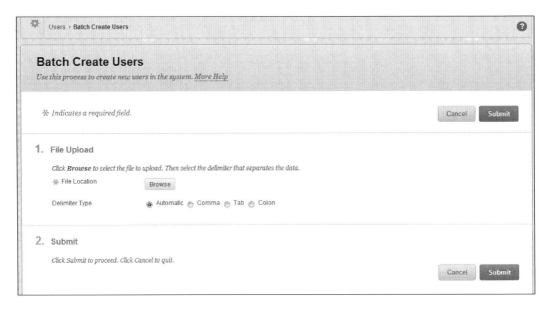

We then see our result's page, which should look similar to the following screenshot. This page not only shows the successfully created accounts, but also any errors that mean our users weren't created successfully, and may suggest alternative usernames if there is a conflict with existing accounts.

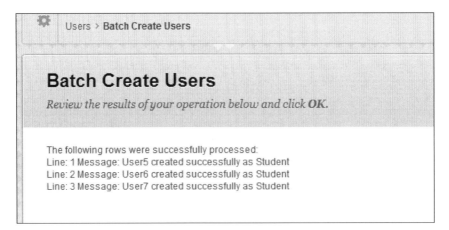

Accessing users in Blackboard Learn

Now that we have created users within our environment, we need to learn about our abilities to search and find users within Blackboard Learn. We can access users within the **Users** link. This area allows us to create and search for a user along with using the batch process to create and delete users on our Blackboard instance. Let's spend a little bit of time familiarizing ourselves with this page.

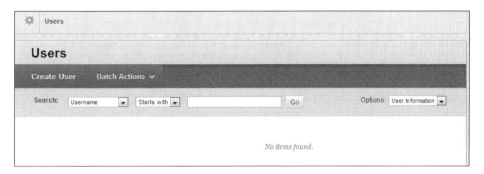

At the top of this page, we find a **Create User** button and a **Batch Actions** drop-down menu. These allow us to create and delete users from our Blackboard instance. We will discuss more on these options later. The next part of this image allows us to search for users within Blackboard Learn. We have several different fields we can search on, including: **Username**, **First Name**, **Last Name**, **Email**, **Student ID**, and **Data Source Key** (we will discuss more about data source keys in *Chapter 10*, *Authentication and Data Integration in Blackboard Learn*). Our search options also include **Starts with**, **Equal to**, **Contains**, and **Is not blank**, which we have seen in our course search options.

We also have some additional options in this area. If we look to the right side of the page, there is a drop-down box with four different options. The default option is **User Information**, which allows our search options for users. Let's go a little deeper into the other three options available.

- **Enrollments**: This option allows us to see how many users are enrolled in courses or organizations. We can search based on less than, equal to, or greater than a set number.

- **Last Login**: When we use this option, we can learn how many system users have accessed our instance before or after a set date or have ever accessed our system.

- **System Roles**: If we ever wonder which users have system administrator, system support, or any other system role, just use this search option and select what roles we want to find. We will learn more about system roles in *Chapter 7*, *Managing Roles and Users in Blackboard Learn*.

Summary

We have just completed our initial look into the world of Blackboard Learn users. This chapter helped us understand the importance of planning when it comes to users. Whether we plan to integrate our environment with other organizational systems or have it run by itself, administrators like us have to do some chin rubbing. We must think about how our decisions and user policies will affect us in the future. Blackboard offers us many controls on what information users can see about themselves and others. Our discussions also reviewed the process to create one or multiple users within our instance.

Our next chapter gets us into the deeper waters of user management within Blackboard Learn. We will start to become the virtual landlord for our tenants, giving out keys and access to different parts of our virtual community. So get ready to learn more about roles and privileges as we move into the next chapter.

7
Managing Roles and Users in Blackboard Learn

In our conversations about courses, we compared the Blackboard Learn course shell to a home or apartment. These virtual spaces serve as a home to our instructors and students. However, they can allow or restrict access, just like their real-world counterparts. In the real world, we have keys or key cards to gain access, and in the virtual world we have enrollments and course roles, which control who can gain access and what they can access within Blackboard Learn and its courses. This chapter will address the following:

- Demonstrating how we can create course, institutional, and system roles
- Reviewing the management options for course, institutional, and system roles
- Demonstrating how to change privileges for roles within Blackboard Learn
- Learning helpful tips when creating policies for users in a Blackboard Learn instance
- Reviewing the steps to disable and remove a user

Our conversation about users continues with a look into course role management.

Roles within Blackboard Learn

Users within our Blackboard Learn environment normally won't find themselves without some type of role attached to their user account. These roles control what a user can do within our instance. There are three different types of roles:

- **Institutional role type**: This role type associates the user accounts with what type of users they are within our organization. As the course role type determines how a course appears to a person, the institutional role type determines how a larger community appears to the user. Most users will be associated with a student institutional role, while some may find themselves in faculty or staff roles. These roles are rarely used to control access within Blackboard Learn, but closely control access to items with the Blackboard Community system.

- **System role type**: Unlike with institutional and course roles, system role types give only specific users the ability to access the **System Admin** tab and portions of the Blackboard Learn environment to administer and support the organization. Different system roles restrict users to only specific tools within the **System Admin** area. We can find a detailed listing of each system role's privilege in *Appendix*.

- **Course role type**: These course roles associate the type of access the user account should have in a course that he/she is enrolled in. These course roles include more than just a standard student or instructor role. We mentioned these role types in *Chapter 5, Enrolling Users into Blackboard Learn Courses*.

These role types provide administrators with the ability to give users enough access to complete their work within our Blackboard Learn instance.

Managing course roles in Blackboard Learn

In *Chapter 5, Administrating Courses in Blackboard Learn*, we discussed the different roles users can have within a course and what users can do with those roles. Our Blackboard Learn instance has a set of default course roles with the following titles.

- **Course Builder**
- **Grader**
- **Instructor**
- **Student**
- **Teaching Assistant**
- **Guest**

We can see a list of these by clicking on the **System Admin** tab. Under the **Users** module, we find the **Course/Organization Roles** link that will take us there, as shown in the following screenshot:

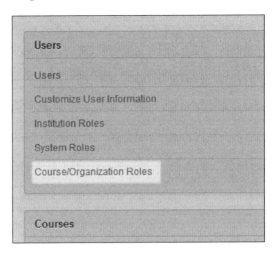

This page gives us a list of our roles and their names in the courses (and organizations, if we have Blackboard Community). We might call these roles by different names within our organization, but for our instance, we will change the title instructor role's name to teacher or professor.

Editing a course role

If we want to make this change, we can do so by moving our mouse over **Role ID**, such as **Course Builder** or **Instructor**. Click on the chevron to display our action menu and then select **Edit**, as shown in the following screenshot:

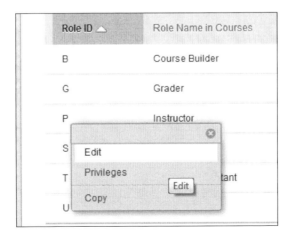

This opens our **Edit Course/Org Role** page.

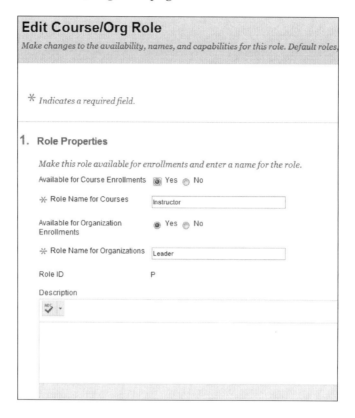

We find that we can change the role name for our courses and organizations at the same time. The page also allows us to set the role to be available for course enrollments. For this option, you can select either **Yes** or **No**. This option will control if the course role will be listed when trying to add users to a course. In the following screenshot, we can see a side-by-side comparison with the **Course Builder** role disabled using this option on the right-hand side.

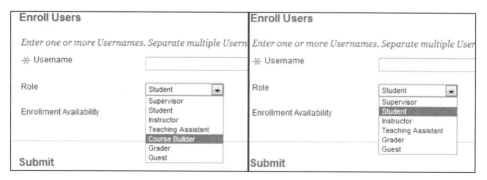

We should note that while we can change the role name, we cannot change the role ID, which we used in the batch course enrollment. This page also allows us to add a description to this role if we want to explain what options and permissions are given to users with this role. This can help users who manage courses or organizations to know what basic actions and abilities this role gives. Please be aware that while you can rename them, currently you cannot edit the privileges or copy the student or guest roles.

The second area within this page allows us to control some of this role's capabilities. The first option asks if we would like our instance to treat users with this role like the Instructor role. This will only affect the options listed on the screen, which are access to unavailable courses, display in the course catalog, and e-mail enrollment requests. We may use this option if one of our course roles will be used to monitor an instructor's work as a supervisor or department head.

The second and third options allow the user role to have full permissions within the course or organization file structure. This means the role would have full access to course and/or organization files. We must have these options set to **Yes** if users with this role are going to be creating and viewing course content. While we have set a few of the privileges within this page, more detailed privilege levels will be discussed later in this chapter. Once we have made any changes, simply click on the **Submit** button and the success or failure option will appear. Note that we can use alphanumeric characters and symbols in our role names.

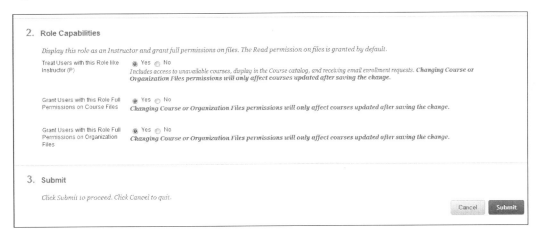

Creating a new course role using the Copy function

While renaming a course role usually works well, sometimes we need to create a new course role to fulfill a need of our organization. Some Blackboard Learn instances have the ability to create new ones by copying existing course roles. We can start this process by selecting a course role's action menu and clicking on the **Copy** option. Note that we should select a role with privileges similar to our planned new user role. This will cut down the number of changes to privileges we will have to make.

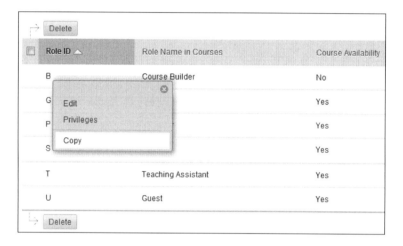

Let's create an example by copying the instructor role.

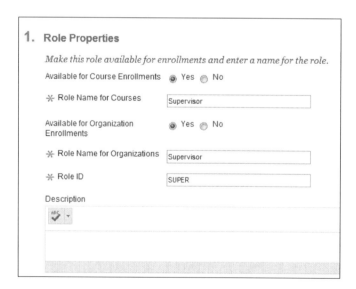

We should notice that our first options are to set the **Available for Course Enrollments** option along with the **Role Name for Courses** option. As we saw earlier, we can have different role names for courses and organizations in our instance by using a different title for the **Role Name for Organizations** field.

Our new role allows us to create a new role ID. This ID can be made up of letters and numbers only—no special characters can be used. We also find the same **Role Capabilities** options that we demonstrated in the *Editing a course role* section.

If we click on the **Submit** button, our Blackboard Learn environment takes us to the **Privileges** page. This page allows us to give and revoke different privileges to users with this role. In our example, this role will have every privilege that the instructor user role requires because we used the instructor role to create this copy. Let's look at a specific privilege within this role; the ability to delete material from a course.

Reasons to create new course roles

Often, our organization will find new needs to create new course roles within Blackboard Learn. These can be as simple as a role to allow an instructor help a new online instructor use the Blackboard Learn environment for a course. Some organizations will create a course role to allow a department head to be able to look into a course being taught by his or her faculty.

These are just some examples of when we might create a course role.

Managing privileges for course roles

We have two ways to find a specific privilege within the six-page list of privileges. Either search page by page for the **delete materials** privilege or use the **Search** tool at the top of the page which will find it for us. Most of us would use the **Search** tool, but sometimes it is good to go through every page and look at what rights the role receives in Blackboard Learn.

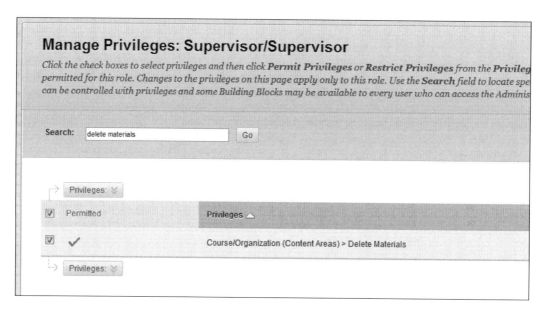

This browsing strategy is also good to use after software updates and upgrades to keep privileges updated.

As seen in the preceding screenshot, our search for the phrase "delete materials" comes up with one privilege. Notice that the privilege has a green check beside it. This lets us know that the privilege is enabled for this role. We would see a red X if the privilege were disabled. Privilege information is displayed in subgroups to help us better understand the impact of our change or changes.

If we want to edit a privilege, we just check the checkbox beside the privilege we want to change and then mouse over the **Privileges** button at the top or bottom of the list. Next, we select either to allow or restrict the privilege, and once we select this option, the change is made immediately. Later in this chapter we will discuss more details about privileges.

Managing system roles in Blackboard Learn

Not only can we manage the roles for users in courses and organizations, but we can also manage the roles that we give other users who help us manage our Blackboard instance. These would be the housekeepers and maintenance staff members who would work in our apartment, complex, or hotel.

Blackboard Learn comes with several default system roles. Back in the **System Admin** tab, we can click on the **System Roles** link under the **Users** module. In the **System Roles** page, there are many system roles available by default; let's go over them.

- **Community Administrator**: Users with this role have the ability to manage items associated with Blackboard Community (if your organization licenses it). These include organizations, discussion boards, brands, and themes.

- **Course Administrator**: This role gives its users the ability to manage courses and enrollments within our Blackboard Learn instance.

- **Goals Manager**: Users with this role can manage the **Institutional Goals** tool within Blackboard Learn.

- **Guest**: This is the default role for users who haven't logged in to Blackboard Learn. We cannot change the privileges given to this role.

- **Learning Environment Administrator**: Users can create institutional tabs, tab groups, and modules with Blackboard Community and can create, import, export, and edit courses and their enrollments within this role.

- **None**: A user will only be able to change his/her personal information in fields that are allowed. Most users will have this role by default.

- **Observer**: Users associated with this role can view materials and interactions for the students associated with the user account. However, observer users have read-only access. This role cannot be renamed.

- **Support**: This role meets the needs of most tier 1 support staff. It gives users basic course, organization, and user functions within Blackboard Learn.

- **Survey Author**: Users can create new surveys and deploy surveys they are allowed to access with this role.

- **System Administrator**: This is the default role for Blackboard administrators and gives all privileges to the user or users. This role's privileges cannot be edited.

- **System Support**: Users have similar privileges as the **System Administrator** role, however some functions are disabled including the **Quick Enroll** privilege.

- **User Administrator**: User creation, editing, enrolling, and deleting can be managed with this role.

Now we know the default roles in our Blackboard Learn instance and what each of them will do. Earlier we discussed how to edit and copy course roles. These options are also available to us with the system roles and work the same way. Let's learn how we can create new system roles within our environment.

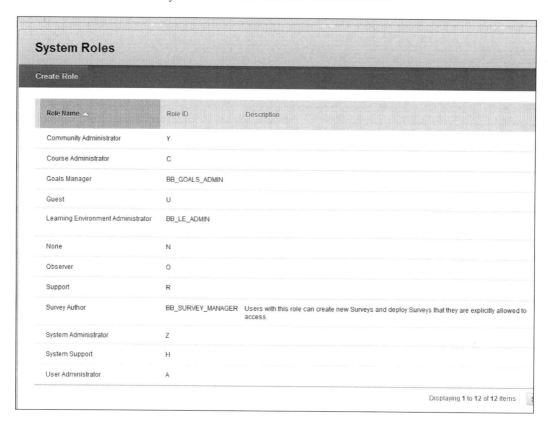

Creating system roles in Blackboard Learn

In our **System Roles** page, click on the **Create Role** button. The **Create Role** page appears. Our first option asks us for a role name and role ID. Remember that our role IDs must be made up of letters and numbers only. We also can put in a description of this role.

After clicking on the **Submit** button, our instance loads the privileges available to a system role. At the time of this writing, a clean install of Blackboard Learn has over 350 privileges to allow or restrict. The more Blackboard Learn changes and other items, such as building blocks, are installed, the more the number of privileges will increase.

As with course roles, we check the boxes beside the privileges and select to either allow or restrict them for this role. Once we complete this, click on **OK** and we are taken back to the **System Roles** page.

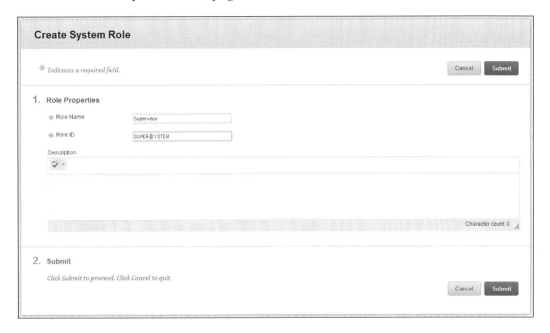

Tips on system roles and their privileges

Most administrators will find some time during their work with the Blackboard Learn application where a mistake by a helpful user with system-level access creates issues. An example might be that a user calls our support team and states they can't log in to Blackboard. The staff member creates a new user within the **System Admin** tab.

If our course or user creation depends on data feeds from the enrollment or student information systems (which we will discuss in *Chapter 10, Authentication and Data Integration in Blackboard Learn*), the creation of a course or user account in this manner could cause issues with the automated enrollment process. This creates more work for us as a system administrator.

If we had removed such a privilege from the system role, this issue would have been forwarded to us, and the time to correct the creation would have been spent finding out why the user's account wasn't created automatically.

Creating custom institutional roles in Blackboard Learn

If your organization has Blackboard Community, you have the ability to create and manage institutional roles. Institutional roles can help control what modules and tabs users can access within a Blackboard Learn instance with Blackboard Community. The creation and management of institutional roles is the same as that of the course and system roles discussed earlier in this chapter.

Managing role privileges in Blackboard Learn

So now we know how to create roles for users on the course, system administration, or institution levels. We even saw what privileges were available to each role and how to permit and restrict them. However, what if we want to look at a privilege and see what roles utilize it? Blackboard Learn gives us that ability using the **Privileges** area.

Unlike most of our role management, we find the **Privileges** link in the **Security** module in the **System Admin** tab.

This link takes us to the **Privileges** page within our instance. This page lists all the privileges available along with a search box. The search box tool can search privileges or roles within the system. If we look at our options, there are many roles that we have already discussed in this chapter, but we might also find other roles. **Unit**, **Program**, **Educational Experience**, **Outcomes Course**, and **Workspace** roles all pertain to Blackboard's **Outcomes** product. We only mention them here so that you can be aware of them.

Earlier we searched for the **delete materials** privilege. Let's use that same search criteria in our **Privileges** search as a comparison. As in our previous search, we get only one result as shown in the following screenshot:

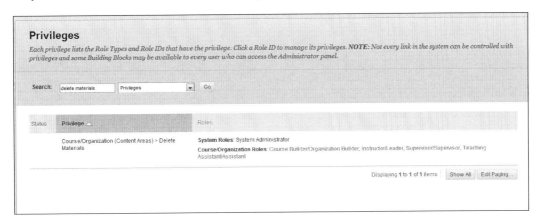

However, now the result is displayed differently. Instead of a check mark or red X, we see the privilege and then the roles that have that privilege enabled. The roles are also organized by type and most are links that allow you to edit the association between roles and privileges, except roles such as **System Administrator**, where the application has disabled this option. We see that the **Supervisor** role, created earlier in this chapter, has this privilege. If we want to remove this privilege from the role we can click on the role. This link takes us to the **Manage Privilege** page. From here we follow our earlier steps to allow or restrict a privilege or privileges for this role.

Developing role privilege policies in Blackboard Learn

So far in this chapter, we have reviewed the user roles available in our Blackboard Learn instance. Our discussions have shown how to create, copy, and manage roles along with how to manage privileges, and have been mainly focused on the how-tos that Blackboard administrators need to know. Now let's talk about what we can do as administrators to manage who has access.

- **Regularly audit users to system roles**: Often, we have more than one person to help administrate our Blackboard Learn instance. As part of any good security policy, it's important that we ensure an annual or semi-annual review of all users who have a system role. We can do this within our Blackboard instance by going back to the **Users** page and selecting **System Roles** from the options. Many administrators keep a spreadsheet listing the users who have roles to compare audits.

- **Regularly review the privileges for roles**: Sometimes system roles will need access to complete a task. But sometimes policies change and that means a role change is needed. If different departments and teams use these roles, it would make sense that we sit down and review these privileges on an annual and semi-annual basis.

- **Record the enabled and restricted privileges for each role**: While role privileges shouldn't change without our knowledge, sometimes changes can happen as the result of an update or patch. Administrators like us might keep a copy of privileges for each role, including which ones are permitted and restricted. At this time, Blackboard doesn't have the ability to import or export role privileges.

Disabling user access to Blackboard Learn

Our discussions so far have focused on creating and managing users in Blackboard Learn. However, sometimes we need to disable a user account within our Blackboard Learn instance. This may be due to someone leaving our organization or taking a sabbatical. While we might want to remove the user immediately and be done with it, most administrators recommend disabling a user first. Why this two-step approach? If we remove the user, the associated content and course work will be lost, which could create issues for instructors; disabling allows for the ability to recover information. Also, if the user comes back (for example, if he/she decides to return to the organization or returns after a long absence), we can simply enable their account.

If we want to disable a user, we first need to go back to our **Users** page. Here we should search for the user we need to disable. Once found, we check the checkbox beside the search result. Then, find the **Availability** button at the top or bottom of the search result. When we move our mouse over this button, we get the options **Make Available** or **Make Unavailable**. Once we select our option, the page will reload and a success or failure bar will appear at the top. Alternatively for a single user, you can make the user unavailable via an option in the action menu. There is no option to disable a batch in the GUI.

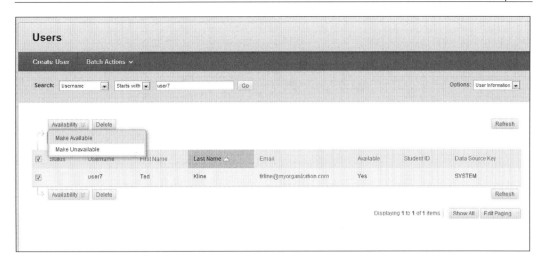

Removing users in Blackboard Learn

If we find that disabling a user doesn't meet our needs, or if a "cooling down" period has passed, we can remove a user. This process is final; once a user account is deleted, it cannot be restored along with all its associations. If the user account is enrolled in a course or organization, their information, such as discussion boards or wikis, will replace the user's information with anonymous data, or completely deletes the contribution. This also means that the user's grades will also disappear. Because of these issues, most administrators will just disable a user and not delete the account. If after that warning we still want to remove a user, it is highly recommended that we archive courses or organizations where the users are enrolled.

Removing a user can be done in two different ways; one at a time or by using a batch file. Let's start our conversation by learning how to delete one user from our Blackboard Learn environment.

Removing a single user from our Blackboard Learn environment starts with us back at the **Users** page in our **System Admin** tab. The search allows us to find the specific user; we then check the checkbox beside the user to be removed. At the top or bottom of our results, click on the **Delete** button and a pop-up box asks us to confirm that we want to remove the user from our instance. After confirming the removal by clicking on the **OK** button shown in the following screenshot, we get the success or failure bar that lets us know the status of our request:

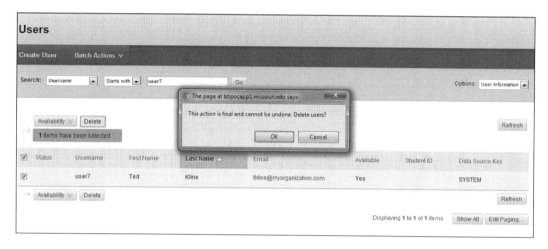

Just like creating and enrolling users in Blackboard, we can batch delete our users by creating a file. Unlike deleting single users, the batch process allows us to remove a larger number of users from our instance at one time. Blackboard Learn accepts many fields in each deletion record and they must be in the following order:

- **Username**
- **Last Name**
- **First Name**
- **Email**
- **Password**
- **Student ID**
- **Middle Name**
- **Job Title**
- **Department**
- **Company**
- **Street 1**
- **Street 2**

- **City**
- **State / Province**
- **Zip / Postal Code**
- **Country**
- **Work Phone**
- **Home Phone**
- **Work Fax**
- **Mobile Phone**
- **Website**
- **Primary Institution Role**
- **System Availability**
- **Other Name**
- **Suffix,Title**

While these fields can be in our batch file, the **Username** is the only required field. We can use a comma, tab, or colon as file delimiters just as in our other batch files. Here is an example of how it should be:

```
User5, Smith, John, jsmith@myorganization.com, jsmith5
User6, Nice, Suzy, snice@myorganization.com, snice6
User7, Kline, Ted, tkline@myorganization.com, tkline7
```

We may be asking ourselves why the file is exactly the same as our users batch file created back in the *Creating multiple users in Blackboard Learn* section in *Chapter 6, Creating Users in Blackboard Learn*. This is a handy way to avoid having to create two separate file formats, one for account creation and one for account removal. This format can be very useful, if we are managing temporary users and enrollments. We can quickly remove these users at once.

After creating the text file and saving it, we go back to the **Users** page and follow the same steps as we have discussed in our other batch processes in *Chapter 6, Creating Users in Blackboard Learn*.

Within the **Users** page, we move our mouse over the **Batch Actions** button and select **Delete Users** from the drop-down menu. Then we upload our file and click on the **Submit** button. After the file processes, we learn if the file causes any errors and get our success or failure notification.

Summary

Users play an important part in our Blackboard Learn environment. Whether they are students, teaching assistants, instructors, support staff, or administrators, like us, each one has a role in the system. These roles require privileges, which allow the users to complete tasks and control access to areas, just like our hotel or apartment complex. We as administrators should develop ways to monitor which users have access to the different parts of Blackboard Learn and when privilege changes allow new roles to gain or lose specific abilities. Our final discussion about users reviewed the ways to restrict access completely by disabling or removing users.

We've mainly talked about courses and users over the past few chapters, but now let's move into some of the important tools for administrators within Blackboard. The application offers numerous tools within courses, but some of these same tools can help us manage and inform our virtual community. Our next chapter gives us a crash course in the tools of Blackboard Learn.

8

Using Tools and Utilities in Blackboard Learn

Our discussions over the past few chapters touched on the management of courses and users within Blackboard Learn. While these play a major role in how our virtual community works, there are many other items that help us (administrators) do our job or ensure that the courses we host operate smoothly. In this chapter, we will discuss the following tools in detail:

- System announcements
- Spellcheck
- Language packs
- System notifications

Our discussions in this chapter will also include brief overviews of other tools within the **Tools and Utilities** module. By the end of this chapter, we will understand how we can use our tools to improve our work as Blackboard Learn administrators.

System announcements

Often, we as administrators need to communicate information to our Blackboard Learn users system-wide. Whether the topic is planned maintenance, campus events, weather closures, or other emergency messages, Blackboard Learn gives us this ability with system announcements. This tool works in the same way as course and organization announcements, but will be displayed to every user when they access our environment.

We access our **System Announcements** area by clicking on the **Announcements** link located under the **Tools and Utilities** module within the **System Admin** tab.

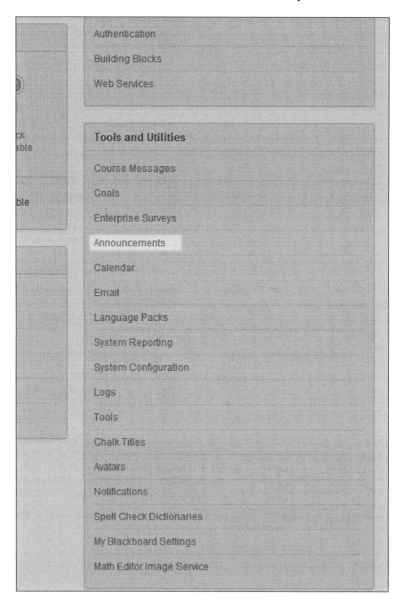

In our **Announcements** page, we see any announcements we previously created. From this page, we can manage our system announcements from creation to deletion. Let's go through creating an announcement for our Blackboard Learn environment.

Creating a system announcement

Within the **Announcements** page, click on the **Create Announcement** button.

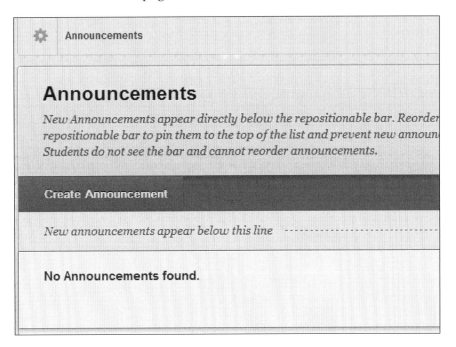

The **Create Announcement** page loads. The first item we need to provide is the announcement's subject line. The subject line should explain the announcement. For example, if we plan to have our instance down on Sunday afternoon, our subject line should read,"Blackboard Down This Sunday Afternoon for Maintenance". We may also want to add the date within the title to clarify when the event will happen.

Our message comes next. Here we explain to the users when the system will be unavailable and when the system will come back up. We can also explain why we need to have the system unavailable at this time and offer an apology or appreciation for the user's patience. Notice that we have the visual textbox editor that will allow us to format our message and include links, images, and even videos if we wish.

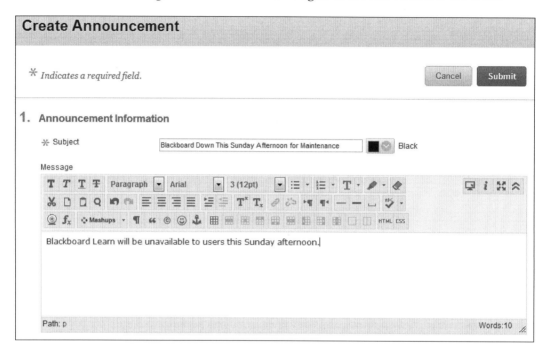

Next we must set the options. Our first option sets the duration of our announcement. Either we set the announcement to be restricted by date by using the **Date Restriction** option, or allow the announcement to display permanently, by using the **Not Date Restricted** option.

If we select **Date Restriction**, we must set either **Display After**, **Display Until**, or both options. Notice that these settings not only require a date, but also a time. We can enter the date and time into the text, or use the calendar and clock buttons to select the information. We should note that these time and date restrictions are based on the server time and date. If we stop here and click on **Submit**, our announcement would display within the **My Announcements** module and in the **Notifications** dashboard, but sometimes we need to make our announcement more visible.

The next two options will help us with our announcement's visibility. First, we can make our system announcements appear on our login page. In *Chapter 3, Setting Up and Customizing Blackboard Learn*, we mentioned this ability when we customized our login page. When we set the **Show at Login** option to **Yes**, our announcement appears on the login page as long as we move it above the repositionable bar, which we will discuss in a bit. Its location will be based on where we placed the announcement's tag within that page.

We also have the ability to have our announcement appear in course and organization announcements. When we set the **Show in Courses and Organizations** option to **Yes**, our system-level announcement will appear in the course or organization announcement. This option is an excellent way to inform students, however course instructors and organization leaders could find it frustrating if the announcement is pinned to the top of the page.

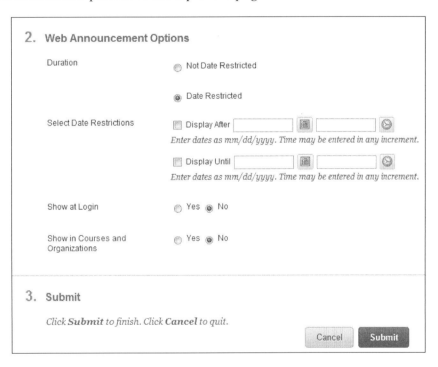

Once our options are set, simply click on the **Submit** button and the **Announcements** page will load along with the success or failure bar at the top of the page. If our announcement was created successfully, we will see it appear below the repositionable bar. This bar is the gray line seen in the following screenshot with the words **New announcements appear below this line**. Any announcements above this bar become pinned to the top of the announcements list, appear on the login page, and have priority over other system, course, or organization announcements.

If we want to move an announcement around, simply place the mouse over the announcement subject. Notice that the mouse pointer changes to our moving compass. If we have multiple announcements that are available at one time, this allows us to drag and reorder the way our announcements appear. Blackboard also gives us this same ability using the button on the right side of our page which has two arrows, one pointing up and one down.

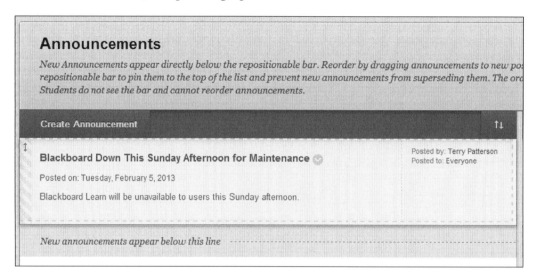

Also note that if the announcement is scheduled to become available later, **Item is not available** will appear below the subject line in our **Announcements** page. In short, if we as administrators really want to inform users about this, our login page option will reach every user who accesses our Blackboard Learn environment. But we do have other options if we need to push an announcement out immediately.

Editing or deleting a system announcement

We can go in and edit or delete our announcements as well. Back in our **Announcements** page, we can open our actions menu by putting our mouse icon over the announcement and clicking on the action button. The action button appears on the right side of the announcement subject. Our menu gives us two options, either to edit or delete the announcement we created. When we select **Edit**, our instance takes us to the **Edit Announcement** page, which allows us to change our announcement with the same information and option areas when we created it. Note that if we do make changes, this may cause our announcement to be moved below our repositionable line. If we select the **Delete** option, a pop-up box appears to confirm that we want to delete this announcement. Once we click on **OK**, the announcement disappears from our instance.

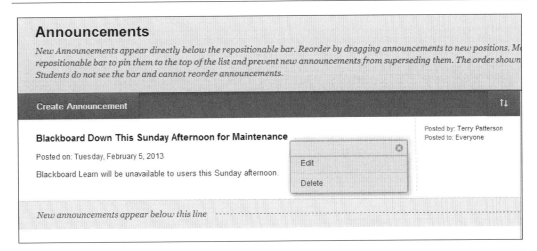

Spell Check Dictionaries in Blackboard Learn

Most computer users, whether novice or experienced, have become dependent on the ability to spellcheck their compositions. Within Blackboard Learn, users who are working in English or Spanish are able to use the default spell check dictionaries by clicking on the **Spell Check** icon within the textbox editor. This checks the written work against a set of words uploaded to the instance. In the latest version, Blackboard now uses the `.dic` file format used in such word processing programs as Microsoft Office, OpenOffice, and LibreOffice.

Within these applications, we can create a customized dictionary or we can use a textbox editor to open a `.dic` file. Either way, we should add words that might be heavily used within our own instance such as our organization's name or location. Once our customizations have been saved in our text file or saved and exported from our applications, we can begin adding the dictionary file into our Blackboard environment.

Back in our **System Admin** tab, we click on the **Spell Check Dictionaries** link within the **Tools and Utilities** module. Note that there are three spell check dictionaries within our instance. From this page we have two options; either add a new dictionary, or manage one of the current dictionaries.

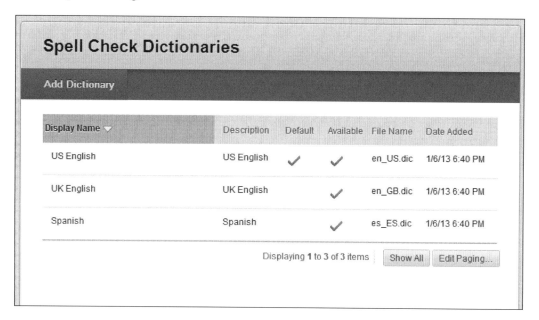

Creating a new spell check dictionary within Blackboard Learn

We mentioned earlier that English and Spanish dictionaries are loaded into Blackboard Learn by default. However, our organization may want to have spellcheck for other languages, such as French or German. This means we need to create a ZIP file that contains the .dic and .aff files associated with our spell check dictionary. The process to find and create a ZIP file requires us to follow a few steps.

1. We must find the dictionary we want to use. Here we use the OpenOffice repository, http://extensions.services.openoffice.org/en/dictionaries, which has numerous dictionaries. We must go to the link and then click on the **Get It** button present at the bottom of the page. This will download the spell check dictionary in an .oxt file format.

2. Now that we have the file, we need to change the extension from .oxt to .zip, as shown in the following screenshot, and then unzip it.

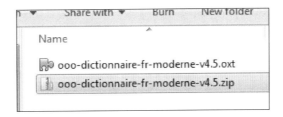

3. We then need to find the `.aff` and `.dic` files within the extracted folder. Once we find them, we can copy them into a new folder.

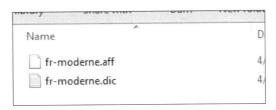

4. Now we can take that folder and create a `.zip` file. This file can now be used to create a new spell check dictionary within our Blackboard Learn environment.

Adding a spell check dictionary in Blackboard Learn

We can create a new spell check dictionary within our Blackboard Learn environment by clicking on the **Add Dictionary** button. Our first item requires us to attach our `.zip` file to this new dictionary by clicking on the **Browse My Computer** button and selecting it. Then add **Display Name** for this dictionary along with an optional description. The next selection allows us to make it available within the system and set this dictionary as the default. Once our options are selected, we simply click on the **Submit** button to apply them.

Managing a spell check dictionary in Blackboard Learn

Within the **Spell Check Dictionaries** page, we can replace dictionary files associated with our current listings and delete dictionaries entirely. Let's go over the process to replace the dictionary file. The process begins with moving our mouse over the selected dictionary name and clicking on the action button. Within the action menu that appears, select the **Manage** option.

The **Edit Dictionary** page loads. Now we must remove the current dictionary file. Note that there is no way to back up or download our current file within our Blackboard instance before removing it. Now simply click on the **Do Not Attach** button to remove the current file and then attach the new file by clicking on the **Browse My Computer** button.

We can also change the dictionary's name, description, availability, and system default on this page as well. Once our changes have been made, click on the **Submit** button to apply them to our instance.

The deletion of a spell check dictionary uses the same process; however, we can only delete spell check dictionaries that we have created, for example, the French spell check dictionary we created earlier. When we move our mouse over the dictionary name, we can see that we have a **Delete** option in our action menu. Simply click on **Delete**, and the selected spell check dictionary is removed from our environment.

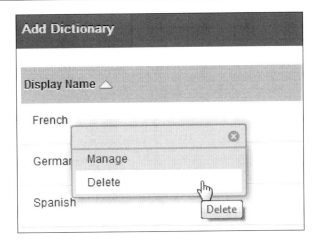

Language packs

Unlike communities in the real world, virtual communities can reside in different locations and bring users from different parts of the world into one classroom. While this is a strength of virtual communities, being unable to navigate using your native language can become difficult. Every Blackboard Learn instance includes language packs, which when enabled, allow the user to display Blackboard-generated titles, links, and information in a selected language.

> We should note before going forward that language packs won't work with user-created content or content from third-party applications or plugins unless the developer has internationalized them.

A language pack for Blackboard Learn is a collection of property files that include every title, button label, sentence, help resource, and so on. They are broken down into multiple folders along with an .xml file. We as administrators have the ability to customize how these items will appear by editing our language pack. In this section, we will show how to add, manage, copy, and edit a language pack within our Blackboard Learn environment.

Within our **System Admin** tab in Blackboard Learn, click on the **Language Packs** link. The **Language Packs** page loads and displays a list of all the language packs installed within our environment. While Blackboard Inc. has produced additional language packs in the past, at the time of publication the company has no language pack repository available for administrators. Once downloaded, we can import a new language pack into our Blackboard Learn instance by clicking on the **Import** button.

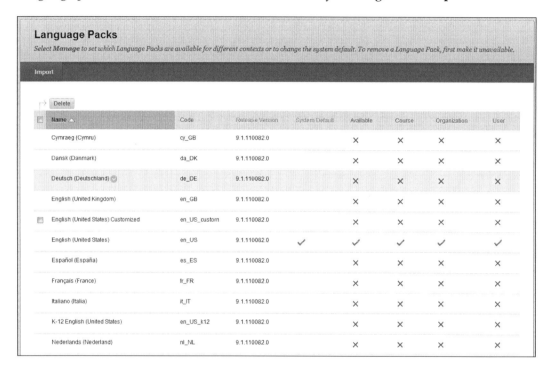

The **Import Language Pack** page has the same type of process for our Blackboard Learn environment. First we need to attach the language pack ZIP file we want to import by clicking on the **Choose File** button. Next we must add **Name** and **Code** for this language pack; we do have the option of using the name and code within the language pack or typing in our own. This information is located in the `bb-lp-manifest.xml` file. Our name and code should be unique from any language packs currently installed. The next step requires us to accept the legal disclaimer about the language pack editor. Once our changes are made, we click on the **Submit** button. We find ourselves back at the **Language Packs** page and we should see our imported language pack now listed.

Once our language packs have been imported, we do have the ability to manage them. Find the action button by placing the mouse on the language pack we wish to work with. When we click on the language pack, a button displays our options, which are **Manage**, **Export**, and **Copy**. If we click on an imported language pack, the Blackboard instance will give us the **Edit** and **Delete** options. Let's review these options:

- **Manage**: Our management page allows us to make the language pack available within our Blackboard instance. We also have the ability to allow or restrict access to this language pack within a course, an organization, or for users.

- **Export**: If we wish to customize our language pack, we can export our current language pack to edit it offline.

- **Copy**: If we want to make language pack customizations online, we can use the **Copy** function to give our language pack a new name and code.

Notifications

Back in *Chapter 4, Creating Courses in Blackboard Learn*, we briefly discussed notifications, but now let's take a deeper look. Notifications are system-generated messages about specific actions within a Blackboard Learn course or organization. These messages can cover a wide variety of notification types and delivery methods. Before we start that discussion, we must learn how to enable notifications within our Blackboard Learn environment.

Setting up general notifications

In the **Tools and Utilities** module, we click on the **Notifications** link. This brings us to the **General Notifications** page. This page allows us to control the general options within our environment. Our first selection allows us to enable or disable the notifications tool entirely. A new Blackboard Learn installation has the notification tool turned off by default. Some organizations might not see a need for this tool and won't enable it.

The most basic way the notification tool sends its messages to users is by e-mail. The **Email Settings** area allows us to apply system-wide e-mail settings. Most administrators set the **Send email notifications as** option to **Allow User Choice** and the Default Email Format option as **Individual**. If our Blackboard Learn instance hosts large courses or organizations, we may choose to only allow e-mail digests. E-mail digests take all the messages that users would get within a 24 hour period from courses and organizations, then put them into one e-mail. This option may be used so that we don't overwhelm our organization's mail servers.

We also must put in an e-mail address where the e-mail notifications will appear to come from. We use that phrase because this address doesn't (and normally shouldn't) exist as an actual mailbox. Often, users will believe that the message or announcement comes from the instructor and reply back with a response or questions to the instructor or leader. These messages will quickly fill up a mailbox, and many administrators just put in an e-mail address such as `donotreply@ myorganization.com` to address this issue. We should also let our e-mail server administrator know the address so that the replies don't bounce back to the user or cause issues within the e-mail server.

If we as administrators or users select to send e-mail notifications in a daily digest format, we need to set a time when those daily digests will be sent out. By default, our instance suggests daily digests be sent out at 11:00 pm server time. We can change this option by either typing in the new time in the textbox, or by clicking on the clock icon and selecting a time.

Our last option on this page allows us to set how long the notifications stay displayed in the user's dashboard within our Blackboard Learn instance.

The first option asks us to set when the system removes important notifications. These notifications are defined as important by default with no noticeable way to change it. These important notifications can be seen by clicking on the **Show Important Notifications** link to the right of the textbox. Normally they deal with the due dates of items, tests, surveys, or assignments. The system default is 120 days, but can be set between 1 to 1000 days.

Other notifications such as the item availability and due dates will use the next option. We can see the list of what notifications fall in this category by clicking on the **Show Other Notifications** link. Our environment automatically sets these notifications to be removed if they are older than 28 days, but can be set between 1 and 1000 days.

3. **Notification Cleanup**

   ※ Remove important notifications more than   `120`   days old.   Show Important Notifications

   Important notifications can be retained in the system for up to 1,000 days. Enter a number between 1 and 1,000.

   ※ Remove other notifications more than   `28`   days old.   Show Other Notifications

   All other notifications can be retained in the system for up to 1,000 days. Enter a number between 1 and 1,000.

4. **Submit**

   *Click **Submit** to finish. Click **Cancel** to quit.*

   [Cancel] [Submit]

Once we have made our changes to the options within the **General Notifications** page, we can click on **Submit** to apply them. Our system-wide notifications' options have been configured, but this is only the first part of the notifications tool's process.

Managing the default notifications settings

Let's go back to our **System Admin** tab and click on the **Course Settings** link within the **Courses** module. We need to click on the **Default Notifications Settings** link. This page, called **Default Notifications Settings**, allows us to set the default notifications for courses created.

Our first setting on this page asks us to set the bulk notification options for different notification methods. By default, our system has two distribution methods, dashboard and e-mail. If we have installed other tools within our instance, such as the Blackboard Mobile Learn Building Block, we may find additional notification options listed. In our example instance, the Mobile notifications will go to the Blackboard Mobile Learn app.

The **Bulk Notification Settings** option turns on notifications within the different distribution methods. The options, **Default Off** and **Default On**, set a user's choice to either off or on, and then will allow the user to change that. The **Always On** and **Always Off** options ignore a user's personal setting and either enable or disable the tool within our environment. Our other option, **Use Individual Settings**, will just allow our users to make the decision.

1. Bulk Notification Settings

Change settings here for each distribution method for all notification types

Dashboard	Default On ▾
Mobile	Default On ▾
Email	Default Off ▾

Our next area, **Settings**, allows us to turn specific notifications available or unavailable to users by checking the **On/Off** checkbox. We can also set the default notification option for the different notification methods. Once we make our changes, we can click on the **Submit** button and the setup of our notifications is complete from the administrator's perspective.

2. Settings

Change setting here for each distribution method for individual notification types

☑ On/Off	Notification	Dashboard	Mobile	Email
☑	Announcement Available	Default On ▾	Default On ▾	Default Off ▾
☑	Assignment Available	Default On ▾	Default On ▾	Default Off ▾
☑	Assignment Due	Default On ▾	Default On ▾	Default Off ▾
☑	Assignment Needs Grading	Default On ▾	Default On ▾	Default Off ▾
☑	Assignment Past Due	Default On ▾	Default On ▾	Default Off ▾
☑	Blog Needs Grading	Default On ▾	Default On ▾	Default Off ▾
☑	Content Item Available	Default On ▾	Default On ▾	Default Off ▾

Now let's briefly review the other tools within the **Tools and Utilities** module.

Course Messages

Course Messages, known as **Messages** in older versions of Blackboard Learn, acts as an internal e-mail system for every course and organization within our environment. If this is enabled in a course or organization, users can communicate using this tool with all messages remaining within their enrolled course or organization, unlike using an external e-mail system where those messages are stored within the user's e-mail account. While we, as administrators, are unable to use the **Course Messages** tool to communicate with users, we must set a few configuration options within our Blackboard Learn environment before this tool can be used by users within a course or organization.

We can review and make changes to our **Course Messages** options by clicking on the **Course Messages** link within the **Tools and Utilities** module. Our page loads and we can now manage the message options within our instance. The first option allows us to enable or disable the sender's ability to attach files to messages across the entire instance. Our second option allows anyone using **Course Messages** to create personal folders to help organize and store old or important messages. If we decide to make any changes, click on the **Submit** button to apply them and then our Blackboard instance takes us back to the **System Admin** tab.

Calendar

We, as administrators, also have the ability to add events to the institutional calendar (or calendar in this context) within our Blackboard instance. The institutional calendar events appear as part of any user's calendar view and within the **My Calendar** module. We access the calendar tool by clicking on the **Calendar** link in the **Tools and Utilities** module, which allows us to add events. Blackboard has recently made improvements to this tool via a building block. In the updated version, we still have the ability to create, edit, and delete an institutional event. However, we have an additional option to get the institutional calendar as an `.ics` download by clicking on the **Get External Calendar Link** button.

The new calendar also includes the ability for users to see not only institutional calendar items, but also course and personal calendar information. These are controlled within their areas respectively. Our discussion about **Calendar** only addressed the institutional one.

E-mails

While our Blackboard Learn instance has many different ways to communicate, such as the notifications and messages tools, e-mail continues to be one of the main forms of communication within organizations. If using the **Announcements** tool doesn't meet our needs, we can send e-mails to our users. We access our **Email** tool by clicking on the **Mail** link within the **Tools and Utilities** module. Within the **Email** tool, we have a few options:

- **All Instructor Users** allows us to send an e-mail to all users who are instructors in at least one course
- **All Student Users** gives us the ability to send users who have the role of student in one course
- **All Users** sends an e-mail to every user within our Blackboard Learn instance

If we click on any of the options, Blackboard Learn loads a page where we compose our e-mail. Notice that the **To:** line shows the group of users to which we will send our e-mail. The **From:** line displays the name and e-mail address from where this e-mail will be sent. If you don't want this e-mail to come to your mailbox directly, you can change your e-mail address by editing your user information. We then need to add a subject line for this e-mail and finally type in our message using the textbox editor. Once we are ready to send our message, click on the **Submit** button.

Enterprise surveys in Blackboard Learn

Enterprise surveys were recently added to Blackboard Learn. While our role as an administrator allows us the ability to create enterprise surveys, we normally provide a survey with an expert access to use this tool.

This tool allows us to create a survey with standard survey question types. After the creation of the survey, we can set up a timeframe for survey responses and select survey recipients by enrollment type (instructors, students, and so on), a specific term, or selected courses. If the users aren't in our Blackboard instance, we can upload a file with e-mail addresses. The survey can also send a reminder e-mail to non-respondents during the survey's timeframe.

Goals

Many organizations have taken initiative to help ensure users complete their academic or training programs. Some of these organizations may use a Blackboard product called Blackboard Outcomes. It allows for very detailed tracking and alignments at the institutional, departmental, and program levels, if needed. Alignments connect the goals to items within courses and organizations. **Goals** is one of the tools, which now come with Blackboard Learn. This tool allows us as the administrator the ability to create or upload institutional goal sets. These goal sets can be created by clicking on the **Goals** link. On the **Goals** page, we can create **Goal Set Name** and categorize it. Within that set, we can create more goals, categorize them, associate them to courses within our instance, and even run reports to see the connections. Instructors can then use these goals and associate them with course items and assessments. An example goal might be to increase active learning activities within courses.

My Blackboard Settings

Let's take a deep breath because this tool and its controls may cause confusion to those long-time Blackboard Learn users. Many Blackboard Learn instances call the main tab, **My Blackboard**. This page includes many modules such as **My Courses**, **My Organizations**, **My Announcements**, and others; but this isn't what we are talking about here. The new **My Blackboard Settings** tool addresses the new **My Blackboard** area created in Blackboard Learn 9.1 Service Pack 10. This area can be accessed by clicking on the avatar and name in the upper-right corner of the web page, as shown in the following screenshot:

Within the **My Blackboard Settings** page, we have the ability to turn different tools on or off that would appear in this area.

Math Editor Image Service

Blackboard Learn 9.1 Service Pack 10 brought a new visual textbox editor to users. This textbox editor improves the management of content items. This new editor also required changes to the math editor. The math editor creates an image of a mathematical equation to insert into the textbox editor. However, we need to configure the application server, or one of the application servers in our instance, that will create these images and host them.

We can edit the configuration by clicking on the **Math Editor Image Service** link. The **Math Editor Image Service** page asks if we wish to use HTTP or HTTPS protocol (especially, if we have SSL enabled system-wide), and then asks for a specific application server. The third option allows us to set the port which would be 80 or 443 based on what protocol we use. Our final configuration sets the path where the Math Editor's renderings will reside. Once our configuration is complete, we can click on the **Submit** button.

Tools

In *Chapter 4*, *Creating Courses in Blackboard Learn*, we discussed setting up course tools. In this page, we are able to set the availability of each tool within a course. This **Tools** area allows us to do that and more. We access the **Tools** area by clicking on the **Tools** link. This page displays all the tools in our Blackboard Learn environment and the different access points for each tool. For example, the **Announcements** tool can be controlled as a system, course, or organization tool. We have the same options as we used in the **Course Tools** page (**Default On**, **Default Off**, **Always On**, and **Always Off**) and some tools have the option to allow guest and observer access. Unlike the **Course Tools** page, any changes we make are applied when we click on the **Submit** button.

Chalk Titles

Course instructors sometimes utilize publisher content from external websites to help instruct student users. Most instructors don't use this tool to add course content because many book publishers use building block integrations and course cartridges as they now give students access to that same content. **Chalk Titles** can bring with them course tools, single sign on to external sites, along with roster and Grade Center syncing.

We can manage the system's chalk titles by clicking on the **Chalk Titles** link. If one of our courses does have a chalk title installation, the course will be listed in this area. Within the **Manage Chalk Titles** page, we have three different options. The **Properties** option allows us to see what courses are using **Chalk Title** and what tools are being used. **View Log** will appear if our Chalk Title fails to install properly and can provide details to help troubleshoot the issue. **Retry** allows us to try the installation process again.

Summary

The tools we covered in this chapter vary in what they do and our role in implementing them. The one common thread is that all our tools help us improve how we communicate and complete our duties as Blackboard Learn administrators. This chapter wraps up the overview of how to manage the day-to-day functions of a Blackboard Learn instance. The rest of our discussions in this book will revolve around the advanced tools.

In the next chapter, we will cover how to keep our Blackboard Learn instance secure and configured to operate optimally.

9
Security, Reporting, and Configuration in Blackboard Learn

Every community in this world has had a time of growth. The addition of new homes and businesses means more need for utilities such as power, water, and gas, which the city or a utility company provides. We may also need to add additional police officers, fire fighters, or medical responders. When our virtual community grows, we must also expand in the same way. This chapter delves into dealing with growth within our Blackboard Learn environment. Our discussions in this chapter will help us understand how we can create a system that is secure and built to serve the needs of our growing user community. We will discuss the following topics:

- Managing security within the Blackboard Learn environment
- Managing application and statistics information within our instance
- How to make changes to our current configuration
- Reviewing how to optimize our servers to meet the needs of our users

Let's start our discussions in this chapter with the current tools and options we have to help secure our Blackboard Learn environment.

Security in Blackboard Learn

One of the important duties for Blackboard administrators is to ensure a secure experience for our users. This means securing not only the input and interactions of users within our environment, but also the content, such as students' work and personal information. We can do this with many different tools such as SSL certificates, guest access options, along with HTML and input validation filters. Let's start our conversation with the process to set up SSL certificates.

Managing SSL certificates

Most websites today use SSL to keep their user's important data secure from Internet prowlers or hackers. **SSL (Secure Socket Layer)** uses a certificate to assure the users that the server they connect to is a trusted server and will encrypt information between the users' browsers and the server. It neither identifies the user nor will it encrypt the data once it resides on the server. Blackboard recommends organizations use an SSL certificate to protect their users. Before we discuss installing and setting up SSL access, we must purchase a certificate from a Certificate Authority or have one created by our organization. Once the certificate is created, it must be installed within our web server, either Apache or IIS depending on our server's operating system. If we don't have experience in installing an SSL certificate, most Certificate Authorities will offer documentation on the installation process. We may also request another system administrator with this experience to assist.

After installing our SSL certificate on our application server or servers, we can start managing the SSL option within our Blackboard Learn environment. Note that we should not make any changes within this area until the SSL certificates are installed. If we enable this before we install our certificate, we will be locked out of our environment entirely. We start our management by clicking on the **SSL Choice** link that is present within the **Security** module on our **System Admin** tab. On the **SSL Choice** page, we have several options to address. Our first option allows us to control how we enable the SSL across the application. We have three options to review:

- **SSL off**: This option disables the SSL service from user interactions. The SSL option is required for credit/debit card processing, secure proxy tools and web services, along with the connected SMS service.
- **SSL system-wide**: Blackboard recommends this option, and this means that every page that comes from our server is SSL encrypted. Some 32-bit Blackboard installations may have given performance issues in the past with this option, but we should find no issues within 64-bit environments.

- **SSL for Selected Areas and Tools**: If this option is selected, we can select specific tools and areas to use SSL. This option is not recommended by Blackboard and has been depreciated in later versions, however if this option is selected, the next options allow us to select what specific areas, tools, building blocks, proxy tools, and web services will be enabled. If we install new building blocks, we can return to this page and select the tool to use SSL.

Once these changes have been made, we click on the **Submit** button. We should notice that SSL is now functioning in the areas selected system wide or nowhere based on our preferences. Most administrators will use the Blackboard recommendation that enables SSL across the entire environment.

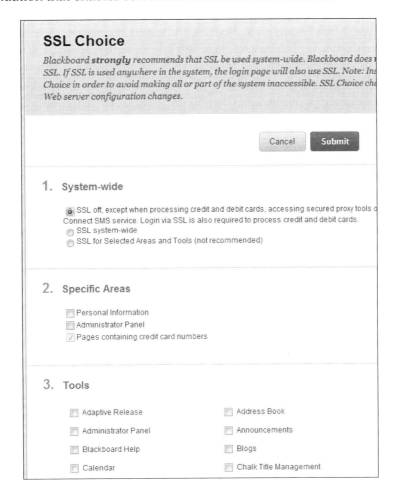

Managing guest access

In *Chapter 3, Setting Up and Customizing Blackboard Learn,* we briefly mentioned the **Gateway Options** area in our **Security** module. This area holds more than just the ability to change where our users can log in to our instance, so let's learn more. The **Gateway Options** page can be accessed by clicking on the link within our **Security** module. We addressed the first option in our previous discussion, but let's continue to review the other options on the page.

If we have the **Gateway page** option selected, our next area offers a few options. This allows us to display a **Course Catalog** link.

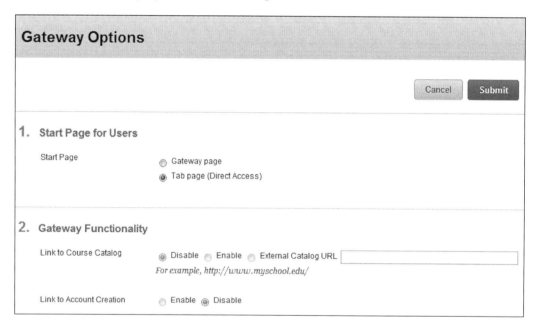

The **Link to Course Catalog** option allows a guest user to see the list of categorized courses within our instance, if we select the **Enable** option. If we want the guest users to review an external catalog, we can select the **External Catalog URL** option and put the URL into the textbox.

The **Link to Account Creation** option gives us the ability to allow guest users to create an account within our Blackboard Learn application. We may find a rare occasion such as a Blackboard Learn environment that hosts several massive online open courses (MOOCs) may want this option enabled. Most of the times, however, it should be disabled. The **Lost Password Functionality** option on our page allows us to give the user the ability to request a forgotten password. The default settings for this option send users to a request page within our Blackboard Learn environment where they can request their password to be e-mailed to the associated address. This option works well if we are using Blackboard's internal authentication process. If we use an external authentication process, such as LDAP, CAS, or Shibboleth, the internal password recovery option won't work. We can replace the default URL, `/webapps/blackboard/password/`, with an external URL that allows users to reset their password or provides instructions on who to contact.

Our **Guest Access defaults** option allows us to set which guest users can gain access within our Blackboard Learn environment without logging in. There are three different suboptions.

- **Allow Guest Access to the System**: This option, if enabled, will create a link that allows an unregistered user, which we are calling a guest user, the ability to access our system. This means the guest user can see into our Blackboard Learn environment. If we are using the **Tab** page (or **Direct Access** start page), this option must be enabled so that registered users can log in.

- **Allow Guest Access to Courses**: This option controls if we allow guest access to courses. If this is enabled, guest users would be able to search for courses using the **Course Catalog** tool (that we mentioned earlier in this chapter). The guest users will be able to access only courses that will allow guest access.

- **Allow Guest Access to Organizations**: Similar to courses, this option controls guest access to organizations within our Blackboard Learn environment. Guest users will be able to find organizations and gain access if the organization allows guest access.

Planning for guest access

Guest access requires that we have the guest user within our Blackboard Learn environment enabled. The configuration of the guest access options within our environment require discussion and planning within our organization. With guest access to courses or organizations enabled, guests have the ability to access copyrighted or restricted materials. Some Blackboard Learn environments use the guest access option to allow incoming students view course information and content items, such as course syllabi, before signing up.

3. Lost Password Functionality

Request Forgotten Password   ⊙ Disable   ○ Enable

URL for Forgotten Password | /webapps/blackboard/password |

Set the URL for the link on the login page that allows users to request that th
in their user information. The default URL is /webapps/blackboard/passw

4. Guest Access defaults

Allow Guest Access to the System   ⊙ Enable   ○ Disable

Allow Guest Access to Courses   ⊙ Enable   ○ Disable

Allow Guest Access to Organizations   ⊙ Enable   ○ Disable

5. Submit

Click Submit to proceed. Click Cancel to quit.

Cancel   Submit

Managing session fingerprints

In addition to the SSL encryption, we can protect users by enabling the session fingerprint settings within our Blackboard Learn environment. A session fingerprint uses information such as the browser type, IP address, and session ID to create the unique fingerprint. Changes in a user's session fingerprint in the middle of a session could arouse suspicion that the session has been hijacked by an attacker. Blackboard Learn can require that if the user's session fingerprint changes in anyway, the user will be forced to log in again. If we use SSL, this option offers little benefits. The **Settings** page allows us to help develop what information makes up the session fingerprint and how our environment will respond to a possible change.

We start configuring this option by clicking on the **Session Fingerprint Settings** link within the **Security** module. Our first option is to enable session fingerprinting within our Blackboard Learn instance, which will allow session fingerprints to be created.

The next line on the page tells us the name of the session fingerprint's log file. We can find the `bb-session-log.txt` file in the `logs` directory. Next, we can select what information will be used to create a user's fingerprint in the **Fingerprint value** option. We have the options to include just the user's IP address, the user agent (or browser), or both. We can select our options based on how secure we want to make our environment.

We also have the ability to exclude specific IP addresses from the **Session Fingerprint** option. These can be trusted IP addresses or addresses that are frequently changed by an Internet service provider. If we want to enable this option, we must first create a text file called `bb-session-fingerprint-excluded-addresses.txt` in the `config` folder. Within this file, we add the IP addresses that need to be excluded from session fingerprints. Once the file is created, the **Filter IP addresses** option will no longer be grayed out and we can enable it by selecting **Yes**.

Our final configuration option, **Create new session when fingerprint changes**, will force the user to log in again if his/her session fingerprint changes, if enabled. This could cause issues if a user's IP address changes often. Once we complete our **Session Fingerprint** configurations, we simply click on the **Submit** button.

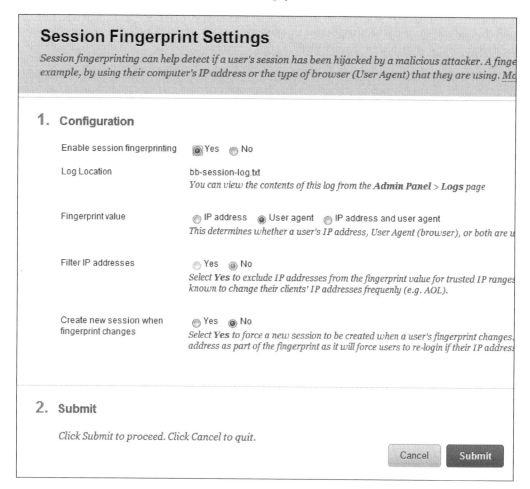

Input Validation Filter

The security features we've discussed so far have been focused on securing the connection and communication process between a user's computer and our server. The next feature focuses on securing the content put into our Blackboard Learn instance.

The **Input Validation Filter** page addresses cross site scripting vulnerabilities. Cross site scripting is an attack where a malicious user selects an input area, such as an announcement title, and injects a script that allows him/her to gain access or privileges within our Blackboard Learn environment. The **Input Validation Filter** tool acts as a firewall between the user's input and Blackboard Learn. Any user input is reviewed by the filter, and if it matches the ruleset, it may be removed.

We can review the **Input Validation Filter** page by clicking on the **Input Validation Filter** link within the **Security** Module. The filter is made up of two different rulesets. The **Default Ruleset** contains validation rules from Blackboard and cannot be disabled. Let's look at a default rule from the Input Validation Filter.

```
<rule path="/webapps/blackboard/execute/announcement"
    parameter="context" constraint-name=
    "alpha" on-fail="HtmlEscape"
    max-version="9.1.100000"/>
```

The preceding path gives the path that this rule will address; in this case it's the submission of an announcement. The parameter called `context` is a variable passed within the processing of an announcement. The `constraint-name` is a constant defined within our Input Validation Filter, which sets what type of information should be within the parameter. This means that a < character will be replaced with `&lt;`. The `alpha` constraint will only allow alphabetic characters in this parameter. If this isn't the case, the `on-fail` parameter, `HtmlEscape`, will escape any special HTML characters within the parameter. The last line, `max-version`, tells the filter to apply this rule only on versions higher than the version number listed. There are several other default rules within the Input Validation Filter, but each one works in a similar fashion.

The information we just reviewed can be found by clicking on the **Default Ruleset** link and then click on the **Download Schema (xsd)** button. We can also click on the **Download Ruleset (xml)** button to get the default ruleset on our computer. Both documents can be opened with any text or XML editor such as XML Copy Editor.

Advantages of using an XML Editor

Our current discussion is the first of many that will have us interact with .xml files. We can edit these file types using text editors. An XML editor will visually help us find errors in our file that could cause it to not function properly within our Blackboard Learn environment.

Just as the default ruleset contains the base ruleset from Blackboard, the custom ruleset gives the administrator the ability to build specialized rules. These custom rules use the same XML structure as the default rules. We can use the schema and default ruleset we downloaded earlier to help us understand how to create a new ruleset. Once we create a custom ruleset, we must save the file in the .xml format. We can then click on the **Custom Ruleset** link on the **Input Validation Filter** page. The **Upload Custom Ruleset** page loads, and then we click on the **Browse** button and select our .xml file. Click on the **Submit** button. We should see a success that our Custom Ruleset was uploaded.

We are taken to the **Custom Ruleset** page, which allows us to upload a new Custom Ruleset by clicking on the **Replace** button. We can also remove the custom ruleset by clicking on the **Delete** button, or download the current custom ruleset with the **Download** button.

While we reviewed the parts of a rule within the Input Validation Filter, we may require more information and assistance to create our own custom rulesets. Most administrators will use a Blackboard Learn test environment and request additional resources from Blackboard Support about creating these type of rules.

Safe HTML Filters

While the Input Validation Filter works to help stop cross site scripting vulnerabilities, the Safe HTML Filters work to protect our system from malicious attacks using the textbox editors and other mainstream input areas accessed by users. Users could try to gain unauthorized access or elevate their privileges within a course or organization by embedding HTML code into blogs, journals, discussion boards, or other locations.

Users affected by the Safe HTML Filters

Before we move further into our discussion, we should note that the Safe HTML Filters only apply to users who don't have the ability to add trusted content. This option is called either **Add/Modify Trusted Content** or **Add/Edit Trusted Content With Scripts** privilege. It can be enabled or disabled within the **Privileges** area, which we discussed in *Chapter 7, Managing Roles and Users in Blackboard Learn*. By default, someone with an instructor, grader, course builder, or teaching assistant will have the trusted privilege within that course or organization. Student users within either courses or organizations will not have that.

The **Safe HTML Filters** tool is a building block provided by Blackboard. We must download it from Behind the Blackboard and then install and enable it as a building block, which we will discuss in more details in *Chapter 11, Implementing Building Blocks in Blackboard Learn*. Once this tool is installed and enabled, we will find the **Safe HTML Filters** link in our **Security** module. We simply click on the **Safe HTML Filters** link. On the **Global Safe HTML Filter** page, we find two options. The first option, **Global Safe HTML Filter**, allows us to turn on the HTML filter within our instance and set the HTML filtering mode to either **Dangerous HTML** or **All HTML**. **Dangerous HTML** would only apply filter controls when content such as JavaScript is found within submitted content. While All HTML will check every type of content submitted, with the content editor. The Global Safe HTML Filter was known in previous versions as the Global Cross-site Scripting Security Control. Blackboard recommends this filter be enabled and the proper filtering mode be selected for our environment.

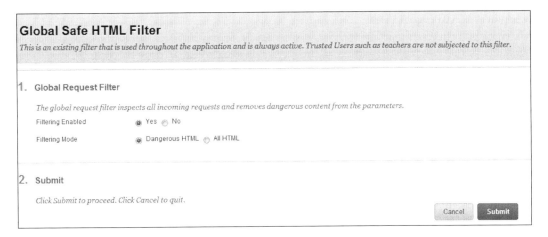

The other option allows us to create additional Safe HTML policies by filtering a widely used tool within the Blackboard Learn environment, the content editor. We can get to the **Safe HTML Filter** area by clicking on the **Safe HTML Filter for Content Editor** link. Blackboard already has one default policy, called `default-policy.xml`. If we mouse over it, our action menu button appears. Once we click on it, the menu appears and allows us to download or test the current policy. We can download the default policy by selecting **Download** from the menu or clicking on the policy name. We can then use a text editor to edit or add more filters to our content editor. We can then upload our edited `.xml` file back to the server by clicking on the **Upload** button.

> While these options are outside of our discussions, they should be done with great care and applied to only a production environment after rigorous testing within on a Blackboard Learn development environment.

As we saw in the action menu, we can also test the policy by clicking on the **Test** menu option. Then we paste our HTML code into the textbox and click on **Submit** for testing.

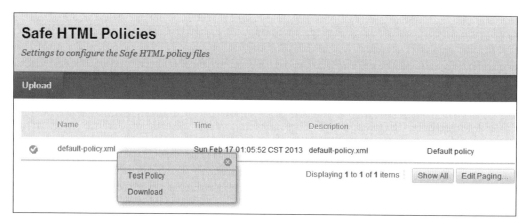

Alternate Domain for Serving Content

While we have protected our Blackboard Learn environment from malicious attacks by injecting malicious code into URLs and content editors, we still need to protect ourselves from malicious files that could attack our Blackboard Learn instance. The **Alternate Domain for Serving Content** option prevents such attacks by forcing files uploaded by the user to be opened from a different domain. If our Blackboard Learn URL is `https://blackboard.myorganzation.com`, and if we enable this option, user content might come from `https://blackboard-user-content.myorganization.com/`, which will use the same original security policy.

This policy, which is enabled in most modern browsers, stops any script from running if it isn't using the same domain name, SSL encryption, or port number. Enabling this option is simple, however we must configure an alternate domain for our Blackboard Learn instance. and if we are using SSL, we should create a new SSL certificate.

Once those items are complete, we simply click on the **Alternate Domain for Serving Content** link in the **Security** module. In the **Set Alternate Domain** field, we would put in our URL. Let's use `https://blackboard-user-content.myorganization.com/` and then click on the **Submit** button.

System information in Blackboard Learn

Now that we have secured our instance, we can now focus on learning more about what is going on within our Blackboard Learn environment. The information we will review in this section can be compared to traffic cameras and sensors in large communities to understand and support traffic as it moves around. Understanding what is going on within our instance will help us create a traffic plan for our virtual community to make sure that things run smoothly.

System configuration

The first thing we should discuss is the configuration of our system. At the beginning of our Blackboard Learn discussions, we talked about making sure our hardware and software would be able to support the number of users that we would need. We then built our Blackboard Learn instance to support those users, however the needs and expectations for applications like Blackboard Learn can change. Many times we find that the tools within our instance can meet needs that we didn't plan for in our initial setup. Normally, we then find ourselves needing to improve our application's performance with little monetary support. If we take the time to understand our system configuration, we can begin the optimization process.

Within the **Tools and Utilities** module, we find the **System Configuration** link. On the **System Configuration** page, we find the **System Information** link. We can think of this area as our system status and history. Click on the **System Information** link and we will find three different items. The first item, **Licensed Module Information**, tells us what parts of Blackboard Learn we have enabled based on our license. We also can find out client ID number, which can be helpful if we forget it and need to contact Blackboard Support. We also find our environment's installation date, number of users, and available users within our instance. The **Current Software Installation** area gives us the details on our Blackboard Learn release number including the system's Xythos Engine version number. Xythos is the name of the product that manages course or organization content. This area also tells us the installation date, type, and description of our last install or upgrade. Our last area, **Installation History**, gives us a historical view to display how our system has progressed from version to version.

System Information

Licensed Module Information

Licensed modules	Blackboard Client ID	Installation date	Number of users	Number of available users
Course Delivery, Community Engagement -		Friday, October 26, 2012		

Current Software Installation

Software release number	Xythos Engine version	Install date	Install type	Install title
9.1.110082.0	7.2.114.2057	Wednesday, January 9, 2013	BB_UPDATER	Updated to Blackboard version 9.1.110082.0

Installation History

Software release number	Xythos Engine version	Install date	Install type	Install title
9.1.110082.0	7.2.114.2057	Friday, January 4, 2013	BB_UPDATER	Updated to Blackboard version 9.1.110082.0
9.1.100401.0	7.2.114.2057	Tuesday, December 18, 2012	BB_UPDATER	Updated to Blackboard version 9.1.100401.0
9.1.82223.0	7.2.96.1019	Friday, October 26, 2012	Initial Install	Installed Blackboard version 9.1.82223.0

Back at the **System Configuration** page, our second link, **Registration Information**, takes us to this page. Back in *Chapter 2, Installing Blackboard Learn*, during our installation, we put in information about our organization to register our product. Within this area, we can update the name, location, and institution type.

The final link on the **System Configuration** page plays a major role in learning about the heart of our system. This link to the **System Performance Settings** area takes the information located within our `bb-config.properties` file within each of our Blackboard Learn application servers and puts it at one place. The information is broken up into groups for us. The first group reviews the settings within the application server, which control our Tomcat and Java processes and performance. Before we move on to discuss other groups, let's touch on some keywords within these settings.

- `appserver.maxthreads` and `appserver.minthreads`: These two configurable terms set the number of threads that one appserver can run. A thread is an execution of a Java Tomcat process within our Blackboard Learn system. The thread can be as simple as doing a user search or as complex as an assessment. The system can only manage a finite number of threads and we can set the minimum and maximum number here.

- `jvm.options.gc`: **GC** stands for **Garbage Collection**. This is a process within Tomcat that looks to reclaim memory from our Blackboard application. This makes the memory available for other threads and processes. Objects or classes that no longer have any references to them can be put into Garbage Collection.

- `max.heapsize.tomcat` and `min.heapsize.tomcat`: Heap size is the amount of space that Tomcat has to create new objects. **Objects** are files within our application that help create and execute tasks. Think of heap size as a cluttered room and objects. The more room we have (heap size) the less cluttered it becomes because we can put and place things properly with space to move around.

Application Server Performance Settings

These parameters control Tomcat and Java performance.

Properties	Summary	Host: bbpocapp1
bbconfig.appserver.maxthreads	Maximum threads	200
bbconfig.appserver.minthreads	Minimum threads	50
bbconfig.jvm.options.extra.tomcat	Additional JVM settings	
bbconfig.jvm.options.gc	JVM GC settings	-XX:+UseConcMarkSweepGC -XX:+ExplicitGCInvokesConcurrent
bbconfig.max.heapsize.tomcat	Maximum heap size	1024m
bbconfig.max.stacksize.tomcat	Stack size per thread	400k
bbconfig.min.heapsize.tomcat	Minimum heap size	1024m
bbconfig.page.results.size.max	Maximum cap for object searches	1000

Our next selection gives details about our collaboration server's performance. Remember the collaboration server can run separately or on board with one of our application servers. This serves our virtual chat and virtual classroom tools within our Blackboard Learn environment.

- `collabserver.http.writethreads` and `collabserver.tcp.writethreads`: These two properties are used within the collaboration server to write messages for output. These threads help take the words that users type into the chat tool and then push that message back to a user or users.

- `collabserver.lwchat.workerthreads` and `collabserver.vchat.workerthreads`: These are worker threads that are activated by the client application (your browser or in this case a Java applet running within the browser). These tools can be used to complete requests, but are not normally a part of pushing text back and forth between the client and the server.

Collaboration Server Performance Settings

These parameters control Collaboration server performance.

Properties	Summary	Host: bbpocapp1
bbconfig.collabserver.http.writethreads	HTTP write threads	5
bbconfig.collabserver.lwchat.workerthreads	Worker threads for lightweight chat	10
bbconfig.collabserver.tcp.writethreads	TCP write threads	20
bbconfig.collabserver.vchat.workerthreads	Worker threads for virtual chat	10

The next group of settings deal with the application's database connections. While we discuss the application's database as one, it actually is made up of three databases. The instance database stores our main data including course's information, users, and enrollments. The admin database contains system configuration and system information that we reviewed earlier in the **System Information** area. The stats database maintains recorded information about our user's activities over the long term. Each of these databases have a pool of connections. Let's go over each of the different terms within the configuration.

- `initpoolsize`: This number determines how many connections are made to the database when the system starts

- `maxpoolsize`: This option configures the maximum number of database connections required to fulfill application requests

- `minpoolsize`: Similar to the initial pool size, this determines the minimum number of connections required to hold application requests

- `timeout`: The amount of time (in seconds) given to database transactions to process before the system times out

Currently, the following database properties are for Oracle databases only:

- `statementcache.size`: The number of SQL queries that are stored in the database's statement cache

- `defaultrowprefetch`: The number of result rows initially delivered to the client while the rest of the result set is populated

Database Performance Settings

These parameters control the allocation of database connections.

Properties	Summary	Host: bbpocapp1
bbconfig.database.admin.initpoolsize	Initial connections	1
bbconfig.database.admin.maxpoolsize	Maximum connections	10
bbconfig.database.admin.minpoolsize	Minimum connections	1
bbconfig.database.instance.defaultrowprefetch	Rows to prefetch	10
bbconfig.database.instance.initpoolsize	Initial connections	1
bbconfig.database.instance.maxpoolsize	Maximum connections	200
bbconfig.database.instance.minpoolsize	Minimum connections	10
bbconfig.database.instance.statementcache.size	SQL statements stored	150
bbconfig.database.instance.timeout	Timeout window	300
bbconfig.database.stats.initpoolsize	Initial connections	0
bbconfig.database.stats.maxpoolsize	Maximum connections	10
bbconfig.database.stats.minpoolsize	Minimum connections	0
bbconfig.database.stats.timeout	Timeout window	300

The next group shows the last time we made changes to our `bb-config.properties` file along with the last time our server was restarted. Our final group reviews the performance settings for our web server, either Apache or IIS based on our operating system. This area may display other information depending on our web server, but the following common values should appear:

- `fileupload.max.filesize`: This number sets the maximum file size for a single file upload. The number appears in megabytes and by default is set at 2,500 MB (or 2.5 GB).

- `webserver.compression`: This setting allows us to turn HTTP compression on within our instance. HTTP compression allows for greater transmission speeds and better use of a user's bandwidth.

If we are running multiple servers across our Blackboard Learn instance, we will see each application server's configuration settings within this page.

Modification History

These parameters provide the date and time that the bb-config.properties file was last updated and that the Blackboard services were last restarted.

Properties	Summary	Host: bbpocapp1
bbconfig.modified.date	bb-config.properties changed	1/9/13 12:42:26 AM CST
bbconfig.restart.date	Blackboard services restart	2/17/13 1:04:10 AM CST

Webserver Performance Settings

These parameters control the advanced webserver configuration settings.

Properties	Summary	Host: bbpocapp1
bbconfig.fileupload.max.filesize	Single file upload limit	2500M
bbconfig.unix.httpd.keepalive	Allow persistent connections	On
bbconfig.unix.httpd.keepalivetimeout	Keepalive timeout	15
bbconfig.unix.httpd.maxclients	Maximum servers	200
bbconfig.unix.httpd.maxrequestsperchild	Maxiumum requests per child	1024
bbconfig.unix.httpd.maxspareservers	bbconfig.unix.httpd.maxspareservers.summary	10
bbconfig.unix.httpd.minspareservers	Minimum spare servers	5
bbconfig.unix.httpd.startservers	Initial servers	10
bbconfig.webserver.compression	HTTP compression	No
bbconfig.webserver.compression.max.filesize	Maximum filesize for compression	0
bbconfig.webserver.compression.max.filesize.mem	Maximum filesize for in-memory compression	10000
bbconfig.webserver.compression.min.filesize	Minimum filesize for compression	600

We've now reviewed the current configuration of our Blackboard Learn instance. But what if the current settings aren't meeting the needs of our organization. Are users experiencing slow load times even when server load is light? Do users report getting 503 or internal server errors when trying to access information within our instance? These types of issues can be a hint that our load maybe too much for the hardware on our server, or that we need to make adjustments to our configuration. Even if we move our current environment to a new server, we will need to make adjustments to take advantage of the possible changes such as increased RAM for example. Later in this chapter we will review what configurations we can change and tune based on information we can collect from our current environment.

System reporting

Now let's discuss how to collect information on the many activities within our Blackboard Learn instance. Within the **Tools and Utilities** module, we find the **System Reporting** link where we can create, run, and view reports for our system.

System Reporting

Statistics Reports

View statistics reports that monitor activity, tracking data, page views, usage, and provide debugging information.

Auto-Reporting Options

Turn on or off automatic reporting of system data to Blackboard, and whether the system collects usage data for event tracking.

Scheduled Reports Queue

*View or delete reports in the scheduled queue to run at the time set on the **Manage Report Schedule** page. Reports can be scheduled by editing them from the **Report Definitions** page.*

Reports Archive

View or edit archived reports, or download a completed report and save it to the Content Collection.

Textbook Reporting

View information on textbooks in use, and filter by course, ISBN number, and/or dates.

Report Definitions

View, import, delete, or edit system report definitions, including report properties, schedule, tags, and system and location availability.

Manage Report Schedule

*Set the time of day to start running automatically scheduled reports in the **Scheduled Report Queue** and the maximum time to commit to running them.*

Disk Usage

Display disk usage data for courses and organizations with recent user interaction.

Refresh Report Data

Refresh report data or view status information about current ETL state.

With the **System Reporting** page, our first option, **Statistics Reports**, gives us the ability to broadly see what users are doing within Blackboard Learn. There are several reports within the application that can collect a variety of information including course activity, page views, tracking reports, and even specifics about the system's Java environment. No matter what report we review, there are similarities between them all.

Every report will have a brief description below the title along with the date and time it was last ran. We also will see if the report is scheduled to run on a regular basis.

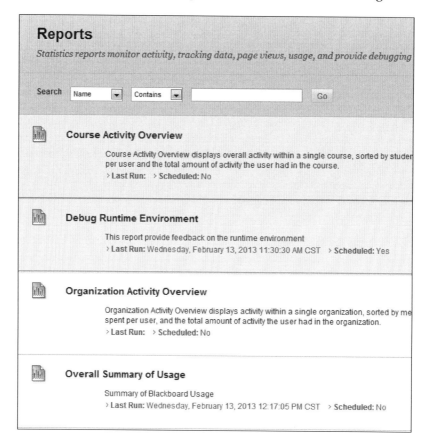

To run a report manually, we open the action menu by clicking on the chevron that appears to the right of the report title. We mouse over the menu and then select **Run**. The **Run Report** page appears along with the name, description, and the time it took to process the last report request. We may also see additional required specifications for our report such as a specific course and the ability to select a timeframe. Some reports will also ask us to select a report format. The system can create reports in PDF, HTML, Microsoft Excel, or Microsoft Word formats. Once these options are selected, we click on the **Submit** button to get the report started. Now the report starts to process. This can take a lot of time depending on the current load on our environment and how much data is collected. Once the report is processed, we have the ability to download this report in our previously selected format or run a new report. We should note that not every report will have every option we reviewed, however this is the basic process and should give us a basic understanding into how to run these reports.

What to do if a report fails…

Sometimes a report will fail to create the PDF, Excel, or Word document you were expecting. If this happens, run the report again and select the report to display in HTML format. If the report fails due to issues within our environment, we should see the exceptions displayed within the web page. These would not be displayed to us in the other formats.

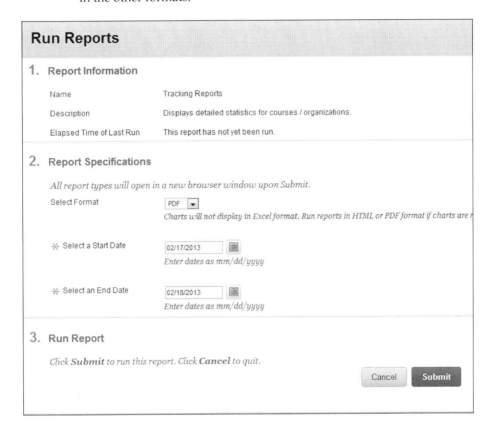

Just like other major software developers, Blackboard has a built-in ability to allow system administrators to send site's statistics information back to Blackboard's servers. Blackboard uses this information to improve and support the product. However, if we can change this reporting option to **No**, this information will not be reported. The other configuration option within this page allows us to turn on **Event Tracking**. Event tracking collects information within our environment and must be enabled for any reporting options to work. While this may seem like a great option, we should make sure that turning this option on will not impact our user's experience negatively.

Within the **System Reporting** page, there are four links that all deal with by taking the statistical reports we briefly discussed earlier and scheduling them to run on our Blackboard Learn instance. Let's go over each of them.

First we have the **Report Definitions** section, which allows us to import, schedule, and make available a report for processing. Not only do we find many of the reports from earlier, but also there are goal, alignment, and content reports as well. Once we have enabled a report or series of reports, we then must schedule them by going to the **Manage Report Schedule** page. This page gives us the ability to not only set the time when our reports should be ran, known as the **Start Time**, but also the duration of the reports. No need to worry if our reports don't complete in the allotted time, the reports will start back at the same place at the next start time. We should note that changes in the **Start Time** will require us to restart Blackboard Learn services.

In the **Schedule Reports Queue** section, we can see what reports are pending and have been completed within our instance. Once a report has been completed, we can find it within the **Reports Archive** page, which allows us to search for a report by name or description.

Disk Usage

Back in *Chapter 4, Creating Courses in Blackboard Learn*, we discussed **Course Size Limits**. This option caps the amount of content that could be stored within a course. This calculation is based on the amount reported by a daily calculation of course sizes. It would also notify the administrator and course instructor or instructors via e-mail that the course was close to its limit. However, what if we as administrators want to see the size of all the courses within our Blackboard Learn instance. This information is found by clicking on the **Disk Usage** link.

On the **Disk Usage** page, we have the ability to use the search tool to find courses or organizations within our instance by the course/organization name or ID. We also have the ability to search based on course sizes. With this search option, we can look at course or organization sizes based on course files, legacy filesystem, protected files, soft limit, and total size. We then can put the numerical size we want to search for based on the greater or less than option in kilobytes, megabytes, or gigabytes.

 Earlier in this chapter, we mentioned the Xythos system, which is where a course or organization's files are stored. The Xythos filesystem uses technology that de-dupes files, which means the system looks to find commonality within stored files to reduce the information it must store. This means that if we add up the size of our course files, legacy filesystem, and protected files, this may not equal the actual size these files take up.

Course ID △	Course Name	Status	Course Files	Protected Files	Legacy Filesystem	Soft Limit	Total Size
TEST-COURSE-001	Test Course A	Available	0 B	0 B	0 B	Unlimited	0 B
TEST-COURSE-002	Test Course B	Available	0 B	0 B	0 B	Unlimited	0 B
TEST-COURSE-003	Test Course C	Available	0 B	0 B	0 B	Unlimited	0 B
TEST-COURSE-005	Test Course - Marketing	Available	0 B	0 B	2.106 KB	Unlimited	2.106 KB

Refresh Report Data

The information we use to create our reports refreshes before the scheduled reports are run. However, if we need to update our data and can't wait for the next scheduled update we can force the system to refresh by going to the **Refresh Report Data** page. We can click on the **Refresh Report Data** button to force the system to refresh and below the button we see the last time when our report data was updated.

When to refresh data

While we can click on the **Refresh Report Data** button at any time during the day, doing so during heavy load times could tax the system to a standstill. If you must refresh data during the day, please do so with caution. We should also note that the **Disk Usage** report will not refresh as its data is collected by a daily task.

Textbook Information

Within each course in our system there is a textbook tool. This tool allows the instructor to insert an ISBN number and Blackboard will post the corresponding textbook information within the course along with a picture of the book. The **Textbook Information** page allows us to search this information. We can search to find what textbooks are listed within courses or organizations or search by a textbook's ISBN number. This search also gives us the ability to restrict it by dates as well.

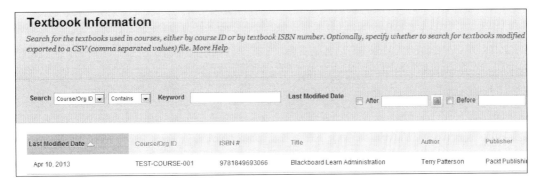

Optimizing our Blackboard Learn environment

So far we've spent much of our time reviewing how to manage our Blackboard Learn system. Now it's time to take the system and its operation to the next level and optimize it. As we discussed in *Chapter 1, Planning a Blackboard Learn Instance*, our hardware and software needs should be a part of our planning. However, after building an instance and allowing user traffic, we begin to learn our virtual community's flows or traffic patterns. Now, we need to look at our environment and search for areas where we can optimize it. Our first option is to look at the series of tasks that run on the system throughout the day.

Blackboard Tasks

Earlier in this chapter, we mentioned the **Disk Usage** task. This is one of many tasks that run on a regular basis within Blackboard Learn. Events such as log rotation, stats purging, cleaning up deleted files, and old notification data are also a part of these. These tasks normally run during the day and normally never cause issues. We can see all the background tasks running on our server by going to the URL `http://applicationservername/webapps/blackboard/admin/view_system_tasks.jsp`. If we are running multiple application servers, we should use the name of the application server. Sometimes, however, we find ourselves in a situation where a task interferes with other events on our servers. Sometimes we have to manage when these tasks run.

Background Tasks

Task Service Started:Sun Feb 17 01:03:50 CST 2013

Key	Period	Delay	Last Started	Last Completed	Duration
bb.connect.usersync	1 hrs	1 min	Mon Feb 18 00:05:22 CST 2013	Mon Feb 18 00:05:22 CST 2013	65 ms
bb.scheduled.report.queuer	1 days	5 sec			not run yet
bb.er.evidence.collection	1 hrs	1 min	Mon Feb 18 00:05:12 CST 2013	Mon Feb 18 00:05:12 CST 2013	12 ms
bb.monitor.cache	10 sec	2 min	Mon Feb 18 00:18:37 CST 2013	Mon Feb 18 00:18:37 CST 2013	12 ms
bb.authentication.log.purge	1 days	1 min	Sun Feb 17 01:04:55 CST 2013	Sun Feb 17 01:04:57 CST 2013	2 sec
bb.portal.channel.update	5 min	50 sec	Mon Feb 18 00:15:03 CST 2013	Mon Feb 18 00:15:03 CST 2013	21 ms
time.cache.update	1 hrs	0 ms	Mon Feb 18 00:07:06 CST 2013	Mon Feb 18 00:07:07 CST 2013	134 ms
bb.task.queue	2 sec	1 min	Mon Feb 18 00:18:43 CST 2013	Mon Feb 18 00:18:43 CST 2013	1 ms

Caution when editing bb-tasks files

Editing the `bb-tasks.xml` or `bb-tasks.xml.bb` files can cause major issues if not done properly. If you wish to edit these files, make sure you submit your proposed changes within a ticket to Blackboard Support to get appropriate feedback. Before editing any system or configuration file within our Blackboard Learn applications, we should always save a backup copy.

We can do this by editing the `bb-tasks.xml` and the `bb-tasks.xml.bb` files. These task configuration files are found in the `config` subdirectory of our Blackboard `home` directory. Both of these files are the same except for their file names. We have two files because when we run the `PushConfigUpdates` process, our configuration files are updated from the template or `.bb` file to create the `.xml` file. Most administrators will make the change in the `bb-tasks.xml.bb` and `bb-tasks.xml` files at the same time.

Now that we understand a little more about why we have two different files, let's look inside them to learn more. We can open either file in our favorite text editor. Within the file, we see multiple items called `task-entry`. Each one corresponds to a different task. Here is an example of the disk usage task entry from one of these files:

```
<!-- Must run on at least one application server -->
<task-entry key="bb.disk_usage" version="60">
  <task classname="blackboard.platform.course.DiskUsageTask">
    <property name="delay"       value="72000000" />
    <property name="period"      value="86400000" />
    <property name="active-days" value="30" />
  </task>
</task-entry>
```

The first line in our example is a comment line. We can notice this because the line begins with `<!--` and ends with `-->`. Blackboard Learn versions prior to 9.1 Service Pack 8 required us to comment out some of the tasks within our `bb-tasks` files, if we had multiple application servers. Current versions require us only to set `bbconfig.server.backend.processor` to on or off within our `bb-config.properties` file. Using this option allows us to set a specific server to run all the tasks for our environment. This option works well if we have already kept a single application server out of our load balancer to run snapshot processes or batch commands. The `task-entry` line identifies the system task, while the task `classname` contains the internal task information. The next lines are the ones we need to focus on.

The `delay` property is the amount of time after the server restarts before the task will start. The value is calculated in milliseconds, so our delay value is 1,200 minutes or 20 hours after our server restarts. This means that if we restart our server at 5:00 am, our disk usage task will run at 1:00 am the following day.

Warning about restarting servers and task scheduling

If we need to restart a Blackboard Learn application server due to an emergency or maintenance, this will reset our task schedule. The restart will adversely affect our bb-tasks. For example, if our restart happens five hours later than a normal restart time, all our tasks will shift an additional five hours. This could put some tasks in the middle of heavy load times, so beware.

The period property sets the time between when the task runs. Our example value, 86400000, equals 24 hours, which means our disk usage task will run every 24 hours after our initial task runs.

Optimizing web services

Now let's review our web service. Our web service can be hosted by either IIS, if our instance resides in a Windows environment or Apache if we use Red Hat or Solaris. Each web service has different ways for us to monitor and optimize it. We will start our discussions with IIS.

Monitoring and optimizing Internet Information Services

We configured our IIS for our Blackboard Learn instance using the information Blackboard provided within the application's release notes. Before we start to optimize our instance, we need to monitor specific parts of IIS. Within our Windows Server, we can click on the **Start** button and type in perfmon. The **Performance Monitor** appears and we need to click on the **Performance Monitor** and then click on the green plus button above our graph. Here we can add specific data types to monitor.

- Memory > Pages per second
- Memory > Available Bytes
- Memory > Committed Bytes
- Processor > % Processor Time
- Process > Thread Count > W3WP
- Thread > % Processor Time > W3WP: Thread #

The last two data types monitor the IIS Application Pool process, known as W3WP in the preceding data types. If we run IIS in worker process isolation mode, we can use the IIS Application Pool process to see the number of threads created and how much processor load is required at various times.

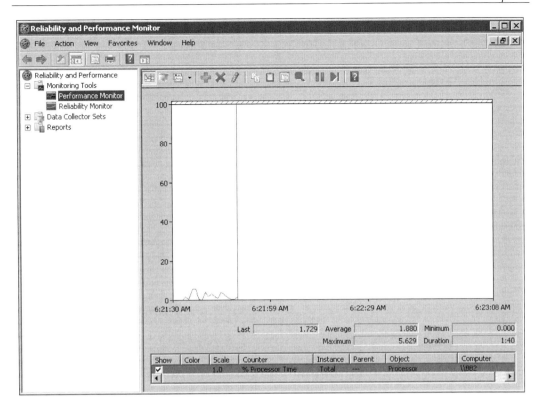

We also have the ability to control some web server configurations within the `bb-config.properties` file. These settings include:

- `bbconfig.webserver.keepalive`: When this is set to `1`, our instance will enable HTTP persistent connections. When this is set to `0`, it's disabled.

- `bbconfig.webserver.keepalivetimeout`: If we have HTTP persistent connections enabled, this numerical value (in seconds) tells IIS how long to wait for another request based on the user's browser and IP address. When installed, the default value currently is 30 seconds. Blackboard recommends changing this to 15 seconds, if we plan to enable it.

- `bbconfig.webserver.compression`: Setting this configuration value to `Yes` allows the compression of website data using GZip compression. This option can decrease bandwidth usage, however heavily used environments will see the most benefit from this option.

Microsoft also provides the ability to set up HTTP compression to dynamic content within IIS. Directions to enable this option can be found on Microsoft's website (`http://technet.microsoft.com/en-us/library/cc753681(WS.10).aspx`).

After we've set up and collected some data on how our IIS works with users accessing the Blackboard Learn application, we can discuss some optimization options. Many experienced web administrators might want to control the number of connections by throttling them. This configuration can create issues between the IIS and Blackboard's Tomcat process. If we tend to see connection or process loading higher than our organization's acceptable levels, we will want to allocate additional hardware or virtual resources for the server.

Monitoring and optimizing Apache

For Red Hat Linux and Solaris administrators, Blackboard Learn comes with Apache 1.3 on board. Apache 1.3 officially reached its End of Life in early 2010, however Blackboard states it does keep the Apache 1.3 up to date. While Blackboard continues to support Apache 1.3, they have recommended Linux and Solaris customers with version 9.1 SP8 or later use Apache 2.2, which continues to be widely supported and updated.

Installing and configuring Apache 2.2 for Blackboard Learn

The transition process from Apache 1.3 to 2.2 is rather simple, once we have Apache 2.2 installed on our server. However, if we compile Apache 2.2, we must choose to enable **multi-processing modules** (**MPMs**). More on that later.

1. Create a symbolic link from the `conf.d` directory within Apache 2.2 to the `blackboard.conf` file in the `config/apache2` subdirectory of your Blackboard `home` folder:

   ```
   cd /etc/httpd/conf.d
   sudo ln -s /usr/local/blackboard/config/apache2/blackboard.conf
   ```

2. Within our `bb-config.properties` file, we must change the `bbconfig. unix.httpd.enable` to `false`.

3. Our changes require us to run the `PushConfigUpdates.sh` command found in the `tools/admin` subdirectory of our Blackboard `home` folder.

4. Once the `PushconfigUpdates` command completes, we must restart Apache 2.2.

Our server is now using Apache 2.2 instead of the 1.3 version.

Now that we have Apache 2.2 as our web server, we need to make some configuration changes to make sure it operates correctly. One of these configuration settings takes us back to MPMs. There are two different multi-processing modules, Worker MPM or Prefork MPM. Blackboard recommends the use of the Worker MPM, which will require changing the default setting, Prefork. Let's review the steps to confirm MPM is enabled in Apache and use the Worker MPM instead of Prefork.

If we want to see which MPM runs in our Apache instance, we can run the following command:

```
/usr/sbin/apachectl -l
```

If MPM is running, we then run the following command to see if the Worker MPM was compiled within Apache:

```
/usr/sbin/httpd.worker -l
```

Here is an example of the output we should see:

```
[bbuser@bbpocapp1 ~]$ /usr/sbin/httpd.worker -l
Compiled in modules:
  core.c
  worker.c
  http_core.c
  mod_so.c
[bbuser@bbpocapp1 ~]$
```

Now we need to go into the /etc/sysconfig/httpd file and uncomment the HTTPD=/usr/sbin/httpd.worker line.

Once we have saved the HTTPD file, we will need to restart the Apache web server.

We've moved to the latest version of Apache to protect us from security vulnerabilities, but now we need to learn more about loading our users to put on our Apache web server. We do this by using monitoring tools. Many organizations may use a variety of different commercial and open source tools, such as AppDynamics or Zabbix. While these tools offer extended monitoring processes, we can start our monitoring with a tool already built within our Apache web server.

Apache's **Server Status** module allows us to monitor the server's performance at several levels. It takes only a few steps to enable this option within our Apache 2.2 configuration. First we need to open the httpd.conf file in our Apache2 (or HTTPD) conf directory.

```
/etc/httpd/conf/httpd.conf
```

We then need to uncomment the `ExtendedStatus On` option.

Next, scroll down and find the `<Location>` section within our file and remove the comments that have it disabled. Note that uncommenting this will open the `server-status` tool world wide (unless we have a load balancer hiding our servers and/ or firewall rules in place). In our example, we only allow the server the privilege to view the page.

```
<Location /server-status>
    SetHandler server-status
    Order deny,allow
    Deny from all
    Allow from 127.0.0.1
</Location>
```

If we need to access it from other IP addresses, simply add more `Allow` statements. Now we save and close the file, and then restart the Apache web server. We should be able to view the **Server Status** tool by going to `http://ServerName/server-status/`.

When we go to the **Server Status** page for an application server, we will see the current time on the server along with the last time our Apache web server was restarted. This area also includes other broad data.

- Averages from the child processes based on requests per second, bytes served per second, and bytes per request
- Processor usage (in percent) broken down by each child process and also displayed as a total
- Total count of clients accessing the server and the amount of bytes served
- Number of children (processes) serving requests
- Number of idle children

Below that area, we find a table which displays all the child processes. This table shows additional information about each one.

- Status of each child process
- Number of requests each child process has performed
- Total number of bytes served by the child process

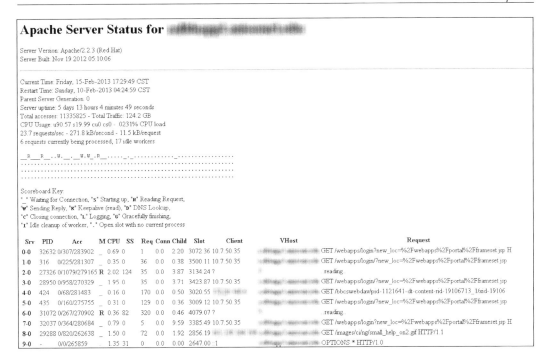

Apache Server Status for ~~[redacted]~~

Server Version: Apache/2.2.3 (Red Hat)
Server Built: Nov 19 2012 05:10:06

Current Time: Friday, 15-Feb-2013 17:29:49 CST
Restart Time: Sunday, 10-Feb-2013 04:24:59 CST
Parent Server Generation: 0
Server uptime: 5 days 13 hours 4 minutes 49 seconds
Total accesses: 11335825 - Total Traffic: 124.2 GB
CPU Usage: u90.57 s19.99 cu0 cs0 - 0.231% CPU load
23.7 requests/sec - 271.8 kB/second - 11.5 kB/request
6 requests currently being processed, 17 idle workers

```
__R___R__._.W.__._.__W.W_.R__....._._..............._................
.....................................................................
.....................................................................
.....................................................................
```

Scoreboard Key:
"_" Waiting for Connection, "s" Starting up, "ʀ" Reading Request,
"ᴡ" Sending Reply, "ᴋ" Keepalive (read), "ᴅ" DNS Lookup,
"ʟ" Closing connection, "ʟ" Logging, "ɢ" Gracefully finishing,
"ɪ" Idle cleanup of worker, "." Open slot with no current process

Srv	PID	Acc	M	CPU	SS	Req	Conn	Child	Slot	Client	VHost	Request
0-0	32632	0/307/283902	_	0.69	0	1	0.0	2.20	3072.36	10.7.50.35	~~[redacted]~~	GET /webapps/login/?new_loc=%2Fwebapps%2Fportal%2Fframeset.jsp H
1-0	316	0/225/281307	_	0.35	0	36	0.0	0.38	3500.11	10.7.50.35	~~[redacted]~~	GET /webapps/login/?new_loc=%2Fwebapps%2Fportal%2Fframeset.jsp
2-0	27326	0/1079/279165	R	2.02	124	35	0.0	3.87	3134.24	?		.reading.
3-0	28950	0/958/270329	_	1.95	0	35	0.0	3.71	3423.87	10.7.50.35	~~[redacted]~~	GET /webapps/login/?new_loc=%2Fwebapps%2Fportal%2Fframeset.jsp
4-0	424	0/68/281483	_	0.16	0	170	0.0	0.50	3020.55	~~[redacted]~~	~~[redacted]~~	GET /bbcswebdav/pid-1121641-dt-content-rid-19106713_1/xid-19106
5-0	435	0/160/275755	_	0.31	0	129	0.0	0.36	3009.12	10.7.50.35	~~[redacted]~~	GET /webapps/login/?new_loc=%2Fwebapps%2Fportal%2Fframeset.jsp
6-0	31072	0/267/270902	R	0.36	82	320	0.0	0.46	4079.07	?		.reading.
7-0	32037	0/364/280684	_	0.79	0	5	0.0	9.59	3385.49	10.7.50.35	~~[redacted]~~	GET /webapps/login/?new_loc=%2Fwebapps%2Fportal%2Fframeset.jsp H
8-0	29288	0/820/262638	_	1.50	0	72	0.0	1.92	2856.19	~~[redacted]~~	~~[redacted]~~	GET /images/ci/ng/small_help_on2.gif HTTP/1.1
9-0	-	0/0/265859	.	1.35	31	0	0.0	0.00	2647.00	:1	~~[redacted]~~	OPTIONS * HTTP/1.0

The **Server Status** tool gives us a well-informed view of how well our Apache instance operates during heavy user loads. If we do find issues in either quantitative or qualitative ways, we will need to improve our current performance settings.

Normally, when we want to optimize our Blackboard Learn instance we go to our `bb-config.properties` file and start our edits from there. However, with our installation of Apache 2.2 being external to our Blackboard instance, any tuning or optimization we do within it must be done within our `httpd.conf` file. We should be able to find that file in our `apache` directory. In our example, the file is found in the `/etc/httpd/conf` directory.

Within our `httpd.conf` file, we scroll down to the Worker MPM area. Earlier we enabled this multi-processing module and we should do so before changing our configuration. Under our `<IfModule worker.c>` area, we have several options. Let's go over each one listed and see how it corresponds to the parameters within our `bb-config.properties` file.

- `StartServers`: This is also known as `bbconfig.unix.httpd.startservers`. This option tells the server how many child processes should be opened at startup. Blackboard recommends this variable be set to `10`.

- `MaxClients`: This is also known as `bbconfig.unix.httpd.maxclients`. This process sets the maximum number of client connections that can be made at one time to this server. We will discuss how to configure this parameter in a bit, but we must make sure that it is larger than the `bbconfig.appserver.maxthreads` parameter. Blackboard recommends this be set to `200` for new systems.

- `MinSpareThreads`: This is also known as `bbconfig.unix.httpd.minspareservers`. This variable sets the minimum number of spare child processes to handle simultaneous client requests. Blackboard recommends this be set to `5`.

- `MaxSpareThreads`: This is also known as `bbconfig.unix.httpd.maxspareservers`. This parameter sets the maximum number of spare child processes and should be set to `50` according to Blackboard.

- `ThreadsPerChild`: There is no known parameter for this, This variable tells our web server the constant number of worker threads within each child process.

- `MaxRequestsPerChild`: This is also known as `bbconfig.unix.httpd.maxrequestsperchild`. Our web server uses this parameter to set the maximum number of requests that a child process handles. Blackboard documentation states this number should be between `1024` and `2048`.

Each of these parameters can be tuned to meet the load and needs of our system. One of the major items we should tune within our Apache web server parameters is the `MaxClients` variable. This will require a little effort and some mathematical calculations on our part. Blackboard recommends that we find the `MaxClients` variable by performing the steps discussed here.

During a time of heavy usage, we should log in to our server and run the following command:

```
ps -ylC httpd --sort:rss
```

Within our output, we should find the largest child process size, also known as the max child process size. Next we need to determine how much RAM memory is reserved for our Apache web server. Lastly, we must get the `bbconfig.appserver.maxthreads` parameter from the `bb-config.properties` file. Now we need to use a formula to find the `MaxClients` variable.

MaxClients = minimum (RAM Memory allocated for Apache web server / Max child process size, bbconfig.appserver.maxthreads)

Our formula asks us to divide our Apache web server RAM Memory allocated by the max child process size. Then, we must compare our formula's quotient to the `bbconfig.appserver.maxthreads` variable and take the lesser of the two to set our `MaxClients` variable.

We also can calculate how much RAM memory we need to have dedicated for our Apache web server by multiplying our `MaxClients` variable with the max child process size.

Apache Web Server dedicated RAM = MaxClients x Max child process size

Before we close our `conf` file, we have a few other configurations to go over. Our first item is to enable `KeepAlive`, which allows persistent connections. This can be done by changing `KeepAlive Off` to `KeepAlive On` in our `conf` file. We then need to set our `MaxKeepAliveRequests` to `100` and `KeepAliveTimeout` to `15` as per Blackboard's recommendations. The `KeepAliveTimeout` parameter tells Apache how long to wait for another request based on the user's browser and IP address. Our last configuration option is compression. This compresses website data using the GZip and can slightly decrease bandwidth usage. Blackboard recommends enabling this option within our Apache web server. We can enable the compression extension within Apache by following the documentation available at `http://httpd.apache.org/docs/2.2/mod/mod_deflate.html`.

Tomcat configuration and optimization

Behind our Apache or IIS server sits Tomcat, the engine of our Blackboard Learn environment. Our configuration and optimization changes for this application allow us to change the environment it runs in and how it communicates with our web and database servers. Before we discuss the configurations that can affect our installation, we should know that making major changes to one part of Tomcat's configuration can negatively impact other areas within our environment. When changes are made, we must do so with caution. Let's review the Tomcat settings found within our `bb-config.properties` file.

- `bbconfig.appserver.minthreads`: This parameter sets the number of threads created when we start our Tomcat server. Blackboard recommends this be set at `100`.

- `bbconfig.appserver.maxthreads`: This variable should be the same number as our `MaxClients` setting for our Apache or IIS instances. It sets the maximum number of Tomcat threads. Blackboard recommends we set this variable between `400` and `800` based on a 4 GB heap size in a 64-bit environment.

- `bbconfig.min.heapsize.tomcat`: Our variable declares the minimum heap size for the Tomcat JVM. Blackboard recommends we make this either half or equal to our `bbconfig.max.heapsize.tomcat` parameter.

- `bbconfig.max.heapsize.tomcat`: A parameter to set the maximum heap size for our Tomcat JVM. (See `bbconfig.min.heapsize.tomcat` for more details.)

- `bbconfig.max.permsize.tomcat`: This variable sets the maximum amount of perm space for the Tomcat JVM. The default Blackboard setting is 256 m.

- `bbconfig.max.stacksize.tomcat`: This sets the stack size for each thread on our Tomcat JVM. It's recommended setting should be between 170 and 300 k.

- `bbconfig.jvm.options.extra.tomcat`: This setting includes numerous variables, which can change between Service Packs. We should review the Service Pack Release Notes for recommendations.

- `bbconfig.jvm.options.gc`: Made up of many different parameters, this variable includes most options that deal with the garbage collection process within Tomcat. It was introduced in Blackboard Learn 9.1 SP9.

 As with our `bbconfig.jvm.options.extra.tomcat`, each Service Pack will have specific recommended performance settings, which can be found within the Release Notes.

The parameters we have discussed so far have dealt with Tomcat and its interactions with our Apache or IIS web server. Next we need to review the settings that connect Tomcat to our databases.

- `bbconfig.database.instance.maxpoolsize`: This parameter sets the maximum connections ready to server database requests for our main database, BBLEARN (or the legacy BB_BB60). Blackboard recommends starting with a conservative maximum, such as 100, and increase it as the number of Tomcat threads increase. Our optimal value for this is normally equal to our `bbconfig.appserver.maxthreads` parameter, but never greater than it.

- `bbconfig.database.instance.minpoolsize`: We set the minimum number of connections available for database requests within this variable. It should be set to 10.

- `bbconfig.database.instance.mssql.initpoolsize`: This is a variable that is only needed for Microsoft SQL database connections. This sets the initial number of collections available for database requests.

- `bbconfig.database.instance.timeout`: The time (in seconds) for database transactions to complete before timing out.

So far we have reviewed many different settings and parameters within Apache and Tomcat. We may expect further discussion about the database server. However, any changes to optimize performance within Oracle or Microsoft SQL should be done with the cooperation of our organization's database administrator. Even slight changes within a database can create major issues for our application and in the end-user experience.

Tomcat thread queuing

Earlier in our introduction to this chapter, we discussed how the web server, Tomcat, and the database serve as power house to our virtual community. Sometimes, however our users will want more than the amount of power that we can provide. Well, what if that happens within our Blackboard Learn application? What can our instance do? We can use Tomcat thread queuing, just as when you queue up for a movie or to checkout, we can line up requests from our IIS or Apache server. While this might extend the user's time for a page to load, it seems better than the page not loading at all. Let's review how to enable this feature in our environment.

1. First we must stop Blackboard Learn services.

2. Then, we must access the Tomcat `config/tomcat/conf` subdirectory, which should be found in the Blackboard `home` directory.

3. If we only want to make the change temporarily, we should edit the `server.xml` file. If we want to make this change permanent, we must edit the `server.xml.bb` file instead.

4. Within the file, we should find `backlog="0"`. Change the parameter from `0` to `10`. This means that 10 requests will be placed in the queue if there are no Tomcat threads available to process a web server request. `10` is the smallest amount recommended by Blackboard.

> We should consider raising this number if users are experiencing 503 errors, which could indicate this issue. However, we don't want to make the queue too large or we could find our users waiting and waiting just like in our movie queue. Gradual increase with this option will be the best bet.

5. Save and close the file.

6. If we select to edit the `server.xml.bb` file, we will need to run a `PushConfigUpdates` command to apply our changes. If we just edit the `server.xml` file, we only need to restart the Blackboard Service.

So far in this chapter, we have reviewed the many different ways to configure our Blackboard Learn environment to improve its performance for our users. While we end our discussion, it should be mentioned that improving the performance of an environment like Blackboard Learn is never ending. Users, content, software, and hardware changes will always have some effect on the performance of this type of web application. We should work to develop some simple processes to monitor our instance so that we know when we need to have another round of performance tuning.

We can start with two different data sets that can help us learn about our system, the number of users on our system and number of assessments given during a day. If we learn when our system has its highest user load, we can look at our performance monitoring tools and see how much load our Blackboard Learn environment handles. Understanding the number of assessments given during a day can also help because those assessments require additional Tomcat threads and database connections.

We can learn this information by querying our Blackboard database. If we use an Oracle database server, we can run the following query:

```
select to_char(timestamp,'mm/dd/yyyy HH24') as "Hour", count(session_
id) from BB_BB60.activity_accumulator where timestamp > sysdate -7
group by to_char(timestamp,'mm/dd/yyyy HH24')
order by to_char(timestamp,'mm/dd/yyyy HH24');
```

If we use Microsoft SQL, we should run the following query:

```
select substring(convert(varchar(19),timestamp,120),1,13) as "Hour",
count(session_id) from activity_accumulator where timestamp >
dateadd(d, -7,getdate())
group by substring(convert(varchar(19),timestamp,120),1,13)
order by substring(convert(varchar(19),timestamp,120),1,13);
```

This query will display the number of users on our Blackboard Learn environment over the past seven days broken down by hour. Now, let's see the same information for assessment attempts by running this query within our Oracle database.

```
select count(pk1) as "# of Assessment Attempts", to_char(attempt_
date,'YYYY-MM-DD HH24') as "Date by Hour"  from attempt where attempt_
date > sysdate - 7 group by to_char(attempt_date,'YYYY-MM-DD HH24')
order by 2 desc;
```

If we use Microsoft SQL, run the following query:

```
select count(pk1) as "# of Assessment Attempts", substring(convert(var
char(19),attempt_date,120),1,13) as "Date by Hour" from attempt where
attempt_date > dateadd(d, -7,getdate()) group by substring(convert(var
char(19),attempt_date,120),1,13)  order by 2 desc;
```

If we don't have database access, we can install the BbStats building block and see the same information. It is available for free and can be downloaded at http://projects. oscelot.org/gf/project/bbstats/. Once we gather this information, we can develop monitoring plans and start to optimize our Blackboard Learn instance.

Summary

Over these pages, we have gained a general understanding of how we can secure, monitor, and improve our Blackboard Learn environment. We discussed how to ensure an encrypted connection between the user's browser and our system. Our conversation also included the new security features that allow us to protect our system from users trying to gain unauthorized access.

We then discussed the system information options available within the Blackboard Learn Administrator Panel including the system configuration and system reporting areas. Our discussions moved into a lengthy review of the monitoring, optimization tools, and parameters available to improve our web server and Tomcat server performances within Blackboard Learn. We also learned how to find the time of day when our system is most heavily used. Our discussion also gave us the basic rule when working to optimize, which suggests we make only small changes in our many configuration parameters.

We have covered some very important and deeply technical information in the past chapter. Our next chapter will continue with technical discussions of a different variety. Many organizations look to integrate their Blackboard Learn environment with other systems, specifically authentication and student information systems. So, let's get ready to learn how we can connect other systems to our virtual community.

10
Authentication and Data Integration in Blackboard Learn

Over the past nine chapters, we have set up a virtual community that can serve our organization's needs. However, we need to populate and allow access to it. Our discussions reviewed how we can do that within our Blackboard Learn environment. In this chapter, the topic turns to helping integrate other systems within our organization to populate, secure, and manage access to our Blackboard Learn instance. We have several aspects of the integration process to cover, including:

- Integrating authentication protocols within Blackboard Learn
- Developing a process to integrate data information systems into Blackboard Learn
- Reviewing the data-integration options available in Blackboard Learn
- Learning how to create a basic data integration within our Blackboard Learn environment

Our integrations will not only challenge our skills as Blackboard administrators, but also require us to work with other administrators, and possibly departments. However, the goal of these integrations is to create a better user experience within our Blackboard Learn system. Let's start our conversation by discussing how we can use external authentication protocols within our instance.

External authentication in Blackboard Learn

In *Chapter 6, Creating Users in Blackboard Learn*, during our review of user creation policy, one of the questions we asked was, would our Blackboard Learn instance use our organization's authentication systems. By using an external authentication system, users will find that their Blackboard Learn login credentials are the same as those used to access e-mail or log in to their workstations. This also removes us and any support team members from dealing with password resets and allows the central authentication system to block user access within our Blackboard Learn environment.

Planning authentication integration

Before we go into our Blackboard Learn instance and connect it to an external authentication provider, we should review the external authentication options that Blackboard Learn supports. Once we review what options can be used within Blackboard Learn, we can select what options to use within our organization.

LDAP

Lightweight Directory Access Protocol (LDAP) has grown to be a major authentication protocol used by numerous organizations. This continues to be the major external authentication protocol used with Blackboard Learn by most organizations. The LDAP process takes the authentication information provided by the user when trying to log in and then sends a query to an LDAP server. The server then searches for the username within the directory and if found, checks to see if the user-supplied password matches the one stored within the LDAP database. If so, the user gains access.

Unlike the Central Authentication Service, LDAP doesn't require a website that will authenticate the user to our instance. It works using its own protocol to gain the information it needs without redirecting the user. In the end, LDAP allows the user to stay within our Blackboard Learn environment to log in; however, our LDAP protocol will only authenticate the user to our instance and is not a Single Sign-On option.

Central Authentication Service

Central Authentication Service (CAS) is increasingly being used as an external authentication system for many organizations as a Single Sign-On option. There are many CAS projects, including OpenID and SAML. A CAS operates when a user tries to authenticate to an application, such as our Blackboard Learn instance. Our environment sends the user to the login server to put in their credentials. The CAS then checks the username and password against a database such as Active Directory. If successful, the CAS issues a security ticket and directs the user's browser, with the ticket, back to our Blackboard Learn instance. Then, the instance authenticates the ticket by using its secure connection to the CAS to verify if the ticket is active.

We can compare this CAS process to going to a movie, theatrical, or a sporting event. We must purchase a ticket from the booth (in this case we purchase it right before the event) and we must offer some identification to get the ticket. Before we are allowed in, we present our ticket to gain entry. Many times these tickets have a barcode on them. The attendant will scan the barcode and the ticket information is sent to a main computer. The main computer checks to make sure the ticket is valid, which approves our entry into the event.

Many organizations use CAS as part of a larger structure. Some organizations use web portals that then allow access to web applications. Users must log in through a CAS login page to access the web portal; this authenticates the user. Within the portal, customized links to web applications pass the CAS ticket and the user immediately gains access.

Shibboleth authentication

Shibboleth authentication has become the major external authentication provider for many academic institutions around the world. It offers a similar function to the CAS we just reviewed since it does use the **Security Assertion Markup Language (SAML)**, as well. Shibboleth, unlike CAS, is an open source software installed on a single server which uses the same "ticketing system" we spoke about earlier to create a Single Sign-On environment. This is based on the shibboleth server which is called the identity provider, and the service provider resides on the same server as our Blackboard Learn environment. Since many organizations using Blackboard Learn may also use Shibboleth, we will review how to prepare our Blackboard Learn instance for Shibboleth.

Blackboard legacy authentication framework

In older versions of Blackboard Learn, our changes were made to `authenticaton.properties`; and in Blackboard Learn 9.1 Service Pack 8, the authentication process then moved to being based on building blocks, which created the external authentication provider tool. However, many instances still require the previous, or legacy authentication framework, to allow users to authenticate to their external servers. These options, such as web-server delegation or Datatel, are supported and configured using the `authentication.properties` file within the `config` subdirectory in our Blackboard `home` folder.

Default

The default authentication option within our Blackboard Learn instance is the internal authentication. Many administrators might think of disabling this option. Why would we need to use internal authentication with the external authentication providers that we may have integrated? What if a scenario kicks in, where we lose the connections with these external authentication providers? What if we want to provide access to users who don't have accounts in our external authentication providers? What if our system admin accounts don't reside in the external authentication providers? These are just a few of the reasons why we may want to keep our internal authentication provider service on as a last resort for logging in.

In case our external authentication options aren't working

If we have our external authentication options available—however, they aren't working—we do have the ability to create a one-time login by going into the `tools/admin` subdirectory of our Blackboard `home` directory. The `AuthenticationOneTimeLogin` script (either `.sh` or `.bat`) allows one time access. We must put in our username, time limit, and entry code, as variables. Here's an example:

```
./AuthenticationOneTimeLogin.sh -u administrator -t 15 -e Letmein123
```

Notice that in this example, we will log in with the username `administrator` and use the entry code `Letmein123`. This option will only be available for 15 minutes after running this command. After running the command, we see this output:

```
One-time Login Successfully Created.
URL to login:http://blackboard.myorganization.com/webapps/
login?action=one_time_login&ticket=b6f51469-868b-45c3-9392-e3ccd61426cb
Entry code:
Letmein123
User to login:
administrator
Ticket will expire at:
Saturday, November 24, 2013 9:29:59 PM CST
```

Now we simply copy this URL (`http://blackboard.myorganization.com/webapps/login?action=one_time_login&ticket=b6f51469-868b-45c3-9392-e3ccd61426cb`) into a web browser. It takes us to a **One Time Login** screen (shown in the following screenshot), where we enter our **Entry Code** and click on the **Submit** button. Now we can gain access with the username and, if the username has access to the **System Admin** tab, fix issues with our external authentication providers.

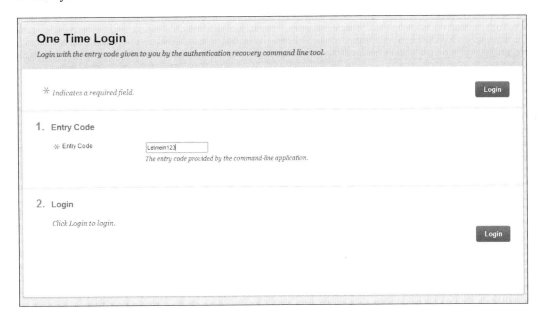

External authentication provider planning

Those are the external authentication providers we have within our instance so far. As new authentication options become available, we will see new providers become available for installation using the building blocks option. Before we start to implement these external authentication providers, let's review the high points:

- Understand the current and future external authentication providers for our organization, and how they might impact the authentication process within our Blackboard Learn environment.

- If using one major external authentication provider, we will want to include a secondary or backup-provider address in case our primary authentication server fails.

- Create a priority list for each of the external authentication providers. This list will help us decide the order in which external authentication providers get our usernames and passwords within our Blackboard Learn environment. We will discuss how to schedule external authentication provider order later in this chapter.

Adding external authentication providers

As mentioned earlier, we now add our external authentication providers within the **System Admin** tab of our Blackboard Learn instance. Here we find an **Authentication** link under the **Building Blocks** module. This link takes us to the **Authentication** page (shown in the following screenshot), where we will integrate our external providers.

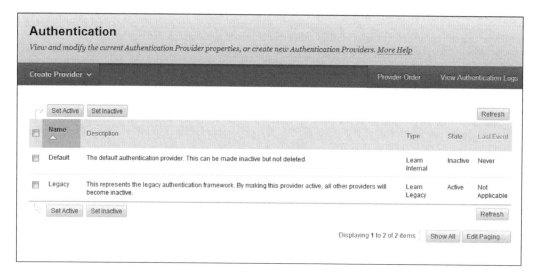

Creating an LDAP provider

Within this page we find two providers, **Default** and **Legacy**, already listed. We add more providers by hovering over the **Create Provider** button and select the type of provider we want to add. In this example, let's create a connection to our external LDAP server. Our **LDAP** selection takes us to the **Create LDAP** page, shown in the following screenshot. As with most creation pages within our Blackboard Learn instances, we need to give our provider a name and then give a description if we wish.

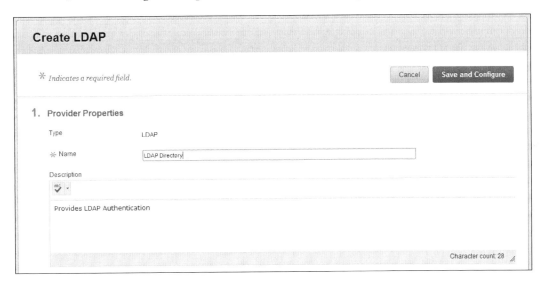

Next we find the ability to allow this provider to be active or inactive. The next item asks us how we should search for our user within LDAP. Most administrators will find that their LDAP directory requires the **Username** to look up information, but some directories might use the **Batch UID**.

Batch UID is normally the same as the username. However, if you use (or plan to use) Snapshot or the SIS Framework for integration, which we will discuss later in this chapter, the Batch UID and username may not necessarily be the same.

Our last option with an LDAP provider is to restrict which hostnames within our Blackboard Learn environment use this provider. We would use this option if we are hosting different domains within our instance, which can be done if our organization has the Community Engagement license. If we have multiple hostnames, we can provide them in the **Restricted Hostnames** textbox. Once our changes are selected, we click on the **Save and Configure** button. This is shown in the following screenshot:

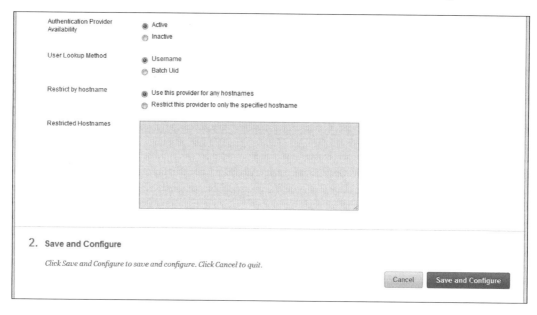

We then go to the **LDAP Settings** page, shown in the following screenshot, where we will add information about our external authentication provider. The **Connection Settings**, **Search Settings**, and **Advanced Settings** should be based on the information provided by the administrator of the external authentication provider. This information will tell our instance where to search for users within the LDAP directory and what **Search Attribute**, such as **username**, will our environment try to match. Some LDAP providers require a privileged user to be able to even search the directory, so we may need to provide this information. Our final configurations will be based on how the LDAP provider has set up the protocol. These advanced configurations set connection timeouts and how our search of the LDAP directory is processed.

If we plan to use LDAPS, our instance will require a commercially-signed SSL certificate or a self-signed certificate, which should be available from the LDAP server administrator. We may use LDAPS if the LDAP request passes outside of our secured network on to public networks. We must then import the certificate into the application server by using the keytool within Java to import the certificate into the JVM truststore. Here's a sample of the command we would run to import the LDAPS certificate:

```
$JAVA_HOME/jre/bin/keytool -import -v -trustcacerts -alias ldaps -file
path-to-the-ca.crt -keystore $JAVA_HOME/jre/lib/security/cacerts
```

Once our certificate is within the truststore, we can continue setting up our
LDAP provider.

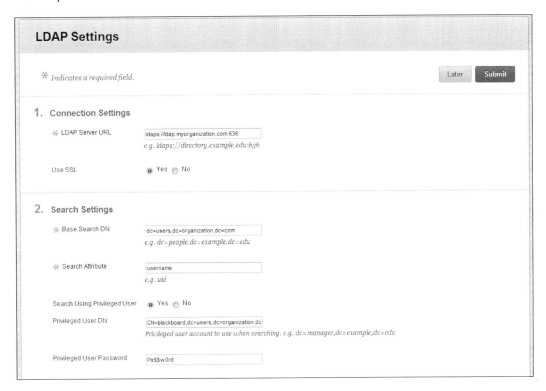

Once we finish filling out our information click on the **Submit** button. If successful,
we find our new LDAP authentication provider listed within our **Authentication** page.

Any provider that we create can't be made active if the **Legacy** option
is active. If we want to disable the Legacy provider, we must either
enable SSL or make a change to the authentication.properties
file by changing the following line from true to false.

```
auth.type.rdbms.use_challenge=true
```

Blackboard recommends enabling SSL if this is our production
instance. However, if we plan to test providers within a development
instance, we can make the above change even though user
information will be passed between the browser and server in clear
(unencrypted) text.

Creating a Shibboleth provider

What if our organization wants to use Shibboleth as an external authentication provider? The configuration process is the same; however, we do have one important process to complete before creating the new external authentication provider. Whether we use Windows, Linux, or Solaris, we must enable or install the tools to allow our IIS or Apache web servers to support this authentication option. Shibboleth 2.0 is not supported by Apache 1.3, which means we must install Apache 2.2. Apache servers need the `mod_shib` module loaded as well to support Shibboleth within our instance. This module must match your version of Apache, for example, `mod_shib_22.so` is the file for the Apache 2.2 version. We will also need to exclude Shibboleth URLs from Tomcat by running the following commands that will allow our Apache Shibboleth module to handle those requests:

```
echo 'ProxyPass /Shibboleth.sso !' > /etc/httpd/conf.d/10_shib_excludes.conf

echo 'ProxyPass /shibboleth-sp !' >> /etc/httpd/conf.d/10_shib_excludes.conf
```

Windows users will find that integration with Shibboleth requires that Shibboleth `ISAPI` module be enabled within their IIS service.

Once we configure our web servers to work with Shibboleth, we must go in and create our Shibboleth Provider. The first step in our process mirrors the information we put in when creating our LDAP authentication provider. However, at the bottom of our screen we are asked to add **Link Text** and/or an **Icon** (shown in the following screenshot) that will be the link to log in using our Shibboleth tool. Now click on **Save and Configure**.

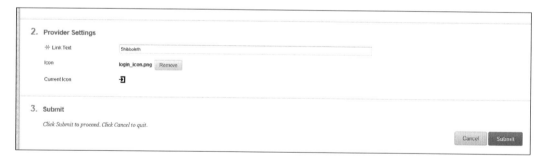

Next we must select where our instance will load the Shibboleth attributes. Linux and Solaris instances use environment variables, while Windows instances will find them in the HTTP headers. We then need to give users a logout page for this specific provider which may provide information on how to end their Shibboleth-authenticated session. Our next two options are very important to note. The first, called **Secure Location URL** (which normally looks like `/webapps/bb-auth-provider-shibboleth-BBLEARN/execute/shibbolethLogin`) is important to us when we configure our Blackboard Learn instance with our Shibboleth Service Provider. The second is the **Single Logout Notification URL**, which some Shibboleth instances use. This information is also important and comes in handy. These options are shown in the following screenshot:

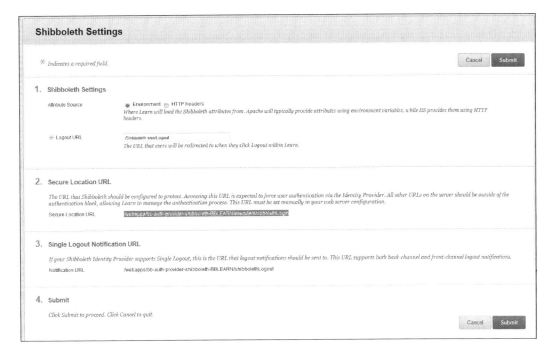

Our next step requires us to install the Shibboleth Service Provider on our instance. This is the time we should bring in our Shibboleth expert to help with the installation and configuration of our service provider. Information on how to install the service provider on our servers can be found within the Shibboleth wiki site, `https://wiki.shibboleth.net/confluence/display/SHIB2/Installation`. There are however two attributes we should use when configuring our Shibboleth Service Provider. When we work with editing the `shibboleth2.xml` file, we need to set the `REMOTE_USER` attribute to the Shibboleth value that will match our Blackboard Learn value, which is normally either the user's username or Batch UID. We must also set an attribute prefix within the file that looks like this—`attributePrefix="AJP_"`.

Windows Server users will need to make some additional changes to the `shibboleth2.xml` file:

- The `<InProcess>` option must set `spoofKey` to be the same as the **Secure Location URL** we spoke about earlier.

- Within the `<ISAPI>` area, we can find the `<Site>` attribute. This must be set to the numeric ID of our IIS site that serves our Blackboard Learn instance.

> If we don't know the ID number of our site, we can find it within IIS.
>
> If we use IIS 6, click on the **Websites** folder in the left pane of the IIS Manager; this will show a list of all the sites. Notice the **Identifier** column. This number is the same as the Site ID.
>
> If we use IIS 7, open the IIS 7 Manager. Once in the manager, click on the **Sites** title. This will show a list of all the sites on our server and the ID number within the **SiteID** column.

- Now we need to look for `<RequestMap>` within the file and find the `<Host>` element. Here we need to add the secure location URL, but remove the first forward slash.

Here's a sample of what our file would look like within our Linux or Solaris instance:

```
<ApplicationDefaults
  entityID="https://sp.myorganization.com/shibboleth"
  REMOTE_USER="eppn persistent-id targeted-id"
  attributePrefix="AJP_"> <!-- config --> </ApplicationDefaults>
```

Windows server administrators will find their `shibboleth2.xml` file look like this:

```
<InProcess logger="native.logger" spoofKey="47690fe2-f5b0-4d2c-
  916c-bfa562f065b7">
```

```
            <ISAPI normalizeRequest="true" safeHeaderNames="true">
                <Site id="1" name="sp.example.org"/>
            </ISAPI>
    </InProcess>
    <RequestMapper type="Native">
            <RequestMap>
                <Host name="sp.example.org">
                    <Path name="webapps/bb-auth-provider-shibboleth-
    BBLEARN/execute/shibbolethLogin" authType="shibboleth"
    requireSession="true"/>
                </Host>
            </RequestMap>
    </RequestMapper>
    <ApplicationDefaults entityID="https://sp.example.org/shibboleth"
        REMOTE_USER="eppn persistent-id targeted-id"
        attributePrefix="AJP_">
    <!-- config -->
    </ApplicationDefaults>
    <Notify Channel="back"
        Location="https://blackboard.myorganization.com/webapps/bb-auth-
        provider-shibboleth-BBLEARN/shibbolethLogout" />
```

Now we are almost ready to test our Shibboleth connection. However, we must enable our shib module within our Linux or Solaris instance. We can do that by logging in as root and copying the shib.conf.orig file:

```
cp /etc/httpd/conf.d/shib.conf /etc/httpd/conf.d/shib.conf.orig
```

Then we must edit the shib.conf file to look like the following sample:

```
<Location /webapps/bb-auth-provider-shibboleth-
    BBLEARN/execute/shibbolethLogin>
AuthType shibboleth
ShibRequestSetting requireSession 1
require valid-user
```

This will ensure that the shibboleth module works with our Blackboard Learn instance.

Once we have made our installations and configurations, we can go back to our **Authentication** page. We can then test our connection by selecting the **Test Connection Settings** option in our action menu. This will go out and try to make a login request with our Shibboleth provider to confirm that the interaction is working properly.

Creating a CAS provider

CAS providers have options similar to Shibboleth providers within our Blackboard Learn environment. After selecting **CAS** from the **Add Provider** button, the **Create CAS** page loads. The options on this page are exactly like the ones on the **Create Shibboleth** page we just discussed. Once we have made our changes and click on the **Save and Configure** button, the **CAS Settings** page loads. This page is shown in the following screenshot. Here we add the **CAS Server URL Prefix**, set our **Global Logout** option, add a **Logout URL Suffix**, and set up credentials for our provider. Our CAS Administrator should be able to share this information with us.

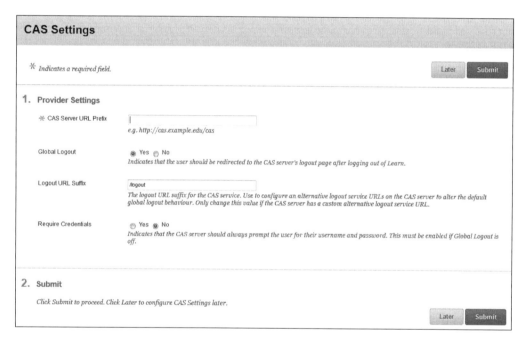

Setting up external authentication-provider order

We've spent time connecting our external authentication providers. Now we need to create an order for our Blackboard Learn instance to use them. We set this by clicking on the **Provider Order** button present at the top of our **Authentication** page. This page allows us to reorder our providers by moving our mouse to the right of the provider name. The mouse pointer will change, letting us know that we can drag that provider up or down the list to change the order. We can also enable the **Continue on error** option. This option means: if one provider sends an error, our instance will try the next provider in the order. Once our changes are made, we can click on **Submit**. This is shown in the following screenshot:

Data integration with Blackboard Learn

Enterprise-level applications such as Blackboard Learn must integrate and be able to process information from external data-sets such as Student Information Systems (SIS). These systems can produce information to create users and course shells. However, creating a robust Data Integration process is the hidden veil for Blackboard Learn administrators. Our coming discussions should lift the veil from this important, and sometimes mystical, process.

The snapshot tool in Blackboard Learn

The snapshot tool consists of three different components: data source, properties file, and the snapshot script. The properties file can be thought of as a map for our snapshot tool. This tells the tool what information is coming in from our external data and how it should be handled within our environment. One important item in the properties file is the data source key.

A **data source key** helps designate different types of data from one another within the snapshot tool. We enter the name of this data source key into the properties file. This will allow the data processed using that properties file to be "tagged". This will stop another snapshot process with a different data source key from mistakenly overwriting or changing the data.

The final item is the snapshot script itself. This script takes the properties file (which contains the data source and rules about how to process the data) along with the data from our external source and puts the information into Blackboard Learn.

We might expect to start the discussion about how we can use the snapshot tool. However, in 2012, Blackboard Inc. announced that the snapshot tool has been deprecated. It is being replaced by the SIS Framework.

The SIS Framework

Snapshot's replacement, the SIS Framework, is a hybrid of the snapshot tool we just spoke about and the IMS Enterprise and Learning Information Services standards set up by the IMS Global Learning Consortium. This standardization of the integration process helps enrollment and user-management tools, such as SunGard or Peoplesoft to name a few, build integration connections within their enterprise applications to our Blackboard Learn instance. While these options may limit the amount of work we must do within our system for full integration, our coming discussions will cover all the different aspects in case we must build an integration from scratch.

Integration options

We begin our SIS Framework integration by understanding the options that we have to integrate within our student information system in our Blackboard Learn environment. We can see these options by clicking on the **Data Integration** link under the **Building Blocks** module in our **Administrator** panel. Once there, we click on the **Student Information System Integrations** link. We see our options by hovering over the **Create Integration** button.

The first three options are part of the IMS Global Standards we spoke about earlier. Firstly, we have the original IMS Enterprise 1.1 standard. If we recently moved from a WebCT Vista instance to our Blackboard Learn environment, we can use the IMS Enterprise 1.1 configuration (from that WebCT instance) in our instance by selecting the IMS Enterprise 1.1 Vista option. IMS Learning Information Services (or LIS 2.0) is the next level of integration for student information systems, supporting web-service integration. The IMS has detailed information about these projects at their website, http://www.imsglobal.org/.

The next two options fall back to the snapshot flat file process. Our SIS Framework allows the development and support of the flat or XML file which many organizations used with the snapshot process. With all these options it may seem overwhelming to decide which version we should use. The process really requires a lot of time to plan out the flow of data from our student information system to the Blackboard Learn environment.

Questions to ask when planning your data integration

Our data integration will only be successful if we take the time and care to work on the details. Sometimes this means charting the process out and getting everyone in a room to work through some of the (following) major questions:

- How long does data live on our Blackboard Learn environment?

- Who has the ownership for the data? Can user data (such as names and e-mail addresses) be changed within the Blackboard Learn system without being overwritten by our integration process?

- Will our integration create course shells for every course or only for those requesting for one within our instance?

- How often will updates be sent to Blackboard Learn?

- How will we test and implement the process?

These type of questions can make us think about the issues and situations we must face. When we get other support personnel in the room, more questions and discussion topics will become apparent. In the end, our discussions will select the best option for our organization. Our example will build an integration process using flat files. This covers the most basic way to implement an integration with any student information system.

In this example, we will have two different integrations—a users integration and a course- and enrollment-integration. Why would we break up our integration into two parts? The discussions we had within our organization found that user data within our instance should stay around much longer than course or enrollment data, which can be archived. We also use a semester-based system within our student information system. So we should use the same system for course and enrollment information within our Blackboard Learn instance to maintain consistency.

 No matter which data integration option we decide, Blackboard Inc. offers us some sample information about how the different integrations work. We can find this information under the **Sample Documents** button within our **Student Information System Integrations** page.

Creating data sources

Earlier we spoke about data sources and their use within the snapshot tool. These still play an important part in the SIS Framework process. Before we start the flat file creation and integration process, let's create some data sources for the information that we will bring in from our external sources. We create our data sources by going to the **Data Integration** page and click on the **Data Sources** link.

Within the **Data Sources** page, we click on the **Create Data Source** button, and the **Create Data Source** page loads, shown in the following screenshot. The page only requires us to create a key name for the data source. Historically, most administrators will give the data source a name that helps define where the information comes from and what type of information will be provided. So for our users integration, we would name our data source **SIS_USERS**. If we want to give more detailed information, we can create a brief description as well. Once we click on **Submit**, we are taken back to the **Data Sources** page, where we learn if our instance created our new data source successfully. There is another way for us to create a data source during the integration process; we will learn how that works later.

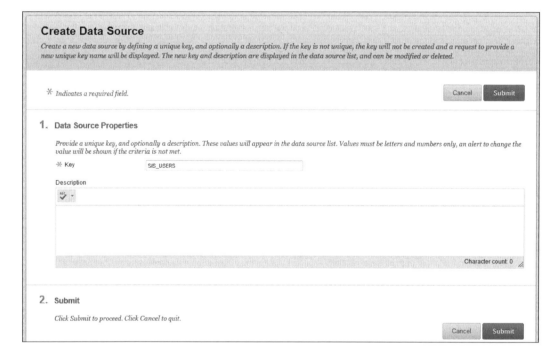

Building a flat file integration

Our flat file integration starts with the development of the file itself. If we are lucky, this process allows us to bring in an administrator or a programmer who understands the student information system to help create the file. We are going to discuss the creation of three main files that any basic integration would need: users, courses, and enrollments. Each of these files has a set of required fields; however, it is hard to find a list of the fields for each file without creating an integration. Our integration will require two different integration points, one for our users and another for our courses and enrollments.

 While our discussion only reviews how to manage users, courses, and course enrollments, many other objects, such as institutional roles, group memberships, and organizations, can be created in the same way.

Creating the flat file

Within the flat file that will deliver our users from the student information systems, there are some required fields. Within the data integration, these fields are called **objects**. These objects are: External Person Key, Username, First Name, Last Name, and Password. The External Person Key object will normally be the primary ID within the student information system. This can be as simple as a student or employee ID number. The external person key will not appear to the user, nor is it searchable within the **System Admin** tab, and only serves to connect the Blackboard users to their user account within our student information system. The titles for each object will appear on the first line of the flat file or what some administrators call the header line. Here is an example of our flat files' first two lines:

```
EXTERNAL_PERSON_KEY,FIRSTNAME,LASTNAME,USER_ID,PASSWD
0123456789,Johnny,Smith,js033,s0meP@$$w0rd
```

In this example, we used commas to separate our different objects (you can choose another separator when you actually start your own integrations). The next file will be our course-creation file. This will create the courses from our student information system within our Blackboard Learn environment. Here's our sample:

```
EXTERNAL_COURSE_KEY,COURSE_ID,COURSE_NAME
4027_123456,SP2012-123456,Underwater Basketweaving
```

As in our user example, we have an external key. This time it is called the **external course key**. Just as our person key was the primary ID within the SIS, the course key acts in the same way for our courses. Here's a sample:

```
EXTERNAL_COURSE_KEY,EXTERNAL_PERSON_KEY,ROLE
4027_123456,0123456789,S
```

Our next example is the enrollment file. This enrollment file uses the external course key and the external person key to process the enrollment. The file must also include the user's role within that course—whether it is a student, a teaching assistant, or an instructor.

Each of the files we just created only have the required fields. We however can add many optional fields to our three files, when we create actual files for production. We should also understand that the SIS Framework supports many different information sets than just the ones we discussed here. These other files can send information to associate courses with terms, categories—even nodes. We can even create and manage organizations in a similar way, but the three files we created give us a good basic understanding of how to create data integrations. The only place we have been able to find the feed file headers is within Blackboard Inc.'s own help area. We can see this information at `https://help.blackboard.com/en-us/Learn/9.1_ SP_10_and_SP_11/Administrator/120_System_Integration/006_Student_ Information_System_%28SIS%29/070_SIS_Feed_File_Headers_and_Object_ Types`, or search for feed file headers.

Creating the integration within Blackboard Learn

Now that we have our files created, we can start the integration process. The process starts back within our **Student Information System Integrations** page, shown in the following screenshot:

Here we select the **Snapshot Flat File** option under the **Create Integration** button. For those of us who have used the snapshot process, this would be comparable to creating our properties file. On this new page, we will create our integration. First we must give this integration a name and an optional description. We then create a shared username and password. We will learn more about how this username and password works within this new SIS Framework process a little later. Since we are sending a flat file, we need to define the file's delimiter to designate how we will separate the different fields. Our next option asks us what the integration status should be upon creation. The active and inactive options turn on and off the integration. The testing option functions like the active option, however, it will not create any of the data. This gives us the ability, as the option states, to test our files. We must also set our default log verbosity for this integration. When testing we should set this to **All Diagnostic and Debug Messages**, but when in production we should reset it to **Errors Only**, as shown in the following screenshot:

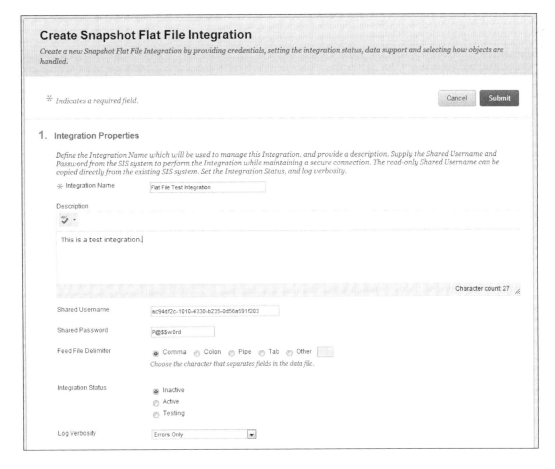

Earlier in this discussion we created a new data source that we would use with our integrations. Here under the **Data Support** area of our integration creation page, shown in the following screenshot, we can select the specific data source that we created earlier, or create a new one by putting the information into the **New Data Source Key** textbox. We can also create a prefix for our Batch UID. The prefix option works best when trying to support different student information systems where the primary person or primary course key could be duplicated. Our next option allows us to attach this data integration to a specific node of our institutional hierarchy, which we touched on earlier in this book.

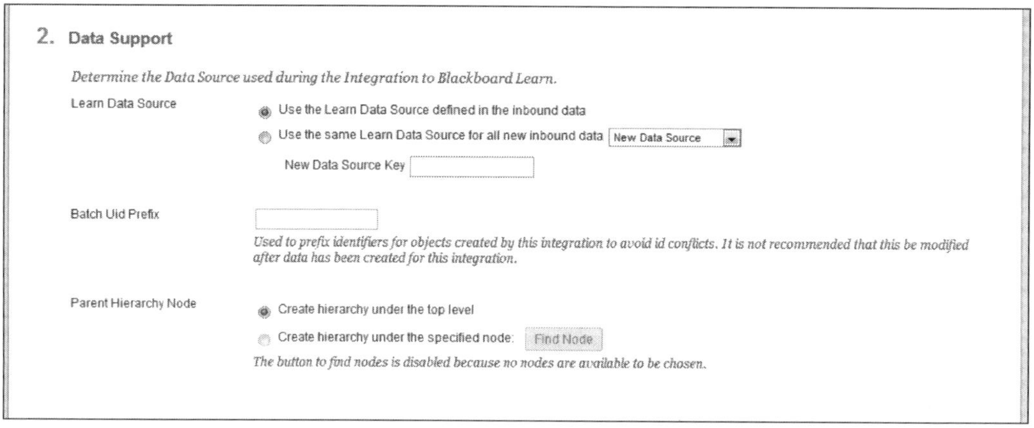

The final option allows us to make advanced configuration settings to our integration and how it handles all the different objects. This area gives us a chance to understand how to compare a Learn object to one from our student information system. In the configuration, we see that the **Users** object term in our Blackboard Learn instance is compared to the **Person** object term from the SIS. This is shown in the following screenshot. Our integration will use the SIS object terms, so we should make sure we understand the association of these terms with our environment.

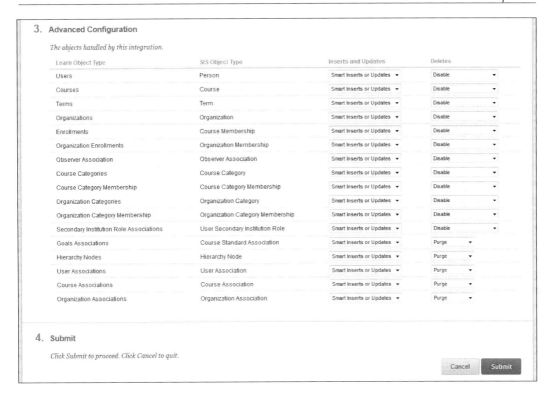

Each of these objects listed require their own separate files to populate and manage. When the file comes over, it can be handled in different ways. This handling is what we configure within this area. The smart updates and inserts will automatically populate the object information in our instance if the information isn't present or is not the same. Also, we can allow only inserts, update, or neither.

While we can insert or update objects, we can also delete them. Many times however, our delete command isn't to delete the object but only disable it so that data isn't lost. We can decide the fate of each object when the delete command is sent, by selecting **Disable**, **Purge**, or neither. Once we complete the advanced configuration, we can now click on the **Submit** button to save our integration within Blackboard Learn. We then go back to the **Student Information System Integration** page and see if our integration was created successfully.

Now that our integration is created, we can enable it for testing. We can do so by clicking on the action menu button at the right of our integration name and selecting the testing option. Our context menu will look different based on whether the integration is inactive, or set for testing, or active. This is shown in the following screenshot:

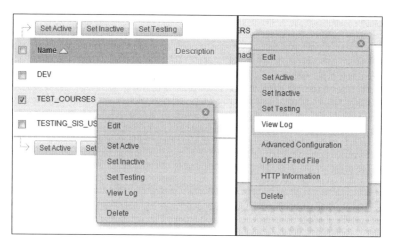

Once we put our integration in the testing level, we gain the ability to test our files against the integration we just created. This helps us make sure that our header and objects within the files will work properly without actually populating our instance with data.

Testing our flat file

We can test our files by selecting the **Upload Feed File** option within the action menu. This will take us to our page where we can select one of our flat files to be processed within our environment. We then select the file type. Remember that during our configuration earlier, we learned that the SIS object titles would be used in our integration. Here is a great example:

- Our users flat file would be a `Person` data type.
- Our course and enrollment files would be classified as the `course` and `course membership` data types respectively.

Once we have told the integration what type of objects will be within our flat file, our next step requires us to tell the integration how to handle the object information provided by using either **Store**, **Complete Refresh**, or **Delete** option (shown in the following screenshot):

- The **Store** option tells our integration that all the information here should be added to our instance. We are not removing object data. However, this will update information from our student information system.

- The **Delete** option tells the integration to delete (or disable, based on our preferences) all the objects listed within our flat file.

- The **Complete Refresh** option accepts the file as a full and complete list of all the objects.

 We can think of **Complete Refresh** as both the **Store** and **Delete** processes, and administrators who used the snapshot tools could compare this to the `Snapshot` command.

Once we have our file ready to be uploaded, we click on the **Submit** button. Blackboard Learn takes us back to our **Student Information Systems Integrations** page where we find a success or failure bar above the page title. However, notice what our success statement says. Our integration works just as the course copy, export, or archive process. Blackboard Learn will work to process records as it also deals with user requests. We no longer must deal with heavy database and processor loads when running snapshot tools because our environment works to spread the load out across the instance.

Sending files to Blackboard Learn

Now we have our integration created within our Blackboard Learn instance. Our files have been tested and don't seem to create any issues. The next step in the integration set up process is getting the file from its current location and into our Blackboard Learn instance for processing.

> The old snapshot process required a two-step process that first required us to make the file available on our environment; then the snapshot tool to process it. The file would arrive on the server either by FTP or by a shared mount point and then be processed. This required us to create cron jobs or scheduled tasks, which delayed the syncing of user, course, and enrollment information. This syncing delay should become smaller using the new SIS Framework HTTP Post process.

The new framework runs a web service that allows our student information system to send our flat file to a specific URL via the HTTP POST method. The URLs that we need to use with our flat files can be found by accessing the action menu for our integration, and click on the **HTTP Information** link. Here we find our integration's shared username and password along with endpoint URLs.

HTTP Information: TESTING_SIS_USERS

Configuration

Username

65bdb0d9-b0dd-437b-a048-65b6696dde1c

Password

pa$$word

Operation	Endpoint Url
Course - Store	https://...../webapps/bb-data-integration-flatfile-BBLEARN/endpoint/course/store
Course - Complete Refresh	https://...../webapps/bb-data-integration-flatfile-BBLEARN/endpoint/course/refresh
Course - Delete	https://...../webapps/bb-data-integration-flatfile-BBLEARN/endpoint/course/delete
Course Association - Store	https://...../webapps/bb-data-integration-flatfile-BBLEARN/endpoint/courseassociation/store
Course Association - Complete Refresh	https://...../webapps/bb-data-integration-flatfile-BBLEARN/endpoint/courseassociation/refresh
Course Association - Delete	https://...../webapps/bb-data-integration-flatfile-BBLEARN/endpoint/courseassociation/delete
Course Category - Store	https://...../webapps/bb-data-integration-flatfile-BBLEARN/endpoint/coursecategory/store
Course Category - Complete Refresh	https://...../webapps/bb-data-integration-flatfile-BBLEARN/endpoint/coursecategory/refresh
Course Category - Delete	https://...../webapps/bb-data-integration-flatfile-BBLEARN/endpoint/coursecategory/delete
Course Category Membership - Store	https://...../webapps/bb-data-integration-flatfile-BBLEARN/endpoint/coursecategorymembership/store
Course Category Membership - Complete Refresh	https://...../webapps/bb-data-integration-flatfile-BBLEARN/endpoint/coursecategorymembership/refresh
Course Category Membership - Delete	https://...../webapps/bb-data-integration-flatfile-BBLEARN/endpoint/coursecategorymembership/delete

Each object file has its own endpoint URL for the **Store**, **Delete**, and **Complete Refresh** actions. Let's look at an example.

Our Users file (which the SIS integration called Person objects) can be sent to these URLs:

- Person Store: `https://blackboard.myorganization.com/webapps/bb-data-integration-flatfile-BBLEARN/endpoint/person/store`

- Person Complete Refresh: `https://blackboard.myorganization.com/webapps/bb-data-integration-flatfile-BBLEARN/endpoint/person/refresh`

- Person Delete: `https://blackboard.myorganization.com/webapps/bb-data-integration-flatfile-BBLEARN/endpoint/person/delete`

When the files are sent to their URL, our integration takes the information and starts to process it just as the uploaded file we used for testing earlier. If our integration is active, the file's contents will be put into a queue and processed based on the file information, the URL, and the integration's configuration. This queue allows our integration to send multiple files at the same time and have our Blackboard Learn environment queue them.

The queue will place all the objects in order based on the time they were sent to the server. If we have more than one server, the server that receives the request will process it. If we want to direct or HTTP `Post` to a specific application server we may do that by altering the URL to direct the post to the specific server. That server will also need to be accessible directly from the server running the cURL process.

We understand where we need to point our file so that it's processed by our integration properly. However, administrators differ on the best way to send the file over. When in doubt, use the tool that Blackboard Inc. recommends for this process. They recommend cURL (pronounced curl), a command-line tool that supports our HTTP `POST` method. We must first download and install cURL. There are several versions of this tool; we want to make sure that we select the version that supports SSL. We must then configure cURL within our system's `PATH` variable.

Once our installation and configuration are complete, we will then run the following command:

```
curl -k -w %{http_code} -H "Content-Type:text/plain"
-u SHARED_USERNAME:SHARED_PASSWORD --data-binary FILE_PATH https://
blackboard.myorganization.com/webapps/bb-data-integration-flatfile-
BBLEARN/endpoint/person/store
```

Notice that we must add our shared username and shared password from our integration creation. Here's how that command looks with that data:

```
curl -k -w %{http_code} -H "Content-Type:text/plain"
-u 65bdb0d9-b0dd-437b-a048-65b6696dde1c:bL@3kb0@rd --data-binary /home/
sis/bblearnfiles/users-store.txt https://blackboard.myorganization.com/
webapps/bb-data-integration-flatfile-BBLEARN/endpoint/person/store
```

Once this command runs, the file goes to our instance and the data is added.

Hopefully, the discussion we've had has lifted the veil off the data-integration process and has given us a better understanding of not only how the process works, but also how we can implement it within our organization. Here are a few tips Blackboard administrators have used during a data-integration process:

- Think of this process in the long term. Don't expect to build a data-integration process and implement it in 30 days. The more time spent looking for issues and problems, the better the integration will be.

- Create a think tank for the process. Bring key people from departments that manage student data and course creation into the discussions about the project and how to implement it. These people can help find issues before they become problems.

- Plan to roll out an integration in phases. Think about how to roll out each SIS object (such as people, courses, and enrollments) in a thoughtful and planned process. If issues happen, we can better troubleshoot them by only rolling out one integration at a time.

In the end, we can turn around and look at our data integration with pride. While we may come away with a few scratches, the process helps to lessen the load within our support team and gives the user a better experience within our system.

Summary

While it may require work installing and configuring our Blackboard Learn environment, external-authentication options help improve user support. Authentication into our instance will use the username and password within existing applications and protocols, and removes the need for an additional username and password to remember. Data integration gives our users an improved experience in the quality of the information within the application itself. Regular near real-time updates keep access to courses and student information up to date, which helps the student and the instructor.

Our next chapter takes us on to the topic of Building Blocks. These, however, are not the stackable toys of our childhood, but they build on to the current structure within Blackboard Learn, hence the name. These provide additional functionality to our virtual community. So let our playtime begin with Blackboard Learn building blocks.

11
Implementing Building Blocks in Blackboard Learn

The tools and options we have within our Blackboard Learn instance will satisfy most of our users' needs; some of our users will push the needs of our system and will want to have additional options. This can also be said of administrators like ourselves who are always looking for new ways to monitor and support our users. When we want to use tools that aren't built into our environment we go looking for building blocks. In this chapter we will learn about the following topics:

- Three different types of tool integration options in our instance
- How to manage building blocks, web services, and LTI tools within our instance
- Where to find building blocks that we might find useful for our organization and users

Some of the items discussed in this chapter are rather new. Developers and third-party vendors are slowly accepting these new options to integrate their products. But first, let's discuss the oldest integration tool within our environment: building blocks.

Blackboard Learn building blocks

Most Blackboard Learn administrators have heard of Blackboard building blocks. Ever since the early days of the Blackboard Learn product, the company has worked to create a set of open APIs that would give developers the ability to create tools that could interact with Blackboard users. From journals and wikis, to data collection, to hosted web tools links, building blocks have been one of the driving forces for new technology integrations.

This has never been more true than today. In 2012, Blackboard Inc. began to release improvements to tools within Blackboard Learn using the building block technology originally created for third-party vendors and developers. This option would allow organizations to decide what tools they want within their Blackboard Learn instance and apply them without waiting for an upgrade. Since this change, understanding how to install, manage, and remove building blocks has become more important.

Installing a building block

Our Blackboard building block discussion starts with the installation of a building block into our instance. Our installation option appears within the **Building Blocks** link found under the **Building Blocks** module. Here we find several options, some of which we will discuss in this chapter. To install our building block we must click on the poorly-named **Installed Tools** link.

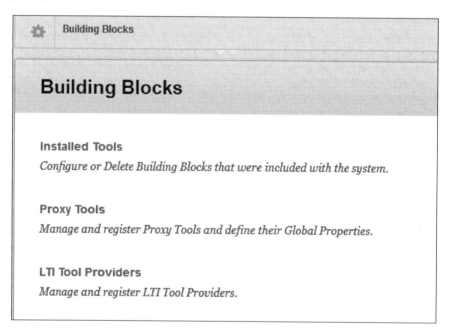

This takes us to the management area for building blocks within our Blackboard Learn environment. Here we find the **Upload Building Blocks** button, which when clicked, lets us proceed further in the installation process.

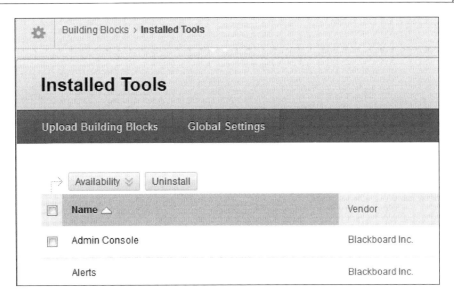

Our building block, which is generally a .zip or .war file, should be saved on our local machine. Later in this chapter, we will learn how to find building blocks for our environment, but for now let's move on to the process. We click on the **Browse** button to find our building block file and select it for upload.

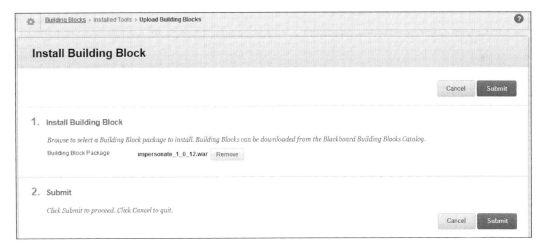

Once the file is uploaded, we may be taken to a page which will ask us to extend Blackboard Learn's database schema, which may be required according to our **Global Settings**. After either page, we are taken back to the building block page, and there we find a success or failure message at the top of the page. By default, building blocks are inactive. We will need to go to the building block itself to enable and configure it. That's our next discussion.

If the building block fails to install, we should either contact Blackboard Support if the building block was created by Blackboard, or contact our third-party developer to report the problem. These sources should help us troubleshoot the installation process.

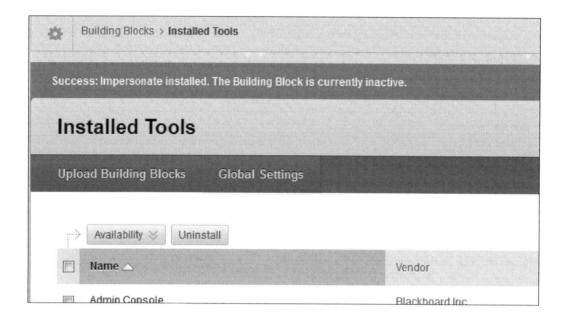

Configuring and managing a building block

Most building blocks require activation within our Blackboard Learn environment and some will need configuration. This is done within the **Installed Tools** or **Building Blocks** page. For our example, we are going to enable the Cookie Disclosure building block. This building block implements user features that will ask for user consent before our Blackboard Learn instance starts to collect user data. This building block is already installed, but it hasn't been enabled. We click on the chevron to open the action menu. We then click on the **Set Available** option.

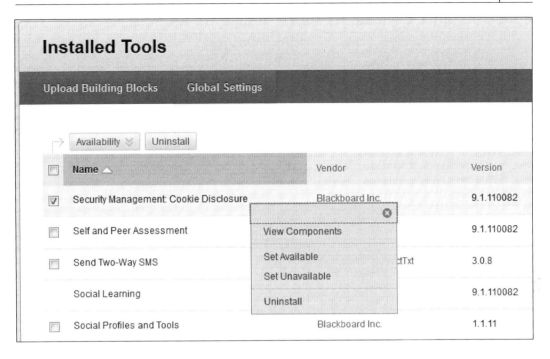

We are taken to the **Make Building Block Available** page. This page shows us just what areas our building block wants access to within our instance. This building block wants to have access to objects within the Blackboard Learn application and its database along with some user attributes. Our last area within the privileges page explains what Java permissions the building block will use, once enabled.

It is difficult to decide if the building block we install needs access to all these areas. If something looks wrong or incorrect, we may want to print this page and cancel making the building block available. Then, we can contact the building block's company or developer and discuss our concerns.

If all these privilege requests are ok, we can click on the **Approve** button and the building block is made available. Notice that we get a success bar, and that the building block is available and it will be displayed within the courses and organizations. If we want to know where and how our building block interacts with our instance, we can find that out by clicking on the **View Components** link within the action menu.

However, similar to the other course or organization tools, we will set the default availability within the **Tools and Utilities** page discussed in *Chapter 8, Tools and Utilities in Blackboard Learn*.

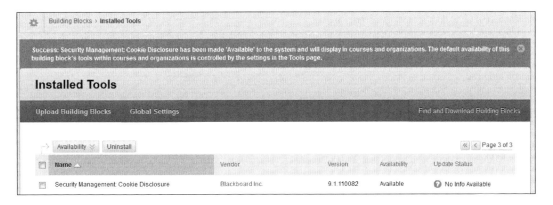

We have made the building block available, but some additional configuration requirements may need to be made. Most building block providers or developers will provide instructions to tell us how to configure them within our Blackboard Learn environment. The configuration or settings can be edited within our building block example by opening the action menu again and selecting the **Settings** link.

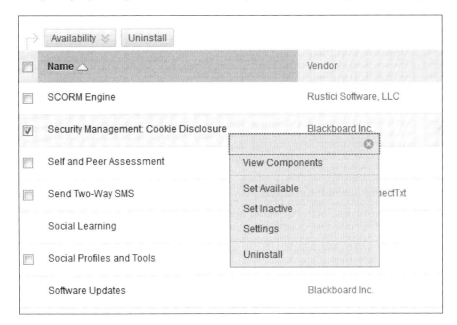

Within the **Cookie Disclosure** building block, our settings ask for optional URLs to explain the cookie disclosure policy. After setting our configurations within our building block, we would click on the **Submit** button.

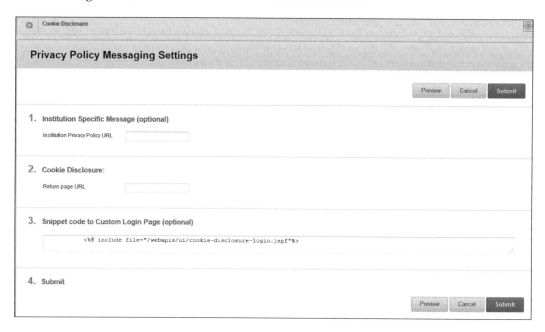

Configurations for some building blocks are simple, while others are complex. If our building block installation has issues, we should contact the building block provider. That can be an institution, open source project, third-party vendor, or even Blackboard Inc. in some cases.

Testing building blocks

While we have reviewed how to install and enable building blocks within our Blackboard Learn environment, we must remember that their installation and testing must be done in a test environment and not in our production instance. This option protects our users and data from being adversely affected by a building block.

Removing a building block

Sometimes, we find that a building block is no longer useful to our users or becomes obsolete because of a new function in Blackboard. Sometimes a building block can even cause issues or not work properly after an upgrade. In these situations we would consider making the building block **Unavailable** or **Inactive**. There is a slight difference between the two modes. The **Inactive** mode disables the building block for users and doesn't allow administrative configurations to be made. The **Unavailable** mode will disable the building block for our users, but we as administrators can still view and edit the configuration settings to work on fixing the issue.

If the unavailable or inactive modes aren't acceptable, we can remove the building block itself by clicking on the chevron and selecting **Uninstall** in the action menu.

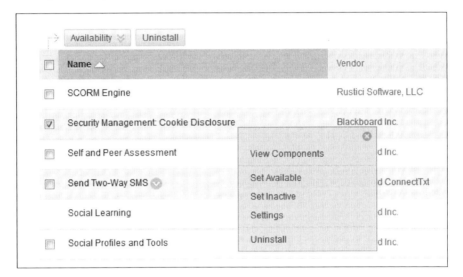

A pop-up box will ask you to confirm that you want this building block to be deleted. Once we select **OK**, the building block will be gone. If this building block was connected or used by courses or organizations for content, that will be gone as well. Most administrators prefer to make building blocks unavailable so user content isn't lost or deleted.

When we look at the **Installed Tools** page, we can change the availability of our building blocks by checking the checkbox to the left of the name and then select what availability level we want. While this option works well, the uninstall feature does not work on most building blocks. The best way to remove several building blocks from our Blackboard Learn environment is one at a time.

Building block manager

While the GUI gives us the ability to manage and control almost every building block within our Blackboard Learn instance, there is an additional option to manage our building blocks using the command line. Some building blocks are installed within our application and cannot be disabled or removed from the GUI interface. If they cause issues within our instance, we need to be able to control them.

B2Manager is a command-line tool (`B2Manager.sh` or `B2Manager.bat`) found in the `tools/admin` subdirectory of our Blackboard `home` directory. This tool can do many of the same tasks as its GUI brother.

Here is an example of how to install a building block in a RedHat or Solaris instance:

```
/usr/local/blackboard/tools/admin/B2Manager.sh -i /usr/repository/b2/
MyBuildingBlock.war
```

Here's the similar installation command for Windows platforms:

```
L:\blackboard\tools\admin\B2Manager.bat -i D:\repository\b2\
MyBuildingBlock.war
```

The syntax of the command will remain basically the same, only changing the filename to the building-block handle. We might wonder what a building-block handle is and how we can find it.

The following command will give us a list of all the installed building blocks for our instance. We also find in the following snippet, one of the following results:

```
B2Manager.sh -v
Plugin: Security Management: Cookie Disclosure
    Vendor: Blackboard Inc. (bb)
    Handle: bb-cookie-disclosure
    Status: UNAVAILABLE
    Setup:  http://blackboard.myorganization.com/webapps/bb-cookie-
disclosure-BBLEARN/execute/settings?admin=false
```

We can also get a list of all the installed building blocks, by replacing the `-v` with a `-l` in our command. There are three other commands we should know about within the B2Manager tool:

- `-c`: This command will change the default status of the building block within courses or organizations. The command must be followed by either the AVAILABLE or UNAVAILABLE statement.

- -r: This option removes the specified building block from our system.
- -s: With this command, we can change the selected building block's status within Blackboard Learn by following the command with either an INACTIVE, UNAVAILABLE, or AVAILABLE statement.

Web services in Blackboard Learn

Blackboard Learn's building block system allows us to interact with new tools and content within our system. However, some integration options won't use a building block but would still want to interact with our Blackboard Learn environment. Web services allow third-party web applications to pull and push data between their environment and instance. One example of using a web service is Blackboard Connect's one-way text-messaging option. The created web service regularly pushes users' mobile phone numbers to a secure server which manages and sends the messages for our Blackboard Learn instance.

We access Web Services by clicking on the **Web Services** link in our **Building Block** module.

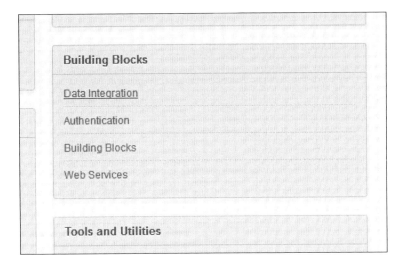

Here we see all the current web services installed within our environment. In our **Manage Web Services** area, we can set the internal secret. This secret is used between the web framework and the web session. We can also upload a ZIP or WAR file that creates a new web service. This operation works like the building block upload process we discussed earlier. If we want to develop a web service for an application, we can download sample tools and documentation within this page as well.

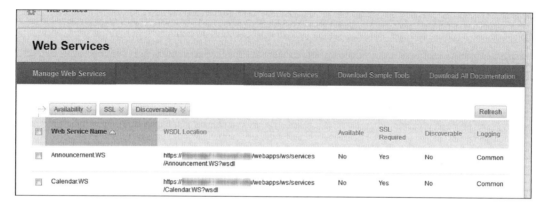

We can also manage our web services individually within this page. We can make our web service available, use SSL, or become discoverable by editing the tool. We get to the edit page by clicking on the chevron that appears to the right of the web service name when we hover over it. Here we select **Edit** to open a page that allows us to make these changes. This menu also allows us to see what controls (within our application) the web service has access to, along with its permissions. Our discussion only skims the web service and its potential; however, these services are not heavily used by basic Blackboard Learn environments.

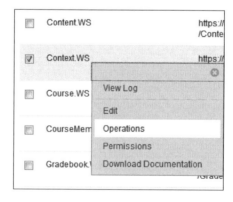

LTI Tool Providers

Learning Tool Interoperability (LTI) is a standard created by the IMS Global Consortium to integrate third-party tools with all major learning management systems, such as Blackboard Learn. LTI tools normally function as external web applications and, when registered within our system, allow instructors to create links to LTI tools within course-content areas. But before we register an LTI provider we must first configure the global properties.

Within our Blackboard Learn **System Admin** tab, we click on the **Building Blocks** link under the **Building Blocks** module. Here we find a link titled **LTI Tool Providers**. This link takes us to our **LTI Tool Providers** page. Our configuration starts by clicking on the **Manage Global Properties** button.

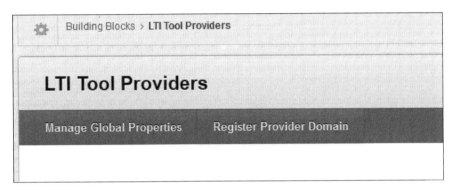

Our first area to set up is the **Feature Availability** section. This allows us to enable the LTI tool options in our courses and organizations. We then must decide how to manage the Tool Provider links:

- If we select the **Allow links to any tool provider that isn't explicitly excluded.** option, it gives our instructor-users the option to add LTI tool links to a course or organization via the web link tool as long as the administrator hasn't excluded this tool from our instance.

- The **Allow links to any tool provider, but require approval for each new provider.** option will allow the addition of an LTI tool link to a course or organization; however, before these links will work, we as administrators must approve them by changing the provider's status to **approved** within the **Register Provider Domain**.

- The **Allow only links to approve tool providers.** option gives the administrator the most control. An LTI tool link cannot be added within a course or organization unless the LTI tool provider has been approved by the administrator.

Manage Global Properties

1. Feature Availability

Enabled in Courses	○ Yes ◉ No
Enabled in Organizations	○ Yes ◉ No
Creation of Tool Provider Links	○ Allow links to any tool provider that isn't explicitly excluded.
	○ Allow links to any tool provider, but require approval for each new provider.
	◉ Allow only links to approved tool providers.
Allow configured tool providers to post grades	○ Yes ◉ No

Our next area configures what information is displayed and sent when an LTI tool link is clicked by the user. Some providers may require user data from our Blackboard Learn instance, such as a course number or student name. If so, we should only send that data over an SSL connection to protect our user information.

We then have three different user fields we can send. If any user fields are required, our LTI tool provider will give this information to us in their configuration instructions. The next item to send is a context identifier which helps the tool provider manage the user. This can be the enrollment primary key or the user's batch UID. Either can be used; however, if a user is removed from a course and then added back in, they will lose the content created within the LTI tool because the connection with the LTI content will be lost.

Our last option allows us to create a user acknowledgement message which can tell the user that they are leaving our Blackboard Learn instance and going to a third-party application which our organization doesn't control. Once our global configurations are made, we click on the **Submit** button to save them.

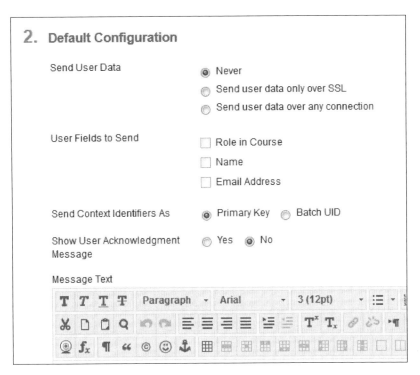

Back within our **LTI Tool Providers** page, we can click on the **Register Provider Domain** button to start the registration process. We must first give the provider domain, such as `tool.mycompany.com`, and then select if it is **Approved** or **Excluded** within our environment. We may also want to add other hosts in case the primary host fails to work properly. We then add the default configuration information sent by the LTI Tool Provider and set the institutional policies for this specific tool provider domain. We click on the **Submit** button and our tool provider has been created and is listed on our **LTI Tool Providers** page.

Once a provider has been created and approved by the administrator, each instructor-user within a course or organization can configure the LTI tool links to their needs and specifications without the need for help from the system admin.

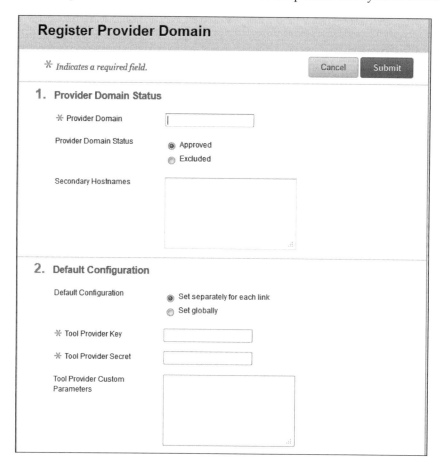

So why don't administrators hear more about LTI tools? Well, most of the third-party tools using LTI already have tighter integrations with Blackboard Learn using building blocks. As these standards start to gain momentum within the learning-technology community, administrators will start to use more tools outside of the current building blocks.

Recommended building blocks

We now understand how to add and manage building blocks, but where can we find them? Searching for the best building blocks can take time, so let's learn about some ways to find them. We'll learn where to search for new building blocks, and learn a few building blocks that are must-haves for any Blackboard Learn instance.

When we want to find building blocks, sometimes the best way is by word of mouth or Blackboard Listservs. However, there are two websites which are great building block resources. The Blackboard Extensions website, `http://www.blackboard.com/Partnerships/Extensions.aspx`, displays building blocks from open source and third-party vendors. Many of the building blocks have a fee or license associated with them and some are outdated or may no longer be supported.

If we want to use mostly open source building blocks, check out the Oscelot Project website at `http://projects.oscelot.org/gf/`. Oscelot is an open source, community-driven organization that supports the development of open source building blocks. Most administrators will find the building blocks here to be a goldmine of tools to help them support users on a daily basis.

These two sites have hundreds of building blocks. We've picked through and selected a few to recommend that we wouldn't want to run a Blackboard Learn environment without the following building blocks:

- **BbStats**: As mentioned in *Chapter 9, Security, Reporting, and Configuration in Blackboard Learn*, BbStats is a building block that collects user activity within our Blackboard Learn instance. We have the ability to learn about how much activity happens within our instance by hour, day, or week. If we want to understand traffic and usage patterns for our environment, BbStats is a requirement. It is available at `http://projects.oscelot.org/gf/project/bbstats/`.

- **LoginAs** and **Impersonate**: Both of these building blocks allow administrators and selected support team members to log in or impersonate another user. Support staff can now reproduce or troubleshoot issues as a user; this can help when staff are unable to recreate the issue within their username. Both building blocks also log when a user uses the tool to access another user's account. LoginAs is available at `http://projects.oscelot.org/gf/project/loginas/`, and Impersonate is available at `http://projects.oscelot.org/gf/project/impersonate/`.

- **Who's Online**: One of the oldest building blocks developed, it remains helpful to administrators. The tool displays what user accounts are still logged in to our Blackboard Learn system and how long they have been online. It is available at `http://projects.oscelot.org/gf/project/senwhosonline/`.

- **Sign Up List Tool**: This building block allows instructors and trainers to create sign-up lists for events which have limited seating. It is available at `http://projects.oscelot.org/gf/project/signup/`.

- **Bboogle**: The project title marries the terms Blackboard and Google, and integrates Google Apps, such as Gmail, Google Drive, and Google Calendars, for Business or Education. This building block's developers recently won an award from Blackboard Inc. for their work. It is available at `http://projects.oscelot.org/gf/project/bboogle/`.

- **Advanced System Tracking and Reporting (ASTRO)**: This building block searches a Blackboard Learn environment and creates large amounts of data which the organizations can use for evaluation, planning, and data-driven decision making. It also gives departments a peek into each course's usage of Blackboard Learn. It is available at `http://projects.oscelot.org/gf/project/astro/`.

Summary

No matter how much we, as administrators, work to provide the best tools and options for our users, someone will always want more. Building blocks, Web Services, and LTI tools are just some of the ways by which we can provide the latest technologies to our instructors and users. These tools require some configuration to allow communication, which should be provided by the developer—whether that is an institution, non-profit organization, third-party vendor, or Blackboard Inc. We can find these tools in a few areas, and often learn about them through word of mouth.

We are near the end of our Blackboard Learn journey, but our final discussions can be the most important to an administrator. Disasters, no matter how small or how big, will happen. We must plan not only for recovery, but also for how long an issue or outage can be present before they start affecting our organization negatively. Also how can we troubleshoot our environment to find clues to what might be happening, and fix it before major issues start? Let's discuss troubleshooting and disaster recovery for our Blackboard Learn instance in the next chapter.

12
Logs, Troubleshooting, and Disaster Recovery in Blackboard Learn

Our final chapter in our long journey with Blackboard Learn takes us into the roles of paramedic, first responder, and detective for our virtual community. Many issues or errors appear to users and the issues land in our e-mail inbox or voicemail. We try to find a solution to the problem, which can sometimes be simple or require detailed analysis. No matter what the issue is, we must try to solve the user's problem.

Sometimes we face a failure in the technology that hosts and manages our virtual community. This happens rarely, but when it does it can create panic, havoc, and an uneasiness about our Blackboard Learn environment from our virtual community. Just as important as the planning and installation of our Blackboard Learn instance, the creation and continuous review of a disaster recovery plan makes us well prepared when disaster strikes and allows us to provide a quick response to our users.

In this chapter we will cover the following topics:

- Learn how to access and read log files within Blackboard Learn
- Review what information each log collects from our system
- Learn tips on understanding and finding important information within the logs
- Understand the importance of disaster recovery
- Gain insights that will help an administrator create a disaster recovery plan

We will start our chapter with a discussion on the issue of logs and troubleshooting. So I suggest you grab your magnifying glass, as we are about to start sleuthing.

Troubleshooting issues in Blackboard Learn

In our role as administrator for our Blackboard Learn instance, we face user issues and problems almost everyday. Some of these issues require the help from Blackboard's support team to resolve. However, there is information within the system that can help us troubleshoot the possible issue or problem. Just as the support team uses the logs and the database to search for clues, we can do the same.

Finding and searching log files

The log files are the first line in the investigation. Often, they give us the first clues, however sometimes it can feel like we are searching for a needle in not just a haystack, but a barn full of hay. Within our **Administrator Panel**, we have several different ways we can work with these log files to help us expedite our search. Let's take some time to learn how to access them.

Locating and accessing log files

Within our **System Admin** tab, we can start our log journey. Under the **Tools and Utilities** module, we find the **Logs** link.

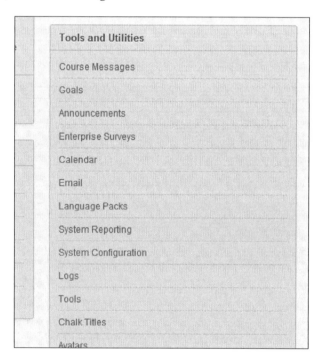

The link takes us to the **Logs** page where we find five different log types for us to explore.

The first is **SIS Logs**. In *Chapter 10, Authentication and Data Integration in Blackboard Learn*, we talked about our integration with **student information systems** (**SIS**). Our next link, **Authentication Logs**, was also discussed in the same chapter. The authentication logs collect this information from not only the internal logins, but also from those that use external authentication providers. The third group, called **System Logs**, holds the log files from Apache or IIS, Tomcat, and our Blackboard application. Our **System Tasks Status** link takes us to a log of actions and tasks that run on our server. Our final group, **Course Cartridge Import Status**, shows the status of any course cartridges that instructors might have installed within their course shells. Now that we have reviewed our five different areas, we can begin a detailed discussion about each one.

SIS Logs

The SIS logs hold a wealth of information when we or our administrator team creates and tests a SIS implementation within our Blackboard Learn instance. When we click on the **SIS Logs** link, we are taken to the **SIS Logs** page, which includes a wonderful search tool.

Here we can use the search field to find detailed information about any data sent within a processed SIS integration file. In the following example, we've searched for the username js033 created with a SIS Framework flat file. Our search returned two results. We click on one of the lines to select it. The line becomes blue when selected. The box below the **Message Detail** header displays information from the highlighted line. It contains details about the process. In the following screenshot, we can see this process created the username js033 in our instance:

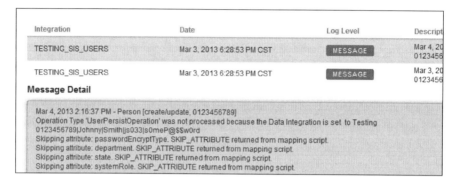

We have the ability to narrow our search results by selecting a specific integration and change the verbosity level, which we want to see. These levels range from debug to error only. This search tool also allows us to select a timeframe to search by checking the checkboxes beside **From** and **To**, and selecting the date and even time that we want to use for our search. When searching the SIS logs, we should note that wildcards and regular expressions will not work as expected.

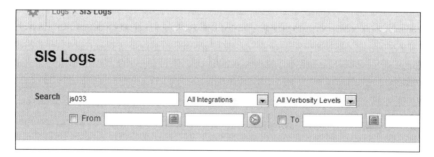

Another great tool within this page is **Log Summary**, which allows a quick glance at the number for messages, errors, warnings, and debug items that have been logged. This summary can be cleared by clicking on the **Clear Counts** button, which can be found on the right side of our page. There we also find the **Refresh** button, which will reload the SIS information from the log file. Instead of hitting the refresh button on the browser, which can kick us back to the **System Admin** tab, we can use this button; a major improvement for any Blackboard administrator.

There is also a **Purge Log** button, which will delete all current data within our **SIS Log**. This cannot be undone, so we should only do this if we no longer need any of the SIS information saved in the log. If we want to download these log files for archiving or storage, we must contact Blackboard Support for assistance at this time.

Authentication Logs

We find similarities in the **SIS Logs** page and the **Authentication Logs** page. Our **Authentication Logs** link takes us to the page that allows us to search the authentication logs. The search tool allows us to search for a username or an IP address within our authentication logs. In the following example, we search for the username user7, and we see how many **Logins**, **Logouts**, and **Login Attempts** we have from this user. If we click on an event, we see its details within the message detail area. Our search query also allows us to specify the authentication provider, event type, and set date restrictions for our search. We also find **Log Summary** as well and our **Refresh**, **Clear Counts**, and **Purge Log** buttons. Just as in our **SIS Logs** page, each event type is associated with a color; a helpful addition when searching through multiple events.

System Logs

If **SIS Logs** and **Authentication Logs** are an administrator's dream, we are about to step into a nightmare. Unlike the **SIS Logs** and **Authentication Logs** pages, we don't have the ability to search within the log file when we access our **System Logs** page.

We get to this page by clicking on the **System Logs** link within the **Logs** page. Here we have the ability to search the log name and description of the log file using the search feature within our page; however, we can't search within the files. Some of our logs may not contain information; we can remove those log files from our search by checking the checkbox beside **Hide Empty Logs**. In our example, we search for the term `java` and it finds seven results. Notice that our examples have an exclamation point within a triangle beside the log name.

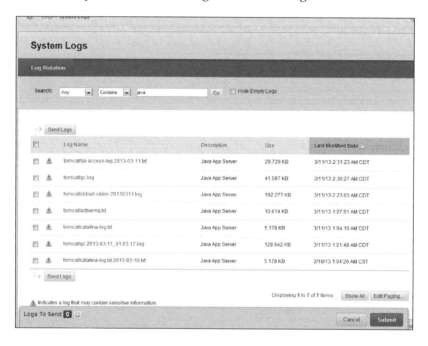

This is an indication that the log may have information that our organization deems sensitive. The log name tells us the location of the log file within the `logs` subdirectory under our Blackboard `home` directory for this application node. It also has a link to download the log file to our local computer; however, we may want to look at the size of the file. An active Blackboard application server can write thousands of lines into a log file during a 24 hour period. These files can grow large, but our search results will also display the size of the log file along with a description.

Our last modified date tells us the last time our application server wrote to this log, which can be helpful if we are looking for a rarely-used log file.

 If we have more than one application server, we must log in to each server to download the log files from it. Sadly, we don't have a single storage location for all log files when we have multiple application servers.

We also have the ability to e-mail logs, but this can create more problems than solutions as we will soon see. First we must select what logs we want to e-mail, then click on the **Send Logs** button. Now we are at the **Send Logs** page. Here we see some of the problems we find with this option, such as the log files only being sent to the System Administrator User listed in the `bb-config.properties` file. So, if our e-mail address isn't listed there, we won't be able to send the files to ourselves. However, if this isn't the case, we can set the subject line and message texts for our log files.

Here we can select additional log files; however, we must beware that attaching large files can cause our e-mail not to be sent or accepted by our organization's mail server. We should make sure that we understand the file attachment size limitations before sending log files. Once we have set our configurations, we click on the **Submit** button to send the e-mail with the log files attached.

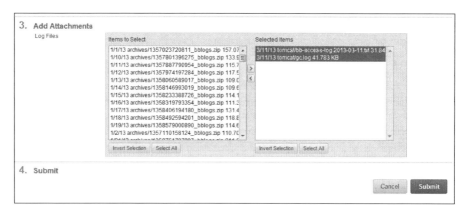

System Tasks Status

During our conversations in the previous chapters, we have discussed many different processes such as batch user creation, batch course creation, course copy, archive, import, and export. Each time one of these actions or tasks happen within our Blackboard Learn instance, its status is documented. Within the **System Tasks Status** page, we can learn if these tasks complete successfully or fail. We access it by clicking on the **System Tasks Status** link within our **Logs** page. The **System Task Status** page differs from the other pages we've seen because we lack any searchable options.

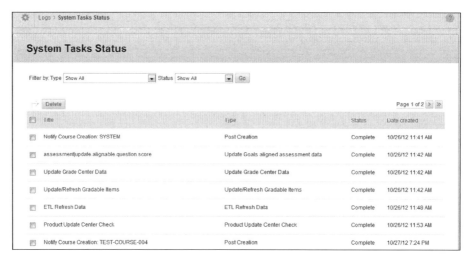

Our search area now changes to a filter option that allows us to see only specific actions or statuses. The filter is applied to our results by clicking on the **Go** button. Here we can see the title of the task, the type of task, its status, and the date that the task was processed.

If we mouse over the task title, the chevron appears. When we click on the chevron, our action menu appears and we can view details about this task or delete it. These system tasks aren't removed automatically and can create a large list. We can delete old system tasks by clicking on the checkbox beside our old tasks, and then clicking on the **Delete** button at the top or bottom of our list.

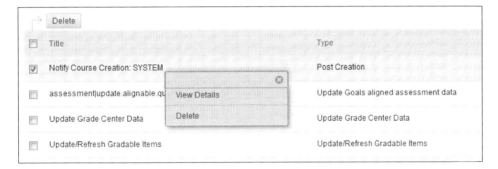

Delete the system task's status using a database query

If we do have a large list of system tasks, we can run a query to delete all system tasks older than today. Most system tasks that complete successfully won't need to be kept. Here is the query in Oracle and Microsoft SQL formats to remove all the system tasks that completed successfully, which is why we have the C status in the following queries:

- **Oracle**: `delete from queued_tasks where dtmodified <= sysdate and status='C';`
- **Microsoft SQL**: `delete from queued_tasks where dtmodified <= GETDATE() and status='C';`

If we really wish to keep our **System Tasks Status** page clean, we might need to create a script that runs this query on a regular basis.

Course Cartridge Import Status

In *Chapter 4, Creating Courses in Blackboard Learn*, we briefly mentioned the topic of course cartridges. While many instructors and publishers are turning towards courses that use web-based content access via a building block, the course cartridge is still used by many instructors. Often, when troubleshooting issues, knowing if a course cartridge has been installed can help us. We do this by clicking on the **Course Cartridge Import Status** link in our **Logs** page. This page offers a simple information set. We find the course ID along with the status of the course cartridge import and we may see a log of the import process. If we mouse over the course ID and click on the chevron, we can reset the course cartridge import if it has failed, or remove it from the course entirely.

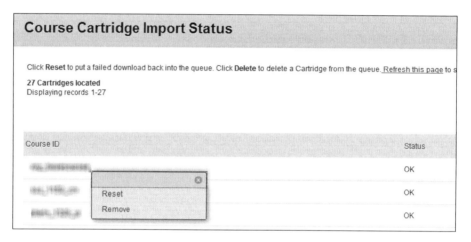

Log Rotation

Earlier in our discussion, we mentioned the growth of Blackboard Learn log files on a daily basis. Logs that grow large make it difficult to troubleshoot issues due to the thousands of lines within each file. When this situation happens, we have the ability to make sure our log file size doesn't get out of hand by using the **Log Rotation** process. This process will save and remove the log files, and then move them to an archive subdirectory for storage. We can manually run the log file by logging in to the application server and running the `RotateLogs` script (`RotateLogs.sh` or `RotateLogs.bat`) located in the `tools/admin` subdirectory of our `blackboard` folder.

The RotateLogs script creates a ZIP file that is stored in a subdirectory of the logs folder called archives. We may want to move these logs to a central archive location, if we have multiple application servers for long term storage.

While we can run this process manually, the automated process is the preferred method to rotate our Blackboard Learn logs on a regular basis. Let's go back to our **System Logs** page. In the upper-left corner of the page, we see the **Log Rotation** button, which takes us to the **Log Rotation** page where we configure the process. There are only two settings for us to configure. The first area, called the **Frequency of System Log Rotation,** allows us to set the number of days between each log rotation. We can set this up to 30 days, however most administrators will have the log rotation process run every day or once a week due to the size we spoke about earlier. Our next configuration option allows us to set when the log rotation happens during the day.

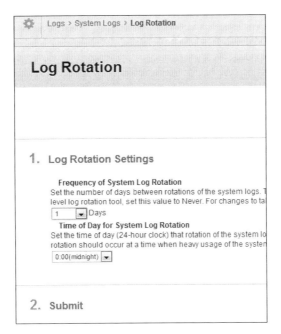

A best practice is to set this rotation process during a time when the server doesn't experience heavy usage. This example instance rotates logs everyday at 12:00 a.m. Once we have set our configurations, click on the **Submit** button and we are taken back to the **Logs** page where we see a success or failure statement. We should note that this script only rotates standard Blackboard logs and not the log files that are written by third-party applications such as Building Blocks. These will have to be rotated manually using a scheduled task or cron script.

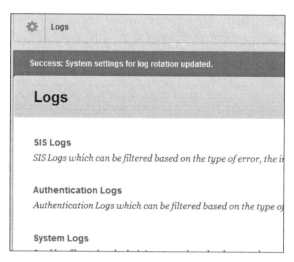

Finding log files within our Blackboard Learn server

While we can use our **System Admin** tab to access many of the logs within our Blackboard Learn instance, we may want to access these log files right from the server. If we log in to our application server, we can go to our Blackboard home directory and go into our `logs` subdirectory. Here we find the same files available to us within the **System Admin** tab. These files can be located within subdirectories and the `log` folder itself.

Locating log files in Blackboard Learn

Our previous discussions have given us the ability to access our log files. However, we haven't discussed how these log files are associated with our Blackboard application. Let's review our log files and learn more.

Apache

For RedHat and Solaris users, Apache creates several different log files. These files are located within the `logs/httpd` directory. Here is a brief description of each file:

- `access_log` and `ssl_access_log`: These logs keep a record of the interactions between the Apache server and a client's browser. It contains the client's IP address, date of the request, request method, and details about the client's browser. If we have SSL enabled, our file will include the `ssl` prefix. See the following example:

```
XXX.XX.XX.10 - - [10/Feb/2013:06:00:26 -0500] "GET / HTTP/1.1"
302 - "-" "Mozilla/5.0 (Macintosh; Intel Mac OS X 10_8_2)
AppleWebKit/536.26.17 (KHTML, like Gecko) Version/6.0.2
Safari/536.26.17" (-) "-"
127.0.0.1 - - [10/Feb/2013:06:02:01 -0500] "GET /server-
status?auto HTTP/1.0" 200 428 "-" "Python-urllib/1.16" (-) "-"
```

- `error_log` and `ssl_error_log`: These logs collect any errors that happen between the Apache server and the client's browser. If we use SSL encryption, our file title will include `ssl` at the beginning. Here is an example from this type of file:

```
[Sun Feb 10 05:47:09 2013] [error] proxy: AJP: disabled connection
for (localhost)
[Sun Feb 10 05:47:54 2013] [error] proxy: AJP: disabled connection
for (localhost)
```

- `mod_deflate.log`: This log file contains a log of when our Apache server has compressed web pages for delivery to users. Here is an example:

```
"GET / HTTP/1.1" -/- (-%)
"GET /server-status?auto HTTP/1.0" -/- (-%)
"GET /webapps/Bb-mobile-bb_bb60/dashboard?course_type=COURSE&with_
notifications=true&v=1&language=en_US&ver=3.1.2 HTTP/1.1" -/- (-%)
"GET /webapps/Bb-mobile-bb_bb60/dashboard?course_type=COURSE&with_
notifications=true&v=1&language=en_US&ver=3.1.2 HTTP/1.1" -/- (-%)
```

IIS

Our log files differ when using the Windows operating system. These log files are still located within the `logs/httpd` directory, however we will find an additional folder that contains our log files.

- u_ex[Date].log: This log file is similar to the access_log file for the Apache server. It contains the date and time, the source IP address, request method, the requested URI, client IP address, and information about the client's browser. Here is an example:

```
2012-11-06 04:33:30 XXX.XXX.211.9 GET /themes/as_2012/theme.css
v=9.1.100401.0 80 - XXX.XXX.XXX.84 Mozilla/5.0+(Macintosh;+Intel+M
ac+OS+X+10_8_2)+AppleWebKit/537.4+(KHTML,+like+Gecko)+Chrome/22.0.
1229.94+Safari/537.4 200 0 0 826
2012-11-06 04:33:30 XXX.XXX.211.9 GET / - 80 - XXX.XXX.XXX.84 Mozi
lla/5.0+(Macintosh;+Intel+Mac+OS+X+10_8_2)+AppleWebKit/537.4+(KHTM
L,+like+Gecko)+Chrome/22.0.1229.94+Safari/537.4 200 0 0 5078
```

- isapi_redirect.log: This log is found in the logs directory. This log collects session exceptions. Here is an example:

```
[Mon Apr 02 03:45:22.910 2012] [1800:2740] [info] ajp_connect_
to_endpoint::jk_ajp_common.c (922): Failed opening socket to
(127.0.0.1:8009) (errno=61)
[Mon Apr 02 03:45:22.910 2012] [1800:2740] [error] ajp_send_
request::jk_ajp_common.c (1507): (root) connecting to backend
failed. Tomcat is probably not started or is listening on the
wrong port (errno=61)
[Mon Apr 02 03:45:22.910 2012] [1800:2740] [info] ajp_service::jk_
ajp_common.c (2447): (root) sending request to tomcat failed
(recoverable), because of error during request sending (attempt=1)
[Mon Apr 02 03:45:24.052 2012] [1800:2740] [info] jk_open_
socket::jk_connect.c (594): connect to 127.0.0.1:8009 failed
(errno=61)
```

Tomcat

The logs for our tomcat application reside in the logs/tomcat folder, which is just a pointer to the apps/tomcat/logs folder. Here we have three common log files that can help us troubleshoot issues:

- catalina-log.txt: This log contains information that involves the application server itself. Here's a sample from this file:

```
INFO 2013-02-10 01:04:14,292 WrapperStartStopAppMain org.
directwebremoting.impl.StartupUtil - - Java Vendor:    Oracle
Corporation
INFO 2013-02-10 01:04:18,280 WrapperStartStopAppMain org.
apache.struts.action.ActionServlet - Loading chain catalog from
jar:file:/usr/local/blackboard/content/vi/BBLEARN/plugins/bb-data-
integration-ss-xml/webapp/WEB-INF/lib/struts-core-1.3.5.jar!/org/
apache/struts/chain/chain-config.xml
```

- `gc.log`: This file logs the garbage collection process that happens throughout the day within Tomcat. Here is a sample of the log file:

```
2013-02-10T01:03:40.211-0600: 7.772: [GC 7.773: [DefNew:
60202K->6503K(76672K), 0.0377360 secs] 60202K->6503K(1040064K),
0.0378790 secs] [Times: user=0.04 sys=0.00, real=0.04 secs]
2013-02-10T01:03:40.249-0600: 7.811: [GC [1 CMS-initial-mark:
0K(963392K)] 6503K(1040064K), 0.0055220 secs] [Times: user=0.00
sys=0.00, real=0.00 secs]
```

- `stdout-stderr.log`: Tomcat will put any information that would be sent to standard output or error into this log file. This file can be a big help when troubleshooting Tomcat issues with our Blackboard Learn environment. Here's an example of what the log file looks like:

```
INFO    | jvm 1    | 2013/03/10 01:01:45 | [2013-03-10 01:01:44.0]
[xyIndex_23376]        Trace Misc      AdminUtil:188    System has
been shut down correctly.
INFO    | jvm 1    | 2013/03/10 01:01:45 | Mar 10, 2013
1:01:44 AM org.apache.catalina.loader.WebappClassLoader
clearReferencesThreads
INFO    | jvm 1    | 2013/03/10 01:01:45 | SEVERE: The web
application [/xythosremoteadmin] appears to have started a thread
named [IndexingThread] but has failed to stop it. This is very
likely to create a memory leak.
```

Blackboard application

Any additional log files come from the Blackboard application or some third-party tools. Unlike the files we have reviewed so far, some of these files and folders will not have sample content because they are either folders, rarely contain content, or the content would be too specific to publish.

- `collab-server`: This folder holds log files associated with the collaboration service within our Blackboard Learn instance. These logs hold informational data about the service's events.

- `content-exchange`: If we ever import, export, or archive a course from our Blackboard Learn environment, a log file from that process is stored here. Each log contains the course ID and the action within the file's title.

- `system-info`: Information about the hardware and software for our Blackboard Learn instance resides within the log files held in this folder. We can get not only specs, but also current folder sizes and other detailed information from within the files.

- `update-tools`: When we install an update to our Blackboard Learn instance, this folder holds logs on the update process and any SQL errors.

- `bb-services-log.txt`: This file is the main log file for the Blackboard Learn application. It collects exceptions including authentication. This file can grow quickly and can become rather large. Here is an example of the log file.

    ```
    2013-02-10 00:07:07 -0600 - Failed to add macro:
    #spellcheckTextbox(  id name label value ) : source = collab/
    collabGrading.vm
    2013-02-10 00:24:48 -0600 - javax.servlet.jsp.JspTagException:
    blackboard.platform.security.authentication.BbSecurityException:
    Either you are not logged in or you do not have the appropriate
    privileges to perform this action.<P><span class="captionText">For
    reference, the Error ID is 0cdf13a3-6478-4394-8946-20ab52a656b2.</
    span> [javax.servlet.jsp.JspException]
    ```

- `bb-sqlerror-log.txt`: If our instance experiences any deadlocks, timeouts, SQL execution issues, or other related issues, these are logged within this file.

- `bb-email-log.txt`: When a user sends an e-mail message to other users from within our Blackboard Learn environment, this log will capture the e-mail. The log will only contain the sender's e-mail address, the recipient's e-mail addresses, and the e-mail's subject line. This, however, doesn't log the body of the e-mail. Here is an example of the log file:

    ```
    2013-02-10 00:32:25 -0600 - SUCCESS: "MessageID:
    <2021012710.9380.1362897145413.JavaMail.bbuser@blackboard.
    myorganization.com>", "Sunday, February 10, 2013", "js033@
    myorganization.com; ", "TEST.COURSE.001: Grades Due", "smithjs@
    myorganization.com John Smith; "
    ```

- `bb-session-log.txt`: Back in *Chapter 9, Security, Reporting, and Configuration in Blackboard Learn,* we discussed session fingerprints. These fingerprints are logged within this log file based on the configuration settings we selected there. Here is a sample of the log.

    ```
    2013-02-10 00:18:15 -0600 - Session fingerprint changed. sessionId
    = 252785892, sessionIdMd5 = C4C4E06CDEFEA592EF59BD3A19E8F74D,
    userName = smithjs, userPk1 = _######_1, ip = XXX.XXX.XXX.31,
    userAgent = "Mozilla/5.0 (iPhone; CPU iPhone OS 6_1_1 like Mac OS
    X) AppleWebKit/536.26 (KHTML, like Gecko) Mobile/10B145"
    2013-02-10 00:18:55 -0600 - Session fingerprint changed. sessionId
    = 252786185, sessionIdMd5 = 0D504AB23F854E2401080BB03B61B33D,
    userName = js033, userPk1 = _#####_1, ip = XXX.XXX.XXX.31,
    userAgent = "Mobile%20Learn/3.1.4 CFNetwork/609.1.4 Darwin/13.0.0"
    ```

These are just a few of the files that we can find within the log files. When trying to troubleshoot an issue, look through all the different log files to see if any might shed light on the problem. Our next discussion allows us to review some tips and best practices for troubleshooting Blackboard Learn issues.

Tips for troubleshooting issues with log files

Any experienced Blackboard Learn administrator will tell you that in the beginning, trying to troubleshoot problems and issues within the application seemed impossible. Even experienced administrators could find themselves pursuing false leads when trying to track down the root of issues. Log analysis, both an art and a science, can easily fill an entire book. We can only hope to convey some tips to help any Blackboard Learn admin improve their troubleshooting skills.

- Logs can be set to different levels of verbosity, such as debug, information, or errors only. We can change the log verbosity by editing the `wrapper.conf` file within the `config\tomcat\conf\` subdirectory of our `blackboard` directory, which affects our Tomcat logs. These changes will require us to restart Blackboard services. If we run the `PushConfigUpdates` script, our changes will disappear unless they are made in the `wrapper.conf.bb` file located in the same subdirectory. We can change the Blackboard log verbosity by editing the `service-config.properties` file within the `config` subdirectory.

- Often, we will get an e-mail with an attached screen capture that shows a red bar with the word `Error` in white lettering. This is one of the main error types that we find within our Blackboard Learn environment, which also include database- and Tomcat-level errors. These errors are normally found within the logs we discussed earlier:

  - Red bar errors appear in `bb-services-log.txt`
  - Database errors can be found in `bb-sqlerror-log.txt`
  - Tomcat errors are found within `stdout-stderr.log`

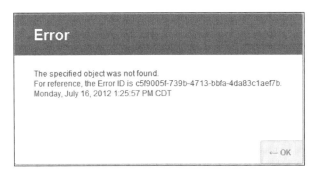

This error will appear within the `bb-services-log` file and appear as follows; note the corresponding Error ID:

```
2013-02-18 00:02:26 -0500 -   <P><span class="captionText">For
reference, the Error ID is c5f9005f-739b-4713-bbfa-4da83c1aef7b.</
span> [java.lang.NullPointerException]
```

```
2013-02-18 00:02:26 -0500 -  <P><span class="captionText">For
reference, the Error ID is c5f9005f-739b-4713-bbfa-4da83c1aef7b.</
span> - java.lang.NullPointerException
        at blackboard.data.course.CourseToolUtil.
isGuestUser(CourseToolUtil.java:131)
        at blackboard.webapps.blackboard.links.LaunchLinkAction$La
unchLinkHelper.handleTool(LaunchLinkAction.java:362)
        at blackboard.webapps.blackboard.links.LaunchLinkAction$La
unchLinkHelper.computeForward(LaunchLinkAction.java:269)
        at blackboard.webapps.blackboard.links.LaunchLinkAction.
execute(LaunchLinkAction.java:63)
        at org.apache.struts.action.RequestProcessor.processAction
Perform(RequestProcessor.java:413)
        at org.apache.struts.action.RequestProcessor.
process(RequestProcessor.java:225)
        at org.apache.struts.action.ActionServlet.
process(ActionServlet.java:1858)
        at org.apache.struts.action.ActionServlet.
doGet(ActionServlet.java:446)
        at javax.servlet.http.HttpServlet.service(HttpServlet.
java:617)
        at blackboard.struts.BbActionServlet.
service(BbActionServlet.java:83)
        at javax.servlet.http.HttpServlet.service(HttpServlet.
java:717)
        at sun.reflect.GeneratedMethodAccessor403.invoke(Unknown
Source)
```

- When investigating the `bb-services-log` file, admins sometimes find long errors, which at first seem very cryptic. These errors contain the thread stack, which gives us a historical path that the Java thread followed before the error shown in the preceding code snippet. When dealing with this log file, there are a few tips such as error lines that start with `at` and contain the word `blackboard` are important. Usually, the error is due to some issue within the Blackboard code. Errors can also contain phrases such as `root cause` or `caused by`, which can help troubleshoot the issue as well.

Let's work through this by using the code from our red bar error. First we can see that we can't find a `root cause` or `caused by` statement within the error. This then means we should start with the first line after our error information. This line will start with the `at` term. Here we see `blackboard.data.course.CourseToolUtil.isGuestUser`, which tells us that the error probably came from the user trying to access a course tool after their Blackboard Learn session had expired or they weren't logged in to our environment. This comes from seeing the `.isGuestUser` statement within the line. This is how we can use the error ID and the `bb-services-log` file to troubleshoot user issues.

- When error messages appear, they normally fall into four different categories:
    - Errors that users find when interacting with Blackboard Learn
    - Errors that find problems with the application's performance
    - Errors addressing broken functionality within the application
    - Informational messages or errors that don't affect the system, also known as log spam

- If we see the following type of errors in our logs, we are experiencing performance issues:
    - Heap space out of memory errors
    - Deadlock errors
    - HotSpot JVM errors
    - Higher than normal full garbage collection errors

> Garbage collection logs normally appear within the Tomcat `stdout-stderr` log and are as follows:
>
> ```
> INFO    | jvm 1    | 2013/02/18 00:02:02 | 2013-04-
> 18T00:02:02.850-0500: 327562.892: [GC 327562.893: [ParNew
> INFO    | jvm 1    | 2013/02/18 00:02:03 | :
> 2933022K->133260K(3495296K), 0.2981040 secs]
> 3893112K->1096869K(16078208K), 0.2989480 secs] [Times:
> user=1.09 sys=0.00, real=0.30 secs]
> ```
>
> These types of garbage collection events happen every few minutes on a normal server; if they start to happen more frequently, there may be an issue.

- Broken functionality errors will normally mention a specific Blackboard component. We can find these by using the following error messages:
    - `NullPointerException`
    - `ClassNotFoundException`
    - `AuthorizationException`

- Log spam can be identified within our files with the following characteristics:
    - Messages posted within the log file don't appear to relate to any special activity in our instance

- The errors are normally very obscure
- The errors can be found again and again within the log file in a repetitive state such that being unable to access a product that is not enabled in our environment such as the content or outcomes systems

- As we continue to troubleshoot issues such as broken functionality, we can use our access logs and the stack trace within `bb-services-log` to create a click-by-click reconstruction that can help us try to recreate the issue.

Disaster recovery

No matter where we are on the planet, disasters happen. Earthquakes, volcanos, tsunamis, and blizzards are just a few of the disasters we can face, not including man-made disasters. Any of these can affect our Blackboard Learn instance and create a nightmare situation for us as administrators. We must discuss how we can prepare for a disaster that affects our Blackboard Learn environment.

Understanding expectations

We as Blackboard Learn administrators can work with other system administrators to create a backup policy and a disaster recovery plan. However, this plan won't be worthwhile unless we know our organization's expectations for our environment. We must discuss these expectations so that we can create a successful recovery plan. Here are a few points to discuss:

- What is the tolerance for data loss?
- Can content or database data be lost with no issue?
- What role does our Blackboard Learn instance play within our organization?
- Who depends on it and how critical is the system being up to our organization's operation?
- How important is our Blackboard Learn environment to our organization's success?

These types of questions will help us decide the expectations, or level of service, that our organization expects from our Blackboard Learn instance. Once we have this information, we can start to create a disaster plan, however sometimes organizations have small budgets when it comes to purchasing software and hardware for disaster recovery. Let's review how to categorize the importance of our information.

The 100 percent recovery bubble

Many admins new to Blackboard Learn expect that the system should be able to recover from a disaster with 100 percent of the data and files still there. Sadly, we must accept that this can be a very hard promise to make and keep. Most Blackboard Learn environments will always have users making changes, whether that is for an assessment, grading, or posting content, and we just can't promise that when a disaster happens everything will be there. The best thing we can do is work to create the best disaster recovery plan based on the expectations, needs, and funding options available within our organization.

Prioritizing Blackboard data

Years of administrative experience has created unofficial levels of data within any Blackboard Learn instance. Let's review them to get a better understanding of how data changes.

- **Application data**: This data includes just about everything within our `blackboard` directory excluding the `logs` and `content` subdirectories. These files don't change much and hold information about only the application itself and its configuration. We should back up these files regularly using our organization's backup method, such as tape backups, and check to ensure our backups are working properly.

- **Course and user files**: These files are kept within the `content` subdirectory of our Blackboard Learn environment. This folder contains user and course files that may play an important part in the course's process and student file submissions. These files can change on a daily and even hourly basis. Our earlier conversation about expectations can help us decide how we want to plan if a disaster affects this area. If our expectations can be met, we may look at incremental backups of this folder with a weekly backup of its contents.

- **Blackboard database**: Experience says that any issue with our database will be costly. Blackboard Learn has evolved to become extremely dependent upon it. Our database contains user, course, and enrollment information. It also holds information that tells the application how to render every page, the location of files within the content subdirectory, and most importantly user grades and activity. This means that if we have to prioritize three different parts of our Blackboard Learn instance, the database sits at the top. We can use failover database options to make sure that our database stays available and uncorrupted.

Example Blackboard Learn disaster recovery plan

While this information can be helpful when developing a recovery plan, there are so many variables based on the organization, size, usage, and planning that don't allow for a one-size-fits-all type of recovery plan. With this issue in mind, let's review the creation of a recovery plan for an organization. This example will hopefully give us a good starting point that can help us develop our organization's personalized disaster recovery plan.

Our organization is a large higher education institution, which has a little over 30,000 students. The institution has several facts about their use and expectations of the Blackboard Learn application:

- Over 4,300 courses use the application

- The institution has several thriving online programs

- Most faculty members use Blackboard Learn to share content, accept assignments, give exams, and post grades

- Users are regularly on the system during a 12 hour period

- Institution administrators have voiced the importance of the application as a part of meeting their goals and the institution's mission

- The institution, through departments and administration, has stated that Blackboard Learn is mission critical and must be up and available to students

So what do these facts tell us? It tells us that if our Blackboard Learn faces a disaster, it can have a major effect on this institution. The system should have complete redundancy that can bring the instance back up in minutes with probably a maximum allowable downtime of an hour. This means our database, course files, and applications must be backed up regularly and incrementally. Now we should discuss the Blackboard Learn instance and its architecture.

The Blackboard Learn environment runs on top of a Red Hat Linux operating system with an Oracle 11*g* database. The environment is load balanced with multiple virtualized application servers and a SAN storage appliance. The institution also has a secondary location, which would be used in case a natural or manmade disaster impacts the institution.

While slightly complex, this environment sounds pretty normal for most mid-size and large institutions. Now we can discuss what our disaster recovery plan could be.

Remember our conversation earlier in this chapter; we defined the three important types of data we must try to recover: database, course/user files, and application files. Our first issue will be the database. Due to the expectations of our mock institution, the information contained in this database must be saved at all costs with students and faculty putting grade data into our environment. We would work with our database administrator to create suggestions such as installing Oracle Data Guard to create a standby site at the institution's secondary site. This would allow us to employ our standby database, which can be brought up in a disaster or can go back to a point in time if the database becomes corrupted.

Our course and user files change rapidly and are an important part of our environment. The easiest way to support these files would be to place the same appliance in our secondary location and schedule a time sync to update the secondary appliance. This works well if we have a great deal of bandwidth to our secondary location, which we are going to assume in this hypothetical situation.

We can follow the same type of route with our application files. Since the servers are virtualized, we can work to have hot backups done on a regular basis which can be brought up within the virtual servers that our institution has in their secondary location.

Solving these problems may have sounded a bit too easy in our hypothetical institution, but it should give us a good process to start thinking about our disaster recovery plan.

Summary

This final chapter took us into the logs to review how we can troubleshoot issues within our Blackboard Learn environment. By understanding the log files and what information each one contains, we have improved our sleuthing abilities. We even learned some helpful tips when trying to troubleshoot user issues. Our final discussion in this chapter took us to the unpleasant discussion of disasters and how to prepare our instance for them. Our successful disaster recovery plan starts by understanding what our organization expects from our Blackboard Learn environment and how we can meet that need. We then must look at the different data groupings within the application itself such as the database, course, and user files, along with application files. We then must take our expectations and craft a customized plan that meets all those needs.

We have taken a long journey learning about Blackboard Learn. I hope that the time that we have spent reviewing the many parts of this application has empowered you to do more with the product. Thank you for your time and I wish you nothing but the best in your work as a Blackboard Learn administrator.

Appendix

This appendix shows the default actions for eight major system roles. We have additional system roles. However, they either work with specific Blackboard products that can be attached to Blackboard Learn, or they are niche roles that are rarely used.

	User Administrator	Course Administrator	Goals Manager	Learning Environment Administrator	Template Administrator	System Support	Support	System Administrator
Access to System Admin tab	Yes	Yes	Yes	Yes	Yes	Yes	Yes	Yes
Courses								
Default Course Design								
Course Catalog		Yes		Yes		Yes		Yes
Course Settings		Yes				Yes		Yes
Courses (Course Search)		Yes	Yes	Yes	Yes	Yes	Yes	Yes
Create Single Courses		Yes				Yes		Yes
Batch Create Courses		Yes				Yes		Yes
Manage Course Availability		Yes				Yes		Yes
Enroll Users		Yes				Yes		Yes
Batch Enroll Users	Yes	Yes				Yes		Yes
Manage Enrollments		Yes				Yes		Yes
Import Course Package		Yes		Yes	Yes	Yes		Yes
Copy Courses		Yes				Yes		Yes
Edit Courses Information		Yes		Yes	Yes	Yes	Yes	Yes
Bulk Delete		Yes		Yes	Yes	Yes		Yes

	User Administrator	Course Administrator	Goals Manager	Learning Environment Administrator	Template Administrator	System Support	Support	System Administrator
Archive Courses		Yes		Yes	Yes	Yes		Yes
Export Courses		Yes				Yes		Yes
Restore Courses		Yes				Yes		Yes
Delete Courses		Yes				Yes		Yes
Manage Terms		Yes		Yes	Yes	Yes		Yes
Course Settings		Yes				Yes		Yes
Course Tools		Yes				Yes		Yes
Users								
User Search	Yes	Yes		Yes	Yes	Yes	Yes	Yes
Create a Single User	Yes					Yes		Yes
Batch Create Users	Yes					Yes		Yes
Change User Password	Yes			Yes		Yes		Yes
Make User Available / Unavailable	Yes					Yes		Yes
Set Institutional / System Role	Yes			Yes		Yes		Yes
Delete a Single Users	Yes					Yes		Yes
Batch Delete Users	Yes					Yes		Yes
System Admin Items								
Add, Edit, Remove Building Blocks						Yes		Yes
Add, Edit, Remove Authentication								Yes
Data Integrations						Yes		Yes
Learning Environment Integrations				Yes		Yes		Yes
Student Information System Integrations								Yes
Web Services						Yes		Yes
Brands and Themes		Yes						
Custom Login Page						Yes		Yes

	User Administrator	Course Administrator	Goals Manager	Learning Environment Administrator	Template Administrator	System Support	Support	System Administrator
Institutional Hierarchy Management						Yes		Yes
Gateway Options						Yes		Yes
Security Management (HTML Filter, Input Validation, Safe HTML, SSL)						Yes		Yes
Tools and Utilities (Unless Otherwise listed)						Yes		Yes
Admin Tools								
Create System Announcements						Yes		Yes
Delete System Announcements								Yes
Send Email to All Instructors	Yes		Yes			Yes		Yes
Send Email to All Students						Yes		Yes
Send Email to All Users						Yes		Yes
Surveys						Yes		Yes
Goals	Yes	Yes				Yes		Yes
Language Packs						Yes		Yes
System Logs			Yes			Yes		Yes
Messages	Yes					Yes		Yes
Notifications	Yes					Yes		Yes
System Configuration						Yes		Yes
System Reporting						Yes		Yes

Index

Symbols

100 Percent Recovery Bubble 293
-c command 264
-f, --force command 45
+ (plus) symbol 61
-r command 265
-s command 265
--silent option 45
-s, --silent command 45

A

action button 106
action menu 106
Active 55
Administrator panel 42
Advanced System Tracking and Reporting.
        See ASTRO
Alt Text for Banner Image field 61
Always Off tool 78
Always On tool 78
Apache 285
Appserver-only installation option 27
architecture, Blackboard Learn
  about 7
  multiple server architecture 8
  one server architecture 7, 8
  selecting 10-13
  two server architecture 8
ASTRO 272
authentication integration plan
  about 226
  AuthenticationOneTimeLogin script 228
  Blackboard legacy authentication
      framework 228

CAS 227
default 228
external authentication provider planning
    230
LDAP 226
Shibboleth authentication 227
authentication Logs 277
Availability button 160

B

Background Color option 55
Background Image options 56
Batch Actions button 163
batch course creation tool
  used, for course creating 94-97
Batch Enrollment page 95
batch enrollment process 111
bbconfig.database.instance.maxpoolsize
        parameter 221
bbconfig.database.instance.minpoolsize
        parameter 221
bbNG
  cssBlock tag 67
Bboogle 272
bbpatch utility 44
BbStats 271
Blackboard
  course setting 74
  courses, searching for 87
  single courses, creating 88-94
Blackboard data, prioritizing
  application data 293
  user files 293
Blackboard Extensions website 271

L

landing page 48
Language Pack option 92
Language Packs page 176
LDAP 134, 226
LDAP provider
  creating 231-233
learning management systems. *See* LMS
Learning Tool Interoperability. *See* LTI
Lightweight Directory Access Protocol. *See*
        LDAP
LMS 49
log files
  accessing 274, 275
  authentication logs 277
  Course Cartridge Import Status 282
  locating 274, 275
  log rotation 282, 284
  SIS logs 275, 276
  System logs 278, 279
  System Tasks Status 280, 281
  troubleshooting, tips 289-291
log files, Blackboard Learn
  Apache 285
  backboard applications 287, 288
  IIS 285, 286
  locating 284
  Tomcat 286
LoginAs 271
loginUI:accessibility tag 67
loginUI:errorMessage 68
loginUI:gatewayButtons 68
loginUI:localPicker 68
loginUI:loginForm 68
loginUI:systemAnnouncements 68
loginUI:welcomeArea 68
Log Rotation process 282
Logs page 275
LTI
  about 267
  links, managing 267-270

M

Manage Package Contents button 103, 117
Math Editor Image Service 184
Microsoft SQL Server database
  installing 20
Module element 58
MPMs 214
multiple server architecture 8, 9
multiple users
  creating, in Blackboard Learn 141-144
multi-processing modules. *See* MPMs
My Blackboard Settings tool 184

N

new course
  content, importing 97-99
Next button 36
notifications
  about 178
  calendar 182
  chalk titles 185
  course messages 181
  default notifications settings, managing 181
  default settings, managing 180
  emails 182, 183
  general notifications, setting up 178-180
  goals 183
  Math Editor Image Service 184
  My Blackboard Settings 184
  tools 185

O

objects 243
one server architecture
  diagram 7
  drawback 7, 8
operating systems 15-17
Oscelot Project website 271

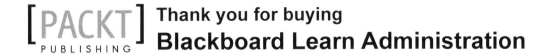

Thank you for buying
Blackboard Learn Administration

About Packt Publishing

Packt, pronounced 'packed', published its first book "*Mastering phpMyAdmin for Effective MySQL Management*" in April 2004 and subsequently continued to specialize in publishing highly focused books on specific technologies and solutions.

Our books and publications share the experiences of your fellow IT professionals in adapting and customizing today's systems, applications, and frameworks. Our solution based books give you the knowledge and power to customize the software and technologies you're using to get the job done. Packt books are more specific and less general than the IT books you have seen in the past. Our unique business model allows us to bring you more focused information, giving you more of what you need to know, and less of what you don't.

Packt is a modern, yet unique publishing company, which focuses on producing quality, cutting-edge books for communities of developers, administrators, and newbies alike. For more information, please visit our website: www.packtpub.com.

Writing for Packt

We welcome all inquiries from people who are interested in authoring. Book proposals should be sent to author@packtpub.com. If your book idea is still at an early stage and you would like to discuss it first before writing a formal book proposal, contact us; one of our commissioning editors will get in touch with you.

We're not just looking for published authors; if you have strong technical skills but no writing experience, our experienced editors can help you develop a writing career, or simply get some additional reward for your expertise.

Blackboard Essentials for Teachers

ISBN: 978-1-849692-92-2   Paperback: 256 pages

Build and deliver great courses using this popular Learning Management System

1. Learn to use the essential features of Blackboard to create and administer great courses

2. Add interaction to your courses with discussion boards, blogs, and wikis

3. Create meaningful tests and graded assignments

Desire2Learn for Higher Education Cookbook

ISBN: 978-1-849693-44-8   Paperback: 206 pages

Gain expert knowledge of the tools within the Desire2Learn Learning Environment, maximize your productivity, and create online learning experiences with these easy-to-follow recipes

1. Customize the look and feel of your online course, integrate graphics and video, and become more productive using the learning environment's built-in assessment and collaboration tools

2. Recipes address real world challenges in clear and concise step-by-step instructions, which help you work your way through technical tasks with ease

3. Detailed instructions with screenshots to guide you through each task

Please check **www.PacktPub.com** for information on our titles

Articulate Studio Cookbook

ISBN: 978-1-849693-08-0   Paperback: 292 pages

Create training courses with Articulate Studio's strong interactivity and rich content capabilities, all within the familiarity of Microsoft PowerPoint

1. Complete your courses by creating Flash-ready presentations through familiar PowerPoint

2. Employ Articulate Engage, Quizmaker and Encoder to make dazzling interaction, asses learners and add full-motion videos

3. Practical recipes to get you moving on a specific activity without the extra fluff

WordPress for Education

ISBN: 978-1-849518-20-8   Paperback: 144 pages

Create interactive and engaging e-learning websites with wordPress

1. Develop effective e-learning websites that will engage your students

2. Extend the potential of a classroom website with WordPress plugins

3. Create an interactive social network and course management system to enhance student and instructor communication

Please check **www.PacktPub.com** for information on our titles

Made in the USA
San Bernardino, CA
24 August 2014